Justice without Borders

The cosmopolitan idea of justice is commonly accused of not taking seriously the special ties and commitments of nationality and patriotism. This is because the ideal of impartial egalitarianism, which is central to the cosmopolitan view, seems to be directly opposed to the moral partiality inherent to nationalism and patriotism. In this book, Kok-Chor Tan argues that cosmopolitan justice, properly understood, can accommodate and appreciate nationalist and patriotic commitments, setting limits for these commitments without denying their moral significance. This book offers a defense of cosmopolitan justice against the charge that it denies the values that ordinarily matter to people, and a defense of nationalism and patriotism against the charge that these morally partial ideals are fundamentally inconsistent with the obligations of global justice. Accessible and persuasive, this book will have broad appeal to political theorists and moral philosophers.

KOK-CHOR TAN is an Assistant Professor of Philosophy at the University of Pennsylvania. He is the author of *Toleration, Diversity, and Global Justice* (2000), which was a joint runner-up for the 2003 Canadian Philosophical Association Book Prize.

Contemporary Political Theory

Series Editor
Ian Shapiro

Editorial Board
Russell Hardin   Stephen Holmes   Jeffrey Isaac   John Keane
Elizabeth Kiss   Susan Okin   Phillipe Van Parijs   Philip Pettit

As the twenty-first century begins, major new political challenges have arisen at the same time as some of the most enduring dilemmas of political association remain unresolved. The collapse of communism and the end of the Cold War reflect a victory for democratic and liberal values, yet in many of the Western countries that nurtured those values there are severe problems of urban decay, class and racial conflict, and failing political legitimacy. Enduring global injustice and inequality seem compounded by environmental problems, disease, the oppression of women and racial, ethnic and religious minorities, and the relentless growth of the world's population. In such circumstances, the need for creative thinking about the fundamentals of human political association is manifest. This new series in contemporary political theory is needed to foster such systematic normative reflection.

The series proceeds in the belief that the time is ripe for a reassertion of the importance of problem-driven political theory. It is concerned, that is, with works that are motivated by the impulse to understand, think critically about, and address the problems in the world, rather than issues that are thrown up primarily in academic debate. Books in the series may be interdisciplinary in character, ranging over issues conventionally dealt with in philosophy, law, history and the human sciences. The range of materials and the methods of proceeding should be dictated by the problem at hand, not the conventional debates or disciplinary divisions of academia.

Other books in the series
Ian Shapiro and Casiano Hacker-Cordón (eds.)
Democracy's Value

Ian Shapiro and Casiano Hacker-Cordón (eds.)
Democracy's Edges

Brooke A. Ackerly
Political Theory and Feminist Social Criticism

Clarissa Rile Hayward
De-Facing Power

John Kane
The Politics of Moral Capital

Ayelet Shachar
Multicultural Jurisdictions

John Keane
Global Civil Society?

Rogers M. Smith
Stories of Peoplehood

Gerry Mackie
Democracy Defended

John Keane
Violence and Democracy

Peter J. Steinberger
The Idea of the State

Justice without Borders

Cosmopolitanism, Nationalism, and Patriotism

Kok-Chor Tan

CAMBRIDGE
UNIVERSITY PRESS

CAMBRIDGE UNIVERSITY PRESS
Cambridge, New York, Melbourne, Madrid, Cape Town, Singapore, São Paulo

Cambridge University Press
The Edinburgh Building, Cambridge, CB2 2RU, UK

Published in the United States of America by Cambridge University Press, New York

www.cambridge.org
Information on this title:www.cambridge.org/9780521542326

First published 2004
Reprinted 2006

Printed in the United Kingdom at the University Press, Cambridge

A catalogue record for this book is available from the British Library

Library of Congress Cataloguing in Publication data
Tan, Kok-Chor, 1964–
Justice without Borders: Cosmopolitanism, Nationalism, and Patriotism /
Kok-Chor Tan.
    p.   cm. – (Contemporary political theory)
Includes bibliographical references and index.
ISBN 0 521 83454 6 – ISBN 0 521 54232 4 (pb.)
1. Distributive justice.   2. Cosmopolitanism.   3. Nationalism.
I. Title.   II. Series.
HB523.T26   2004
172'.2 – dc22   2004049662

ISBN-13 978-0-521-83454-4 hardback
ISBN-10 0-521-83454-6 hardback
ISBN-13 978-0-521-54232-6 paperback
ISBN-10 0-521-54232-4 paperback

For Karen

Contents

Preface

One central challenge to the cosmopolitan idea of distributive justice is that it is unable to accommodate and appreciate the special ties and commitments that characterize the lives of ordinary individuals and that are of value to them. Among these special ties and commitments that cosmopolitan justice seems to rule out are those associated with nationalism and patriotism. My aim in this book is to defend cosmopolitanism against this challenge. I will argue that, properly understood, cosmopolitan justice can allow for special concern and obligations on nationalistic and patriotic grounds, and that it can do so without forfeiting the cosmopolitan commitment to global egalitarianism. This work is, therefore, largely defensive, so to speak. But in clarifying the bounds of cosmopolitan justice in light of the special demands of nationalism and patriotism, I hope to present a distinctive understanding of the cosmopolitan idea of justice.

The literature on cosmopolitanism is rapidly growing. Yet this increasingly well-worked area remains rather untidy. Defenders of the cosmopolitan position themselves are not always clear or united on what their position is with respect to nationalism and patriotism. Although few, if indeed any, cosmopolitans would reject nationalist and patriotic practices altogether, some do give the impression that nationalist and patriotic commitments must be justified by reference to cosmopolitan goals, and that these partial commitments are morally defensible only if they serve the ends of cosmopolitan justice. Other cosmopolitans hold that cosmopolitanism can indeed accommodate patriotic and nationalist concerns because, so they argue, cosmopolitan justice does not require global equal concern for all persons. So one position takes a reductionist view of nationalism and patriotic concern, the other holds a revisionist view of cosmopolitan justice. These attempts to reconcile cosmopolitanism with nationalism and patriotism are unsatisfactory. The first is unsatisfactory to many proponents of nationalism and patriotism because it fails to fully appreciate the moral worth of these ideals. The second is unsatisfactory to those cosmopolitans who see a central motivation of cosmopolitan justice to be that of addressing the problem of global inequality. My aim in this work is to try to clear up some of these ambiguities and disagreements in the cosmopolitan position.

While this work is foremost a defense of cosmopolitan justice, it also provides a defense of patriotism and nationalism against a charge often raised against these ideals. This is the charge that patriotism and nationalism foster a certain narrow-mindedness and parochialism with regard to people's understanding of their moral obligations. My reconciliation of cosmopolitan justice with nationalism and patriotism, if successful, will dispel this concern. It will show that nationalism and patriotism are not necessarily at odds with taking the global point of view. In this regard, I think the arguments in this book will also be of interest to readers primarily interested in the topic of nationalism and patriotism.

Although this book is intended as a research monograph, I also want it to be accessible to students and scholars newly approaching the topic. To this end, chapters 2 and 3 provide background material to the cosmopolitan idea of justice, although they also set the stage for my arguments to come. Also I would like readers to find in other chapters useful, even if brief, introductions to topics such as Rawls and global justice (chapter 4), liberal nationalism (chapters 5 and 6), and patriotism (chapter 7). I hope I am able to achieve this dual aspiration of contributing to an important debate as well as introducing readers to it in the pages to follow.

Acknowledgments

The bulk of this book was researched and written during the years 1999–2001 when I was a postdoctoral fellow in the Department of Philosophy, Queen's University. I want first to thank Will Kymlicka, who supported my postdoctoral research from the very beginning, generously provided extensive comments on different drafts of this work, and offered friendly and helpful advice throughout the publication process. Numerous conversations with him and participation in his graduate seminars on nationalism and minority rights during my time at Queen's helped shape many of the central ideas in this book. My intellectual debt to Will is clear from the references alone. I also want to thank Idil Boran, Alistair Macleod, and Christine Sypnowich for many friendly discussions on topics covered in this work and on political philosophy in general. Thanks are also due to the Social Sciences and Humanities Research Council of Canada and the Department of Philosophy, Queen's University, for supporting my research.

I completed the first draft while I was on a Faculty Fellowship at the Center for Ethics and the Professions, Harvard University (2001–2). I thank the participants in the weekly Fellows' Seminar for sharing their insights and knowledge on various topics in moral and political philosophy, some directly related to the work at hand, others less so but relevant nonetheless: Arthur Applbaum, Nomy Arpaly (who also offered kind encouragement and support through the year), David Brendel, Margo Schlanger, David Sussman, and Bob Truog. Thanks also to Simone Sandy and Allison Ruda for help with copy-editing and library research, to Jean McVeigh and her capable staff for unceasingly supporting the visiting Fellows in a myriad of ways, and to the affiliates and associates of the Center for granting me this unique research year. Most of all, thanks to Dennis Thompson, who not only chaired and contributed to our seminars, but also showed a personal interest in the work and progress of each of the Fellows (and continues to do so beyond their affiliation with the Center). Dennis's combination of intellectual rigor and personal generosity has helped make the Center a peerless place of research and learning.

Final revisions were made while I was a lecturer in the University of Pennsylvania, and I am grateful to members of the Department of Philosophy (chaired by Scott Weinstein) and to the affiliates of the Philosophy, Politics, and Economics Program (directed by Samuel Freeman) for generously arranging teaching opportunities for me, and to the University of Pennsylvania for welcoming me into its community.

Two chapters of this book were discussed at the Ethics in Public Life (EPL) "Young Scholar" conference held at Cornell University. I am grateful to all participants of the conference for their support and for their interest in my work. I should mention by way of special thanks the following for their continuing interest: Chuck Beitz, Marilyn Friedman (both of whom provided written comments during the conference), Henry Shue, Dick Miller, and Michele Moody-Adams. They personify the generous spirit of mentorship that inspired the EPL Young Scholar program.

To the readers and editors at Cambridge University Press for the detailed and insightful comments I received on the proposal and the first draft, I express my thanks. I am especially grateful to Andrew Linklater, Thomas Pogge, and Ian Shapiro for their thoughtful comments and suggestions, and to John Haslam for his interest in the work and for expertly moving the project along. I should like to thank Frances Nugent for her expert and thoughtful copyediting of the manuscript.

Parts of this book have been presented at various conferences and meetings, including American Philosophical Association meetings (San Francisco 2001, Minneapolis 2001, and Philadelphia 2002) and Canadian Philosophical Association meetings (Edmonton 1999, Halifax 2003), as well as at different institutions. I thank those who commented on my work in these sessions, fellow presenters, and members of the audience for their contribution.

For their written comments on parts of the manuscript and/or helpful discussions on various occasions, I thank (at the risk of leaving out some names): David Brown, Gillian Brock, Deen Chatterjee, Anna Cremaldi, David Dyzenhaus, Samuel Freeman, Michael Green, Charles Jones, Erin Kelly, Mika Levaque-Manty, Catherine Lu, Darrel Moellendorf, Mark Navin, Matthew Price, David Reidy, and Scott Woodcock.

But my greatest debt is to Karen Detlefsen, who discussed the work with me from beginning to end, read various chapters in their draft form, and provided much needed encouragement throughout. More importantly, her presence not only made the writing of a philosophy book less lonely than it otherwise would have been, but is also a constant reminder of the other important things in life. This book would not have been written if it was not for her for a variety of reasons, and it is to her that I dedicate it.

Chapter 4 is a revised version of "Critical Notice of Rawls, *The Law of Peoples*," *Canadian Journal of Philosophy* 31/1 (2001): 113–32.

Chapter 5 draws on arguments first presented in "Liberal Nationalism and Cosmopolitan Justice," *Ethical Theory and Moral Practice* 5/4 (2002): 431–61, Kluwer Academic Publishers ©.

Part III of the book relies and expands on arguments presented in "The Limits of Patriotism," forthcoming in a special volume of the *Canadian Journal of Philosophy*, and "Patriotic Obligations," *Monist* 86/3 (2003): 434 53.

I am grateful to these journals and their respective publishers for permitting me to reproduce the arguments in these works here.

1 Introduction

The problem

Cosmopolitanism, as a normative idea, takes the individual to be the ultimate unit of moral concern and to be entitled to equal consideration regardless of nationality and citizenship. From the cosmopolitan perspective, principles of justice ought to transcend nationality and citizenship, and ought to apply equally to all individuals of the world as a whole. In short, cosmopolitan justice is justice without borders.

On one cosmopolitan interpretation, this impartiality with respect to nationality and citizenship applies also to *distributive* justice in that a person's legitimate material entitlements are to be determined independently of her national and state membership (e.g., Beitz 1999a; Pogge 1989, part III). But, as some cosmopolitans themselves have come to recognize, one serious weakness of the cosmopolitan position is its perceived inability to acknowledge and properly account for the special ties and commitments that characterize the lives of ordinary men and women (Beitz 1999b, p. 291). Among the special ties and local attachments typical to most people's lives are those of nationality and patriotism.[1] While the process of globalization in recent decades seems to lend some credence to the cosmopolitan ideal, the last decade has also witnessed the rise of nationalism which seems to contradict the aspirations of cosmopolitan justice. Thus Samuel Scheffler observes that "[b]oth the particularist and globalist ideas have become increasingly influential in contemporary politics, and one of the most important tasks for contemporary liberal theory is

---

[1] The issue of partial concern and justice is naturally not confined to the case of global justice and conationals. Partial concern among family members, friends, and other groupings poses potential problems for justice in general, as well as for the special case of global justice. But in international discourse, the form of partial concern most often invoked as an objection to global equality is that of conational partiality (although, as I note later, this is sometimes used to mean, more generally, favoritism towards fellow citizens). This does not mean that partiality between friends, family, and so on may be ignored by global egalitarians. But the general structure of my response to conational partiality, with appropriate modifications, applies also to these different cases of partiality. That this is so should be clearer in due course.

to address the twin challenges posed by particularist and globalist think-ing" (2001, p. 67; also Shapiro and Brilmayer 1999, pp. 1–2). In this regard, Andrew Vincent concludes his study on nationalism wondering if the universalist aspirations of contemporary political philosophy can properly account for the particularist attachments that are basic to any meaningful human life (Vincent 2002, pp. 240–1). While Vincent advises due vigilance against nationalism and other forms of group-based alle-giances, he also rightly worries that universalist political philosophies tend too quickly to "dismiss groups [and group-based claims] as irrelevant or incoherent" (Vincent 2002, p. 2).

A satisfactory defense of cosmopolitan justice must, therefore, be able to define certain principled limitations on nationalism and patriotism without, however, denigrating these particularist ideals. To borrow the form of a remark by W. K. Frankena, we want a cosmopolitan justice made for humanity, not humanity for cosmopolitan justice.[2] Conversely, and importantly, a satisfactory cosmopolitan defense must be able to accommodate these special attachments *without* surrendering its basic commitment to global equality – a defense of cosmopolitanism would be a pyrrhic victory otherwise, for it would abandon what is commonly believed to be the *raison d'être* of the cosmopolitan ideal.

Obviously, cosmopolitan theories do not claim to be compatible with all classes of nationalist and patriotic demands. Illiberal forms of nation-alism, like Nazism to take an extreme case, will certainly be ruled out by cosmopolitan justice, and the claim can hardly be made that it counts against cosmopolitan justice that it cannot accommodate these illiberal nationalist and patriotic demands. What is challenging for cosmopolitan justice is that there are supposedly *liberal* forms of nationalism and patri-otism that have come to receive growing support in the current literature, and that seem to ground special commitments that can be reasonably endorsed and expressed by individuals. The problem for cosmopolitan justice is that it seems to also rule out these more reasonable kinds of nationalism and patriotism, and hence seems to be an idea of justice that is morally rigoristic and out of touch with what is of value to ordi-nary human beings. It is these liberal forms of nationalism and patrio-tism that this book is concerned with. My aim is to assess the demands of cosmopolitan justice against the demands of *liberal* nationalism and patriotism.

The central claim of this work is that cosmopolitan justice, properly understood, can provide the limiting conditions for nationalist aspira-tions and patriotic commitments, and that it can do so without denying

---

[2] Frankena writes that "morality is made for man, and not man for morality" (quoted in Railton 1993, pp. 98–9). Frankena, in turn, is presumably adapting a remark attributed to Jesus in Mark 2:27 – "The Sabbath was made for man, and not man for the Sabbath."

the moral significance of such particular ties and obligations. Specifically, I hope to show (i) that cosmopolitan justice is compatible with liberal forms of nationalism, once we get clear on the built-in limitations of liberal nationalism and the exact demands of cosmopolitan justice, and (ii) that the patriotic ideal that people have special obligations to their compatriots can be taken seriously without threatening the global egalitarian commitments of cosmopolitan justice.

The claim that cosmopolitans can accommodate certain forms of nationalism and patriotic concern has been made before. Some cosmopolitans deem these special ties and commitments to be worthy only because they provide an efficient strategy for meeting global obligations. But these attempts have often been criticized for being "reductionist." That is to say, these attempts fail to give any independent moral value to the ties and feelings of nationality and patriotism. Yet most nationalist theorists hold that attaching independent moral value to nationality and patriotism is inherent to any meaningful account of nationalism and patriotism, and it is this irreducible value of nationality and patriotic concern that is seen to pose a serious challenge to cosmopolitan justice. One of my aims in this book is to take up this challenge. I want to show that cosmopolitanism can in fact recognize the moral independence of nationalism and patriotism, albeit setting limits on these ideals at the same time.

This work is thus limited in its objective. Its primary aim is not to offer new positive arguments in support of cosmopolitan justice, but to show how cosmopolitan justice can accommodate, in a non-trivial way, the claims of nationalism and patriotism while maintaining its global egalitarian commitments. It hopes to offer a systematic way of reconciling cosmopolitan justice with the demands of nationalism and patriotism that satisfies the conditions stated above. By clarifying the boundaries of the demands of cosmopolitanism, nationalism, and patriotism, I hope to provide a clearer and perhaps distinctive way of understanding the cosmopolitan position. Given the criticisms and even controversies the cosmopolitan position has generated in the contemporary debate on global justice, I believe that clearing the ground of some of the confusions surrounding the cosmopolitan idea in this well-worked but untidy area is an important first step for moving the debate forward. If successful, my arguments will not only provide a defense of cosmopolitanism against nationalist and patriotic theorists, who reject the cosmopolitan view on account of its alleged inability to recognize particularist commitments, but it will also provide a response to those cosmopolitans who think that the cosmopolitan ideal of justice cannot include global equal concern because of the moral significance of such particularist commitments.

The challenge that has been issued is that cosmopolitanism cannot take seriously liberal nationalist and patriotic demands. In accepting this challenge, I have thus largely taken for granted the liberal nationalist and patriotic positions. But to the extent that the doctrine of liberal nationalism is sometimes rejected as an oxymoron on the ground that nationalism compromises the universal egalitarian commitments of liberalism, a successful reconciliation of liberal nationalism and cosmopolitanism will provide a defense of liberal nationalism against this serious objection. Similarly, to the extent that the patriotic ideal is sometimes rejected on the ground that it contradicts the idea of equal concern for individuals, a successful reconciliation of patriotism and cosmopolitan justice will remove this source of concern against patriotism. So although my motivating goal is to defend cosmopolitanism, the success of my project will provide a partial defense of the nationalist and patriotic ideals. For this reason, I believe that the discussion in this book will be of interest not just to cosmopolitans, but also to theorists seeking morally defensible forms of nationalism and patriotism.

The scope and focus

A complete account of justice has to cover two aspects of justice – "political" justice and "economic" justice (Beitz 1999b).[3] Political justice is concerned with protecting the political and civil liberties of persons. On a cosmopolitan conception of political justice, individuals are entitled to an equal range of political and civil rights regardless of where they happen to live. Economic justice is concerned with the equal distribution of material goods such as wealth, income, resources, and so on in a social scheme. On the cosmopolitan view, or at any rate on the interpretation of the cosmopolitan view that I will defend, principles of distributive justice ought to apply equally and impartially to all persons and ought not to be constrained by the borders of countries. It is worth noting that neither cosmopolitan political justice nor economic justice necessitates a world state or government. What cosmopolitan justice calls for fundamentally is the creation of the necessary forms of global institutions in which the basic rights and liberties of persons can be equally protected and secured and in which persons are treated with equal concern. But, as I will argue later (in chapters 4 and 5), the cosmopolitan commitments to protecting individual rights and liberties and to treating all individuals with equal concern do not depend on the existence of a world state. While

---

[3] The distinction between political justice and economic justice parallels the two International Covenants on Human Rights (the first pertaining to civil and political rights, the second to social and economic rights). John Rawls's first principle of justice covers political justice, and the second covers economic justice. For Rawls's principles of justice, see Rawls (1971, pp. 60–1).

cosmopolitan justice will require that we assess and evaluate our global institutions, it is ultimately a normative claim about how individuals are to be regarded and is not tied to the ideas of a world state and global citizenship.

The subject of this book is economic justice. This particular concern with economic justice does not imply that political justice is irrelevant for economic justice, nor does it mean that political justice is secondary to economic justice. On the contrary, the fact of frequent violations of basic political and civil rights in our world shows that it is hard to overstate the importance of defending and protecting these basic human rights. Moreover, given the interdependency of these two aspects of justice, a concern for one must involve a concern for the other. Yet much of the public concern with global justice in the West has tended to focus narrowly on political justice, and relatively little attention has been given to the question of social and economic justice. For instance, violations by nonliberal regimes of the civil and political rights of their own citizens receive more attention from the media, human rights groups and the general public in Western democracies than the persistent problem of global poverty.[4] Indeed, given that poverty afflicts many nonliberal countries, the lopsided focus of the West on political and civil rights to the relative neglect of economic and social rights has prompted leaders and even erstwhile local critics in many nonliberal countries to question the sincerity of the West's efforts to defend and promote human rights globally. Kishore Mahbubani, an outspoken critic of the idea of universal human rights, protests as follows:

[F]rom the point of view of many Third World citizens, human rights campaigns often have a bizarre quality. For many of them it looks something like this: They are hungry and diseased passengers on a leaky, overcrowded boat that is about to perish. The captain of the boat is often harsh, sometimes fairly and sometimes not. On the river banks stand a group of affluent, well-fed and well-intentioned onlookers. As soon as those onlookers witness a passenger being flogged or imprisoned or even deprived of his right to speak, they board the ship to intervene, protecting the passengers from the captain. But those passengers remain hungry and diseased. As soon as they try to swim to the banks into the arms of their benefactors, they are firmly returned to the boat, their primary sufferings unabated (Mahbubani 1998, p. 52).[5]

---

[4] For example, the noted human rights scholar Philip Alston worries that Amnesty International, while to be commended for its efforts, continues to "focus [only] on a very specific range of civil and political rights" (Alston 1990, p. 8). But note recent debate within Amnesty International regarding expansion of its mandate to cover economic and social rights.

[5] The so-called "Asian Values" opposition to human rights is partly a political reaction to this perceived Western cultural imperialism (e.g., Moody 1996, p. 189). See also Bell (2000) for more discussion on Asian Values and global justice.

Thus, as important as political justice is, a sincere commitment to a more just world must also seriously address the issue of global economic justice. This book hopes to contribute to the discussion on this aspect of global justice, though, of course, where political justice is relevant, it will be addressed (see, e.g., chapter 4). "Justice" henceforth, unless otherwise specified, will refer specifically to economic or distributive justice.[6]

It is a common view that any plausible political philosophy, as Ronald Dworkin has pointed out, must begin from the premise that citizens are entitled to equal respect and concern (e.g., Dworkin 1977, chap. 12). What equal respect and concern entails is, of course, open to contest, and different political philosophies may provide different answers to this question. But any defensible political philosophy must endorse this so-called "egalitarian plateau" (Dworkin 1977; also Kymlicka 1990a). Yet it is also a basic assumption of most political philosophies that principles of justice apply primarily to individuals in the context of a "closed society" (i.e., to citizens) rather than to individuals taken as such (e.g., Rawls 1971). The cosmopolitan ideal makes the stronger and more controversial (though defensible, as I hope to show) claim that the ideal of equal respect and concern applies globally to all individuals and not just to citizens within bounded groups.

But just as there are different interpretations of what it would mean to treat citizens with equal respect and concern, so will there be different cosmopolitan interpretations as to what it would mean to treat individuals as such with equal respect and concern. Depending on which conception of justice we begin with, we can arrive at different conceptions of cosmopolitan justice. Presumably, a cosmopolitan position derived from a Marxist perspective will be quite different from a cosmopolitan position with a libertarian starting point. But I will not be arguing for a particular starting point, i.e., a particular conception of justice, in this work. This will be outside the scope of the book. Rather, taking for granted a given conception of justice, I want to show why *that* understanding of justice has to take a cosmopolitan form, and must apply to individuals and not only to citizens in a single society. The theory of justice I assume here is that of egalitarian liberalism which holds that to treat persons with equal respect and concern involves going beyond respecting their basic liberties, and includes ensuring that they have equal access to resources or

---

[6] I discuss the problem of global "political" justice, specifically the tension between human rights protection and cultural toleration, in an earlier book, Tan (2000); also Tan (1998). The present work can be seen then as a supplement to my first book. One might say that my first book deals with the sorts of problems that Amnesty International is traditionally concerned with (i.e., civil and political rights), the present book with the sorts of problems that Oxfam is concerned with (i.e., economic and social rights).

goods with which to exercise these liberties (Rawls 1971; 1999b, p. 49). For the purpose of discussion, I will adopt John Rawls's egalitarian principle – that resulting social and economic inequalities between persons are acceptable only against a background of equal opportunity and a social arrangement in which the worst-off representative person is best off – as the distributive principle that we would want to apply globally. But accepting Rawls's principle is not necessary to the discussion to come. With minor adjustments in the appropriate areas, one could replace my Rawlsian model with other egalitarian liberal models, e.g., Ronald Dworkin's equality of resource model, without undermining my substantive arguments (Dworkin 2000, chap. 2). My starting claim is that if one accepts egalitarian liberalism in its general form, one ought also to be a cosmopolitan liberal.

To avoid misunderstanding, it is worth stressing, then, that a defense of global egalitarianism need not be understood as a defense of the view that all persons are to be equal in well-being or a defense of equality of outcome. Global egalitarianism, as a general ideal, holds that social and economic inequalities between persons across borders pose a moral concern; but different egalitarian theories will offer different approaches with respect to these inequalities. On the Rawlsian view that I am beginning with, the egalitarian requirement is that inequalities are permitted on the condition that there is fair equality of opportunity and that the worst-off persons benefit most under this arrangement, in spite of the inequalities, compared to alternative social arrangements. One of the aims of this work is to see how this ideal of equality can be globalized in light of nationalistic and patriotic claims. References to global equality in this work should be understood to refer to forms of social arrangements (i.e., institutions) under which resulting inequalities are mitigated and justified, rather than to an equality of outcome as such. The reader may wish to keep the Rawlsian "institutional" egalitarian approach in mind when references to global equality are made.

My focus on liberal justice may appear to some to be unhelpfully narrow, on the one hand, and too straightforward, on the other. It might be seen as narrow because most countries in the world today are not (even purportedly) liberal, and so an attempt to derive a global justice on liberal terms seems to leave too many countries out of the global dialogue on justice altogether. But this worry is somewhat misplaced. Given our special concern with global economic justice, paying special attention to what liberals should be committed to will in fact address the main protagonists to the debate. It is an empirical fact of our world that most of the affluent countries, the countries that would be asked to assume the burdens of distributive justice, and from whom resistance to attempts at equalizing resource and wealth distribution globally is most likely to come, are liberal countries. On the contrary, nonliberal countries, which tend to be less well-off economically, have historically been the advocates for greater global redistribution of wealth and resources.[7] So while the demands of political justice are directed primarily at nonliberal countries, the demands of economic justice are directed primarily at liberal countries.[8] A dialogue on the implications of liberal principles for global equality is thus not one which nonliberal developing countries would necessarily find exclusive, but is in fact one which they would actively encourage.

To be sure, nonliberal countries could resist the imposition of liberal political values on them even if they are amenable to the liberal egalitarian distributive ideal. While the failure on the part of liberal countries to take economic justice seriously has the effect of making the universal enforcement of liberal political values seem hypocritical at best and hostile at worst, correcting this failure need not necessarily have the effect of making liberal political values more acceptable to all nonliberal countries which might benefit from the increased global redistribution of wealth. They may still resent the global imposition of liberal values even as they stand to economically benefit from the global implementation of liberal distributive principles. Indeed, I will later suggest that globalizing liberal distributive principles can involve reforming traditional modes of redistributive practices and political practices within nonliberal countries. Nonliberal countries may thus raise the charge of cultural imperialism against attempts to globalize liberal ideas of justice, political or economic. For this reason, some liberals worry about extending liberal values beyond the borders of liberal states. I have tried to argue elsewhere that this concern can be assuaged (Tan 2000, chaps. 6 and 8); and I will argue later in this work (chapter 4) that it is consistent with the

---

[7] Nonliberal countries are the ones that are calling for reforms in global economic practices, more development assistance from rich countries, technological transfers, the recognition of development as a right, and so on. As a counter to the "Universal Declaration of Human Rights," the developing world has also proposed a "Universal Declaration of Human Responsibilities" that includes provisions for development assistance. If developing countries were to reject the debate within liberal terms, it would be that liberal egalitarianism was not egalitarian enough.

[8] So it is not the case that nonliberal countries are off the hook entirely – they are subject to liberal standards of political justice. This shows that a full commitment to cosmopolitan justice not only imposes conditions on nonliberal regimes (to reform their domestic political arrangements), but also imposes conditions on liberal societies to support global redistribution. If the burdens of justice are thus symmetrically assumed, the common perception that liberal justice is a form of cultural imperialism, a one-sided imposition "to cut nonwestern countries down to size," can be corrected. The phrase in quotes is from Lee Kuan Yew, cited in Huntington (1996, p. 197).

ideal of toleration to extend liberal commitments beyond liberal borders. What I am suggesting here is only that the criticism that liberal countries are hypocritical and inconsistent in implementing liberal values (as illustrated in the quote from Mahbubani) can be assuaged if liberals take global economic justice as seriously as they take political justice.[9]

On the other hand, this focus on liberalism may be seen to be too straightforward or a case of preaching to the converted because it is commonly thought that liberalism naturally entails the cosmopolitan perspective. After all, contemporary liberalism is an egalitarian political morality that takes individuals to be "self-originating sources of valid claims" (Rawls 1980, p. 543), and hence is thought to be consistent with the cosmopolitan principle that individuals are the ultimate units of moral worth and are entitled to equal consideration regardless of nationality or citizenship. Indeed, as I will recall later on, many contemporary liberal theorists have argued for the cosmopolitan idea (e.g., Beitz, Nussbaum, Pogge, Shue). But, in recent years, there has been an increased opposition from liberal theorists themselves to the cosmopolitan view. John Rawls himself has famously expressed a reluctance to endorse the cosmopolitan approach in his recent writings on international justice (1999a). More to the central concern of this book, among other liberals, this opposition is prompted in part by their endorsement of the doctrine of liberal nationalism. Besides increasing theoretical opposition to cosmopolitanism among liberals, there is also, in practice, widespread opposition to the demands of cosmopolitan justice on the part of many liberal states. Historically, many affluent liberal regimes in the real world have tended to resist proposals for greater global equality (by way of increased development assistance to developing countries, fairer trade laws, etc.).[10] So a special focus on the cosmopolitan commitments of liberals is neither too narrow nor too easy: it addresses the group we most urgently need to convince of the cosmopolitan ideal.

The cosmopolitan position has a rich philosophical history, and has been variously argued for by the Greeks, the Stoics, and the Enlightenment philosophers.[11] Although I shall make glancing references to some of these historical views, I am concerned primarily with the cosmopolitan position as it is understood and defended in contemporary political philosophy. My goal is to see what contemporary political philosophy can

[9] For one account of how cosmopolitanism is not imperialistic, see Catherine Lu (2000).
[10] Note, for instance, the rejection by the various US administrations of international proposals to further development aid (such as the resolutions on "The Right to Development" and "The Freedom from Hunger").
[11] For some historical accounts, see Kleingeld (1999); Nussbaum (2000c, 1996); Schlereth (1977); Toulmin (1992); and Waldron (forthcoming).

tell us about the problem of justice, nationalism, and patriotism in our current world.

Preliminary distinctions: types of cosmopolitanism

To anticipate the cosmopolitan position I shall be defending, it might be helpful to identify some common classifications of the cosmopolitan ideal in the contemporary literature, and then try to situate my account relative to these classifications. We can identify four overlapping cosmopolitan distinctions in recent writings on the subject. These distinctions will have to be further elaborated on in the chapters to follow, but let me make preliminary remarks about them here.

First is the distinction offered by Charles Beitz between cosmopolitanism as a moral ideal and cosmopolitanism as an institutional claim (1999b, p. 287). Second is the distinction introduced by Samuel Scheffler between cosmopolitanism as a claim about justice and cosmopolitanism as a claim about culture and individual social identity (2001, pp. 112–13). The first distinction, between cosmopolitanism as a moral ideal and cosmopolitanism as an institutional ideal, distinguishes, respectively, cosmopolitanism as a set of moral commitments that (morally) justifies the kinds of institutions we may impose on individuals, on the one hand, and, on the other, cosmopolitanism as a system of global institutions and organization that represents a world state of some sort. This is an important distinction because cosmopolitanism is commonly associated with a world state and thus often rejected on that basis. But, as a moral ideal, cosmopolitanism is not necessarily committed to the notion of a world state and global citizenship; rather it is premised on an account of the equal moral status of individuals, and the kinds of reasons, consequently, that must be given to them for the global arrangement that we expect them to share. To be sure, one might think that taking the cosmopolitan moral ideal seriously would require the creation of a world state, perhaps because any global institutional order short of a world state would fail to treat individuals as the ultimate units of equal moral worth irrespective of their particular nationality or citizenship. But this must be argued for, and indeed I will support the contrary view in the pages to follow. What is important to note now, however, is that a defense of cosmopolitanism is not straightaway a defense of world statism.

On the second distinction, cosmopolitanism as a claim about culture or identity denies that membership in a *particular* cultural community is constitutive of a person's social identity and a condition of her individual autonomy. Cosmopolitanism about justice, however, is concerned with quite a different subject, namely, the scope of justice. Cosmopolitanism about justice holds that social boundaries (for example, the boundary of nationality) do not impose "principled restrictions on the scope of an adequate conception of justice" (Scheffler 2001, p. 112). It rejects the view that principles of justice may be fundamentally limited by boundaries such as those defined by nationality or citizenship. In short, cosmopolitanism about culture is a thesis about the irrelevance of membership in particular cultures for personal identity formation and individual autonomy, whereas cosmopolitanism about justice is a thesis about the irrelevance of boundaries for the scope of justice considered at the fundamental level.

The third distinction worth noting is that between "weak" cosmopolitanism and "strong" cosmopolitanism. Following David Miller, this distinction captures the contrast between a conception of global justice that "respects the conditions that are universally necessary for human beings to lead minimally adequate lives" on the one side, and a conception of global justice that takes inequalities as such between persons across borders to be a concern of justice on the other (D. Miller 2000, p. 174; 1988, pp. 164–7). Weak cosmopolitanism is still a form of cosmopolitanism because it recognizes the equal moral worth of individuals; but it is a weak form of cosmopolitanism because it takes the respect for the equal moral standing of individuals to be discharged by ensuring that individuals are able to live minimally adequate lives (however that may be defined). Once this goal of ensuring minimal adequacy is achieved, any remaining inequality between persons is not a concern of cosmopolitan justice. Strong cosmopolitanism, in contrast, takes the ideal of equal concern for persons to entail a commitment to some form of global distributive equality, and will aim to regulate inequalities between persons, even above the threshold of minimal adequacy, against some appropriate distributive principle.

Finally, the fourth distinction is that between "extreme" cosmopolitanism and "moderate" cosmopolitanism (Scheffler 2001, pp. 115–19). Extreme cosmopolitanism takes cosmopolitan morality to be the sole and unifying source of value in the sense that all other moral commitments must be justified by reference to cosmopolitan principles or goals. Thus special concern, say, between compatriots is justified, on the extreme cosmopolitan account, on the ground that this special concern offers a useful division of moral labor for realizing cosmopolitan goals, or that this special concern is derived from certain fundamentally cosmopolitan commitments (e.g., the principle of reciprocity or fair play). On either explanation, however – whether patriotic concern is taken to be derivative or instrumental – extreme cosmopolitanism denies that patriotic concern has any moral worth that can be understood without reference to cosmopolitan principles. Extreme cosmopolitanism thus holds a reductive view of special concern and obligations. Moderate cosmopolitanism, on the other hand, acknowledges the normative independence of certain special obligations, and does not insist that cosmopolitan values are the only fundamental values by reference to which all other values must be justified. Moderate cosmopolitanism, thus, does not take a reductive view of special obligations, accepting that there may be moral reasons for certain kinds of special obligations that are not ultimately explainable in cosmopolitan terms. It recognizes that treating all special obligations as being worthy only because they promote, or are derived from, cosmopolitan principles, misrepresents and devalues some of the special ties and commitments that matter to people.

It is important not to run together the distinction between moderate and extreme cosmopolitanism on the one side, and between weak and strong cosmopolitanism on the other. The latter refers to the strength of the principles required by cosmopolitan justice; the former speaks to how these principles are to be philosophically understood in relation to other noncosmopolitan commitments. That is, one concerns the normative requirements of cosmopolitanism, the other concerns the moral conceptualization of these requirements. Thus understood, a weak moderate cosmopolitan is not a redundancy; nor is a strong moderate cosmopolitan a contradiction.

My focus in this work is on cosmopolitanism as a *moral* claim about the scope of *justice*. I am less directly concerned about cosmopolitanism as a claim about individual identity (though this may have, as we will see, indirect implications for how we are to think about justice for minority cultures), and I certainly am not attempting to defend a cosmopolitan system of law and government such as a world state. More substantially, I intend to support strong cosmopolitanism (about justice) as opposed to weak cosmopolitanism. That is, I will argue that cosmopolitan justice requires that we take equality between persons as such to be of concern. However, I reject extreme cosmopolitanism, and, consistent with the moderate cosmopolitan view, accept that patriotic ties and commitments have a certain normative independence and worth that are not fully reducible to cosmopolitan ideals. That is, I will argue that a cosmopolitan commitment to global distributive equality need not deny the independent moral significance of patriotism and shared nationality. In short, my goal is to propose a "strong" but "moderate" *moral* cosmopolitanism about *justice*.

The approach

I begin, in part I of the book, by providing some background to the cosmopolitan ideal in contemporary political philosophy. Chapter 2 explains the motivation for the cosmopolitan project by elaborating on the necessity for a cosmopolitan approach to global justice in light of the persistent problem of global poverty and the challenges of economic globalization. Chapter 3 presents a survey of different liberal accounts of cosmopolitan justice. This will serve the dual purpose of providing an overview of the contemporary discussion on cosmopolitan liberalism for readers unfamiliar with the topic, and laying out the liberal approach that I will adopt for my purpose, namely, the liberal theory of John Rawls. But because Rawls himself has rejected the cosmopolitan ideal in *The Law of Peoples* (Rawls 1999a), chapter 4 will attempt a defense of cosmopolitan justice against Rawls's concerns. The substantive aim of the first part of the book is to introduce the view that liberals ought also to be cosmopolitan liberals.

But the cosmopolitan aspiration of liberalism has recently come under siege by another idea from within liberalism itself, and this is the idea of liberal nationalism. The resurgence of nationalist movements the world over in the post-Cold War years has prompted a renewed interest among liberal theorists on the topic of nationalism, and liberals have suddenly found themselves having seriously to confront a problem that they had hitherto largely ignored in contemporary debates. One outcome of this grappling with nationalism is the growing acceptance among many prominent liberal theorists that, far from being contradictory ideals, liberalism and nationalism are mutually reinforcing ones. As we shall see, it is argued that as nationalism needs liberalism to tame it and to limit its manifestation within the bounds of justice, liberalism needs nationalism in order to successfully achieve its ends (Kymlicka 2001a; D. Miller 1995; Tamir 1992). For the latter reason, Yael Tamir suggests that "most liberals are liberal nationalists" (Tamir 1992, p. 139).

Yet it is a common perception that nationalism and cosmopolitanism are diametrically opposed ideals – nationalism is essentially a boundary-making enterprise whereas cosmopolitanism is a boundary-transcending aspiration. So, if liberals are liberal nationalists, they cannot also be cosmopolitan liberals. Or, conversely, as some opponents of liberal nationalism have charged, if liberals must be cosmopolitans, then the idea of liberal nationalism is an incoherent one, for it cannot support international egalitarianism. My conclusion in part I, that liberals must be cosmopolitans, is thus threatened by this recent development in contemporary liberal theory.

Part II of the book explores this alleged tension between nationalism and cosmopolitanism. In chapter 5, I argue that once the demands of cosmopolitan justice and the parameters of liberal nationalism are clarified, the perceived conflict between the two ideals disappears. Chapter 6 goes on to make the stronger claim that liberal nationalists must indeed be committed international egalitarians if they want their nationalist aspirations to be legitimate on liberal terms.

But cosmopolitanism is allegedly problematic for another, more general, reason. This is that the cosmopolitan principle of *impartial* concern for individuals regardless of nationality or citizenship seems to run against the commonsense view that people form special ties and attachments and that these ties and attachments may generate certain special claims among individuals so related. Among such ties and attachments are those based on shared nationality and citizenship, and it is commonly thought that, within certain limits, individuals have special obligations to their compatriots that have precedence over the needs of strangers. This belief that compatriots take priority is integral to the idea of patriotism, and the cosmopolitan ideal that distributive principles ought to ignore considerations of nationality or citizenship is thought to be inconsistent with the partiality of patriotism.

Some cosmopolitans might be tempted, in the face of this challenge, to reject the idea of patriotism altogether as groundless. But such a defense of cosmopolitanism risks being criticized as a *reductio ad absurdum*, for it seems to present cosmopolitan justice in terms that fly against commonsense understanding of the ties and commitments that matter to people. In chapter 7, I try to show how and why cosmopolitan justice does not preclude patriotic concern as such, though it can impose principled limitations on the exercise of such special concerns. That is, a defense of cosmopolitan justice need not make the controversial and counterintuitive claim that patriotic concern is altogether indefensible. It need only make the more modest and more easily defensible claim that any expression of patriotic concern must be limited against the demands of cosmopolitan justice. Chapters 8 and 9 go on to show that the common arguments for patriotic obligations do not subvert this subordination of partial concern to cosmopolitan justice. Chapter 8 focuses on arguments that appeal to the institutional and administrative aspects of shared *citizenship*, and tries to show that these arguments, to the degree that they do successfully ground patriotic obligations, must presuppose the priority of cosmopolitan justice. Chapter 9 focuses on the presumptive shared *nationality* that underpins common citizenship (as argued for by some nationalist theorists), and argues that this cultural argument for patriotic obligation does not undermine cosmopolitan justice. A central claim in part III is that from the perspective of cosmopolitan justice, what is relevant, ultimately, is not how patriotic commitments are rationally justified, but whether and how such commitments can be subordinated to the demands of justice. That is, cosmopolitan justice provides the constraints on patriotic commitments without treating these commitments as reducible to cosmopolitan principles.

Besides offering very *schematic* sketches of some global distributional schemes we could establish to realize the ends of global justice – in part to illustrate the discussion and in part to suggest the feasibility of my normative proposals – I do not provide a detailed *economic* theory of global distribution. Working out the practical and technical details of a just global distributive scheme is beyond the scope of this work, and certainly outside the domain of philosophy and best left to experts in other fields,[12] Nonetheless we can begin to seriously consider the practical details of the cosmopolitan alternative to our current global order only when we are convinced of the moral force and coherence of the cosmopolitan vision. Articulating and defending a plausible vision is the role and responsibility of philosophy, and it is the quest of this book to propose one plausible vision of global justice.

[12] For one economist's alternative to the present neoliberal global order, see DeMartino (2000).

Part I

Cosmopolitanism

2 The need for cosmopolitan justice

Introduction

The cosmopolitan idea of justice, as I am defending it, holds that distributive principles are not to be constrained or limited by state or national boundaries. In this chapter, I want to provide some reasons why we need a *cosmopolitan* conception of global distributive *justice*. I stress here both "justice" and "cosmopolitan" because I want to show both (a) why we need to talk about global *justice* as opposed to humanitarian assistance (and what is distinctive about the two), and (b) why global justice must be *cosmopolitan* in its conception.

My claims here will be largely familiar, I believe; but I think it is worth reminding ourselves of the relevance and importance of a cosmopolitan approach to global justice for the following reasons. First, some theorists argue, or at least give the impression, that we do not need principles of global distributive justice, but only principles of humanitarian assistance to tackle the problem of global poverty.[1] Yet focusing on humanitarian duties as opposed to justice does not fully locate the source of global poverty, and hence falls short of offering a complete solution to it. Second, the surging interest in the theory of nationalism in recent political philosophy has brought on a renewed skepticism concerning the cosmopolitan ideal. Because nationalism and cosmopolitanism are often thought to be mutually incompatible ideals, the resurgence of nationalist claims in the world has put the cosmopolitan idea on the defensive.[2] It is thus important, before we too hastily renounce the cosmopolitan view in favor of noncosmopolitan alternatives, that we remind ourselves of the motivation for the cosmopolitan ideal of justice and its objectives so as to better appreciate its appeal and to better evaluate the competing positions. I shall not attempt a defense of the cosmopolitan view against the nationalist and patriotic challenges here (a task that is left for later

---

[1] One notable recent proponent of this view is John Rawls (1999a, part III).

[2] See, e.g., D. Miller (1995, 1999b, 2000). The challenge of nationalism will be discussed in part II of the book.

20   Justice without Borders

chapters), but shall simply recollect why the cosmopolitan view is morally attractive and worthy of our attention.

The challenges

Almost half of the world's population of 6 billion people live on less than $2 a day, and 1.2 billion (a fifth of the world's population) live in absolute poverty on less than $1 a day. In developed countries, fewer than 5 percent of children under five are malnourished, whereas in poor countries as many as 50 percent are. Infant mortality rates vary across the world. In Sub-Saharan Africa, it is fifteen times that of developed countries. Life expectancy for people living in countries with "high human development" is on average 77.3 years; for those living in countries with "low human development" it is 52.6 years. Seventeen million people in developing countries die each year from curable infectious diseases; 800 million do not get enough food; and 500 million are chronically malnourished.[3]

Moral philosophers have, therefore, long argued that the debilitating poverty and its resultant human miseries described above are pressing universal concerns, and that it is a moral obligation, and not just a matter of charity, that affluent countries should do much more than they are currently doing to assist poorer ones (e.g., Singer 1972; Shue 1996; O'Neill 1986, 2000). The scope of our moral concern, they argue, should not cease suddenly at the borders of our country.

But the crucial question remains: what is the content of this obligation? Do we simply need an account of humanitarian assistance that can ensure that all individuals are able to meet their basic needs? Or do we need to go beyond humanitarianism and critically assess the distributive aspects of the global order against certain principles of justice? The battleline, so to speak, in the philosophical discourse on ethics and international relations has shifted over the past decade. The central dispute, it seems to me, is now no longer between those who think that the scope of our moral concern ought to extend beyond our borders and those who do not – few theorists today seriously urge that we have no humanitarian duties to foreigners absent some compelling national interests for helping. This important and positive shift in theorizing about international ethics is due in no small measure to the force and influence of the writings of O'Neill, Shue, and Singer among others.[4] The new debate, as I see it, concerns the content of this moral concern and whether it is grounded on justice.

[3] See World Bank (2000, pp. 3–4); also UNDP (2001, p. 144); and see UNDP (1997) for figures on deaths due to curable diseases.
[4] Garrett Hardin is an example of an antagonist in the old debate. See his famous "Lifeboat Ethics" (Hardin 1996). The writings of Shue and others were in large part responses to positions like those of Hardin's.

That is, the interesting dispute is now between those who think that we only have humanitarian duties to foreigners, and those who think that we have, in addition to humanitarian duties, duties of distributive justice.

Justice and ethics

As John Rawls puts it, "the primary subject of [social] justice is the basic structure of society, or more exactly, the way in which the major social institutions distribute fundamental rights and duties and determine the division of advantages from social cooperation" (1971, p. 7). A theory of global justice would thus not only be concerned with the particular actions and foreign policies of individual countries, but, very importantly and more fundamentally, it would be concerned also with the background global institutional context within which countries interact.

Duties of global justice would be, thus, more encompassing and would operate at a more fundamental level than what we may call duties of humanitarian assistance.[5] Instead of only demanding that richer states (through direct income transfers, technology transfers, relief funds, and so on) provide needy states with development aid and assistance, duties of justice call for standards by which to evaluate, and to correct if necessary, the "distributive aspects" (Rawls 1971, p. 9) of our global institutions. A crucial difference between humanitarian duties and justice is thus that of focus with respect to the root of the problem. One assesses the inter-action between agents (individuals and/or states), the other assesses the institutional context that shapes and determines "probabilistically" the nature of this interaction (Pogge 1986, p. 68). Adapting the standard (and stylized) distinction that ethics is mainly concerned with personal con-duct and decisions at the interactional level, whereas justice is concerned primarily with institutional arrangements (and their underlying norms and principles), we may say, for the purpose of a schematic contrast, that a theory of global *ethics* has an interactional focus while a theory of global *justice* has an institutional focus.[6]

---

[5] For a recent discussion on international relations that stresses this contrast, see Rawls (1999a, pp. 105ff).

[6] This contrast between ethics and justice follows roughly Dworkin and Rawls, among others. See also Pogge (1988a, pp. 227–31). But by an institutional focus, I mean some-thing quite different from what Pogge has called the "institutional approach" (Pogge 1992b). Pogge's institutional approach not only has an institutional *focus*, but it also has an institutional basis of *justification*. It holds that "[w]e are asked to be concerned about human rights violations [and deprivations] not simply insofar as they exist at all, but only insofar as they are produced by social institutions in which we are significant participants" (Pogge 1992b, p. 93). I do not share the justificatory claim in Pogge's approach that we have duties of justice *only* in so far as we are causally via our institutions responsible for injustices, but I will leave this point aside here. I discuss the relationship between the demands of justice and the fact of institutional practices below.

It is sometimes believed that a global ethic is sufficient to counter global poverty, that an appropriately defined and enforced duty of humanitarianism can adequately meet the subsistence and developmental needs of the worst-off individuals of the world. For example, it might be thought that if developed countries were to fulfill their official development assistance (ODA) obligations and contribute a determined percentage of their GNPs to underdeveloped ones (say the 0.7 percent as determined by the United Nations, or possibly more), then much of the poverty-related human suffering and misery in the world would be alleviated. For example, in *The Law of Peoples*, Rawls explicitly rejects the idea of global distributive justice, and demands only that better-off "peoples" offer assistance to societies that are burdened by unfavorable circumstances, with the aim not to reduce inequality as such (this is explicitly not the goal), but to ensure that "burdened societies," as he calls them, can attain the requisite level of economic and social development for sustaining well-ordered and decent institutions so as to be able to become members in good standing in "the Society of Peoples." As he writes, "once the duty of assistance is satisfied and all peoples have a working liberal or decent government, there is no reason to narrow the gap between rich and poor" (Rawls 1999a, p. 114). According to this view, if basic subsistence can be met through the duty of assistance, then there is no moral reason for worrying about global institutional inequalities as such.[7]

Now one might think that because Rawls grounds the duty of assistance on the goal of helping societies become members in good standing in the Society of Peoples, the duty of assistance is not really humanitarian in motivation. But I think there is also a humanitarian argument at work here. As Rawls puts it, it is a matter of decency that decent and liberal peoples protect basic rights, and this, presumably, can require assisting societies hobbled by unfavorable conditions, for basic rights are likely to be threatened under such conditions (cf. Rawls 1999a, p. 81). He also explicitly speaks of the importance of "mutual assistance among peoples in times of drought and famine" to ensure that individuals' basic needs are met (Rawls 1999a, p. 38), and this is clearly a humanitarian argument. Indeed, his point that under proper political leadership citizens of well-ordered societies can come to recognize that they have a duty to assist foreigners, and can be moved to do so not "by self-interest but by mutual concern for each other's way of life and culture" (Rawls 1999a, p. 113), can be read without distortion as a humanitarian argument.

It is worth stressing, then, that duties of humanitarian assistance as described above (and as understood by Rawls) are not mere charity; like

---

[7] This position is also found in D. Miller (1999a, 1999b).

duties of justice, they are morally required duties.[8] Indeed, implementing Rawls's duty of assistance will mark a vast improvement over the current global situation in which the basic needs of many people are not met and in which affluent countries see themselves to be acting charitably when they do provide assistance to the global needy. But duties of assistance differ from duties of justice in two interrelated ways: first, duties of humanitarian assistance are limited-term commitments with a definable goal (e.g., to raise developing societies to a level necessary for sustaining functioning well-ordered social institutions) as opposed to duties of justice that would aim to regulate inequalities between societies and hence be ongoing without a cut-off point. In other words, duties of assistance cease to be binding once all societies acquire a defined critical level of development, whereas duties of justice are ongoing, and apply so long as inequality persists between societies.[9] Second, and as already mentioned above, duties of humanitarian assistance do not, consequently, directly address the global structural context within which countries *interact*, whereas duties of justice apply directly to the background *structure*.[10] This difference in focus is the fundamental distinction between a humanitarian approach and a justice-based approach to global poverty, and, as we will see, lies at the crux of the question as to whether we should adopt a justice-based or a humanitarian approach.

This distinction between duties of humanitarianism and duties of justice is schematic, and it is important to note that, at the level of policy in the short term, both approaches may be in agreement. Yet the difference between humanitarianism and justice, as Rawls has made clear, is not merely a semantic one, but highlights for us the different and real ways of approaching and conceptualizing (and addressing in the long term) the questions of development, equality, and poverty. It also allows us to recognize the subtle point that those who defend a global ethic need not necessarily be defending some account of global distributive justice, and that those opposing global distributive justice need not be opposed to global ethics. It is thus a distinction that merits more attention than it has traditionally received in the literature on global ethics and justice in which the terms "global ethics" and "global justice" tend to be used quite interchangeably, thereby obscuring the important differences between those advocating for global justice and those for global ethics as such.

[8] Again, see Rawls (1999a, pp. 105ff).

[9] These particular differences are noted by Rawls (1999a, pp. 106–7).

[10] To illustrate the difference: the duty to provide relief for persons imperiled by natural disasters (such as famine or drought, to use Rawls's own examples) or recent warfare would be a clear example of a duty of assistance; duties of justice are akin to a permanent taxation scheme whereby transfer payments of some form are continuously provided to poorer countries from richer ones.

It seems that much of the earlier important philosophical writings on global poverty have tended to offer theories of global ethics rather than global justice (e.g., Singer 1972; Shue 1980). To be sure, far from being too lax, some of these writers argued for duties of assistance that far exceeded the prevailing modest expectation (let alone practice) of assistance; in fact, a common criticism of Singer is that his recommendations are far too demanding for ordinary people, a point to which I shall return in the next chapter. But the stress here had been on the sorts of duties that people (either individually or, more often, collectively as citizens) have *directly* towards foreigners who are less fortunate. The global institutional context within which countries interact and compete was largely ignored in these earlier accounts.[11]

Humanitarian concern can, of course, call for the creation of certain global institutional mechanisms in order to facilitate and coordinate the distribution of humanitarian aid. But institutions are seen on this account as merely instrumental for discharging ethical duties, and are not themselves the direct subject of concern.[12] So it is not that a humanitarian or ethics approach cannot address institutions and that only a justice approach may focus on institutions. The point here is that, on the ethical approach, institutions are seen only as means towards humanitarian goals and not themselves the basic source of injustices, and hence not in themselves the primary subject of critical evaluation.

In recent years, there has been a noticeable move towards an explicitly institutional focus in writings on global poverty and international relations.[13] For instance, Andrew Kuper objects to what he calls the "individualist 'practical ethics'" of Singer, and argues instead for a political philosophical approach to global poverty that focuses on institutions

---

[11] As mentioned, the distinction I note between ethics and justice is stylized, and neither Singer nor Shue ignored institutions altogether (e.g., Singer 1979, pp. 179–80; and Shue 1996, pp. 17–18), but their main focus was on individual actions (Singer) or US foreign policy (Shue).

[12] See, e.g., Shue (1988) for how institutions can "mediate" duties and provide a means of dividing our moral labor. Shue has in recent writings noted more explicitly the need to adopt an institutional focus, and how that is implicit in his earlier accounts of duties of assistance. See "Afterword" (Shue 1996 [1980], pp. 166ff). Singer's recent book, *One World*, also more explicitly pays attention to institutional causes of poverty. See Singer (2002, chap. 3).

[13] Charles Beitz was one of the first, if not the first, to apply a systematic justice consideration to the global context (1999a [1979]). See also Pogge (1989). This focus on institutions is a corollary to extending *political* philosophy, as opposed to *ethical* philosophy, to the world as a whole. Thus Beitz was also the first, to my knowledge, to provide a full-scale extension of contemporary political philosophy (which is generally conceived domestically) to the global context, when he attempted to show that Rawls's theory of justice (1971) should apply globally (Beitz 1999a [1979]). See Brilmayer (1990) for more arguments in favor of extending political philosophy to international relations.

as both the root cause and the site of reform in the fight against poverty
(Kuper 2002, p. 108). This shift in focus is due to the growing recognition that to effectively tackle global poverty and inequality we need
to address the global background context within which countries interact, and not simply take this context as a given. Some global egalitarians
have argued, for instance, that as long as the global economic structure
remains fundamentally capitalistic, citizens of developing and underdeveloped countries will continue to be exploited and deprived of their basic
human needs (e.g., Belsey 1992; Nielsen 1991; Kiely 1998, pp. 34–5).
Others, while less hostile in principle to a global free market, nonetheless
argue that we need to reexamine its basic operating assumptions – especially those pertaining to state sovereignty and resource ownership, fair
competition and free trade, and citizenship and legitimate entitlements
(e.g., Barry 1982; Beitz 1999a; DeMartino 2000; Pogge 1989, 1992a,
1992b; Sen 1999, chap. 5). Such differences in detail notwithstanding,
the general agreement is that the current global economic structure, and
the norms and principles that drive and regulate economic practices, pre-
cipitate and perpetuate gross inequality and poverty.[14]

It must be noted that the structural roots of global injustices go beyond
the economic sphere narrowly understood. Indeed, they permeate much
of the current global background context. Existing international law has
tended to work against disadvantaged and needy individuals, while maximizing the interests of the privileged and rich. For example, the principle
of state sovereignty which underpins international law grants legitimate
ownership of a country's resources to whatever regime happens to gain
power, and hence entitles it to transfer ownership of these resources to
multinational corporations, regardless of the implications of such transactions for citizens in the country.[15] Consider, also, more specifically international patent laws, as defined by the World Trade Organization (WTO)
agreement on Trade-Related Aspects of Intellectual Property Rights
(TRIPS), that tend to favor industrialized and research-oriented countries, but "pay scant attention to the knowledge of indigenous peoples.

---

[14] For a quick overview of the history of the current international economic order starting
from the establishment of the Bretton Woods institutions in 1944 (which include the
IMF and the World Bank, among others), and how that has impacted on poor countries,
see Alfred B. Zack-Williams et al., "The Long Road to Structural Adjustment" in Mohan
et al. (2000, pp. 14ff).

[15] Pogge refers to the case of the Abacha regime in Nigeria and its internationally sanctioned
dealings with foreign oil companies (Pogge 1999, p. 29; also Beitz 1979, pp. 148–9).
Pogge also notes how certain specific international conventions like the Law of the Sea
Convention were also tailored to suit the interests of dominant powers, as when the
proposed clause that seabed mining technologies be shared with developing countries
was voted down by industrialized countries (Pogge 1999; also 1998).

These laws ignore cultural diversity in the way innovations are created and shared – *and diversity in views on what can and should be owned*, from plant varieties to human life" (UNDP 1999, p. 6, my stress).[16]

Structural global inequalities are reflected and perpetuated not only abstractly in terms of global norms and principles, but at a more concrete level as well through the policies and method of operation of specific established institutional bodies. Global financial organizations like the International Monetary Fund (IMF), the World Bank, the G-8, and the World Trade Organization have been criticized in recent years, and not unduly, for their policies of structural adjustments, conditionalities on loans, their emphasis on economic liberalization and open trade, and their autocratic decision-making procedures. As current events have shown us, such policies, though carried out ostensibly in the name of assisting developing countries, have tended to kill the patient while entrenching the interests of big businesses and affluent countries.[17]

Given the institutional and structural bases of global poverty and inequality, an interactional focus alone does not go far enough. Even if all countries were to fulfill their obligations of humanitarian assistance (which is, of course, far from being the case in our world),[18] we would still not get to the root of poverty and inequality if we did not address the global economic structure that brings about and, importantly, legitimizes global maldistribution in the first place. An institutional focus, in contrast, will call on us to reevaluate the guiding norms and assumptions of the global economic arena, including our current definition of "what justly belongs to a country" (Barry 1982, p. 248). The significance of such a "paradigm shift" in how we understand ownership and entitlements is not to be underestimated. To take just one example, we will no longer say that rich countries are required to assist poorer ones by giving away

---

[16] Thus the complicated roles of the WTO and international patent laws have set the price of AIDS medication beyond the budget of most African countries (see, e.g., Palast 2000). The force of public opinion has since forced drug companies and their supporting governments to relent. Indeed, the readiness of the US and Canadian governments to override patent rights during the anthrax scare in the fall of 2001 shows a certain double standard in these governments' defense of the patent rights of pharmaceuticals. For one report, see *The New York Times*, Sunday, 21 October 2001, section 3, 1.

[17] The many failures and flaws of the IMF and World Bank are well documented. For some examples, see Cornia et al. (1987), Mohan et al. (2000), Kiely (1998, pp. 33–4), DeMartino (2000), Sachs (1998), and Stiglitz (2002). For a brief history of the development of the structural adjustment program, see Milward (2000).

[18] To see how far most developed countries are from meeting their ODA obligations, see UNDP (2000, table 14, p. 190). The figures show a general decrease in ODA contributions between 1990 and 1999. During this time, ODA contributions fell from 0.34 percent of GNP to 0.24 percent on average for members of the Development Assistance Committee (DAC).

some of their resources but that such transfers are required to restore an antecedently unjust resource allocation.[19]

At the concrete level of institutional design, an institutional approach will clearly demand that we reexamine the objectives, policy goals, and decision-making procedures of organizations such as the IMF, the World Bank, and the WTO. It is well known, for example, that there is the problem of who decides for the IMF, and who speaks for IMF client states. Reforming the IMF would call for democratizing its decision-making procedures and making them public, holding decision-makers accountable, and increasing and improving participation in decision-making for the citizens of countries participating in IMF programs.[20] Also the institutional approach can call for the creation of new institutional distributive schemes and agencies to facilitate and coordinate, say, a global taxation program (like the Tobin Tax), or to regulate the activities of multinational corporations and currency speculators.[21]

Thus, as we need principles of justice to regulate the domestic basic structure whose impact on people's lives is "profound and present from the start" (Rawls 1971, p. 7), so there is a *global* basic structure, whose impact on people's lives is as profound and present, that must likewise be regulated.[22] This domestic–global basic structure analogy is obviously not airtight. There is no global government, nor are international economic norms and regulations as fully enforceable as those in domestic society. But what is relevant here is that global institutions and practices do significantly constrain and shape a person's life chances and options. Like the domestic basic structure, global institutions define people's various social positions, and consequently their expectations in life (cf. Rawls 1971, p. 7). As described above, the practices and operating assumptions of the global economic arena determine a person's chances and goals just

---

[19] There are many other claims we now take for granted that will be challenged by a paradigm shift in our idea of ownership. Concerning the debt crisis, we will focus not so much on the debt that is to be forgiven, but say that since "1984 there has been a real transfer of resources – and wealth – from poorer countries to richer ones" in the form of interest payments (O'Cleireacain 1990, p. 3). See also cases of offering assistance to needy countries to help their poor purchase medication: we will not say that such acts are charitable acts but that a combination of unfair patent and trade laws have put needed medication out of the poor's reach in the first place.

[20] See, e.g., Palley (1999, p. 108), and Stiglitz (2002).

[21] The Tobin Tax was proposed by the economist James Tobin in 1978. The proposal was for a worldwide tax on all foreign exchange transactions. Such a tax would reduce exchange rate volatility; more to our present concern, the tax would also generate revenue for international development programs. Given the size of the daily net turnover in foreign exchange (approximately $1.8 trillion per day presently), some economists predict that a modest 0.01 percent to 0.5 percent tax on each foreign exchange transaction could generate $150–300 billion annually.

[22] See Buchanan (2000) and Jones (1999a, pp. 7–8).

as profoundly and presently as domestic economic practices and norms – indeed more so, one could say, given the more pronounced global disparity in wealth, and the more limited degree of mobility between countries than between classes within most liberal countries. A mere accident of birth, such as a person's citizenship (that is made morally salient by the norms regulating citizenship, migration, state sovereignty, global trade, and territorial and resource ownership), can drastically affect her entire life expectations and opportunities.[23] The absence of a world government notwithstanding, Beitz notes that there is, nonetheless, an informal "constitutional structure of the world economy" to which considerations of justice can and must apply for the same reasons they apply to our domestic constitutional structure (Beitz 1999a, p. 149; Buchanan 2000, pp. 705–9).

So there is a global basic structure in the significant sense that the global institutional context serves as the framework against which people's legitimate entitlements are identified and pursued. And as we need principles to regulate the "deep" inequalities present in the basic structure in domestic society (Rawls 1971, p. 7), so we need principles to regulate these pervasive inequalities in the global basic structure. Rawls writes that "[t]he role of institutions that belong to the basic structure is to secure just background conditions against which the actions of individuals and associations take place. Unless this structure is appropriately regulated and adjusted, an initially just social process will eventually cease to be just, however free and fair particular transactions may look when viewed by themselves" (1996 [1993], p. 266). This comment, I am arguing, applies equally to the global context.

None of the above should be thought to imply that humanitarian assistance and aid are unimportant or superfluous – to the contrary. But on the institutional view, humanitarian assistance treats only the symptoms of global poverty, and as important and urgent as this is, it does not address the basic cause of poverty – that of structural injustice. To use the words of Andrew Belsey, "of course, in the face of hunger and starvation both development aid and relief aid should be provided, but the *cause* of justice is best served by *a structural transformation* away from unequal global relations based on exploitation and towards equality based on recognition of common similar needs" (Belsey 1992, pp. 47–8, my stress; also Kuper

---

[23] While our increasingly global mobility may seem to make one's citizenship at birth irrelevant, this privilege of movement and migration belongs primarily to those who are relatively well-off to start with. As the UNDP notes, "The global, professional elite faces low borders, but billions of others find borders as high as ever" (UNDP 2000, p. 32, box 1.2).

2002). It would be absurd to think that a *complete* account of justice is concerned *only* with the justness of institutions while remaining completely indifferent about interaction at the inter-state or -personal level. Indeed, the reason why political philosophers are concerned about institutions is that institutions, as mentioned, determine "probabilistically" the nature of individual interaction and conduct (Pogge 1986; Rawls 1971, p. 7). My claim here, thus, is that a focus on interaction alone, while important, is not sufficient. Or, to put it conversely, it is not that an institutional focus is sufficient, but that it is necessary. We need more than a theory of global ethics; we need, as well, a theory of global justice. We need, in other words, principles of justice to assess the background conditions against which individuals and associations interact.

Thus Rawls's recent refusal to propose a global distributive principle is rather striking once we acknowledge the existence of a global basic structure and the importance of regulating that structure by some distributive principle (see Beitz 2000; Buchanan 2000). I will turn more closely to Rawls's international theory in a later chapter. What I want to suggest here is that the difference between humanitarian duties and duties of justice does not concern only the issues of a target level of development and a cut-off point (as Rawls points out), but also the more fundamental one of identifying what rightly belongs to whom. And this is a question of the basic structure, of how that structure allocates benefits and burdens, which in turn is a question that can only be addressed fully by a theory of justice, and not just by a theory of humanitarian ethics.

Globalization and justice

An institutional focus has become all the more urgent in the context of what is normally called globalization. Globalization, in popular parlance, is often employed as a convenient catch-all phrase for a wide range of social phenomena, from multiculturalism and migration, to the universalization of ideals such as human rights. But, for our purpose, we will take globalization to mean specifically *economic* globalization, which describes the process of increasing integration and interdependency of national economies, the increasing mobility of capital and labor across traditional boundaries, the creation of new global markets and products (i.e., financial markets), and the creation of international organs and regulations to facilitate and to govern these interactions (e.g., the WTO). In short, economic globalization refers to the existence, or at least the approximation, of a single encompassing global economy in which all individuals of the world are participants.

The concept and reach of globalization, and its implications for international relations, are currently much debated topics (e.g., Mayall 1998). Some have argued that globalization has spelt the end of the nation state as traditionally conceived; others respond that this claim is exaggerated, and that states have reacted in a variety of ways to counter the threat of globalization to national sovereignty (e.g., Sassen 1998; Clark 1999, p. 144). Some have said, to borrow Roland Rich's apt phrase, that globalization has brought about "a single global space" (Woodiwiss 1999, p. 28); yet others have argued that the idea of an all-encompassing single global economy that has rendered national economic boundaries redundant is rather overstated (e.g., Hirst and Thompson 2000).

But I will leave these important questions aside. What is relevant here, and less open to dispute, is that the advent of new technologies, new global markets, and new global economic institutions and regulations in recent decades has brought about a global economic space in which decisions and actions in one corner of the world have rapid and profound effects in another. Increased capital mobility, modern communications and transportation, increased interdependency through increasing trade, and new global regulations established to facilitate this interdependency have rendered traditionally domestic fiscal policies like interest rates, social policies like tax laws and labor laws, and domestic agricultural subsidies, as well as domestic social patterns like consumption habits, into global ones with worldwide reverberations.[24] So while the phenomenon of economic interdependency itself is not unique to the modern era, what is unusual about globalization is the intensity and profundity of this interdependency, the presence of newly established global markets, and the new global regulations and institutions that it has engendered (UNDP 1999, p. 30, box 1.1).[25] If it is an exaggeration to say that we now live in a single global economy, it is only a slight one. There is a single global economy in the morally relevant sense, in that we are, more so than ever, vulnerable to each other's economic decisions and activities irrespective of borders. Our earlier claim that there exists a basic global structure is all the more salient in the face of globalization.

But it is also indisputable that the benefits and burdens of economic globalization are far from being equitably distributed and shared among the world's population. In spite of globalization (or perhaps because of it, some would say), global income disparity has widened rather than

---

[24] See, e.g., the essays in Kiely and Marfleet (1998); also Stiglitz (2002), pp. 9–10.

[25] For some statistical evidence of the increasing interdependency brought on by globalization, see figures in UNDP (2000, p. 25). For instance, world exports increased from 17 percent of GDP to 21 percent from the 1970s to 1990s; and foreign direct investment increased seven times in real terms over the same period.

narrowed. Between 1960 and 1997, the difference in income between the top 20 percent of the world's population (in the richest countries) and the bottom 20 percent has risen from thirty to seventy-four times (UNDP 1998, p. 36). Moreover, the need to stay globally competitive has forced some developing countries to cut back on public subsidies, liberalize their domestic markets, and undercut labor standards, resulting in increased inequality within these countries.[26]

There is no need to describe in detail the commonly offered reasons why globalization has failed the world's needy.[27] Economic globalization is currently driven along by the principles of laissez-faire capitalism, or neoliberalism as it is commonly called. As some economists have observed, "neo-liberalism might be better conceived as the, often unspoken, ideology that has actively promoted, and to a certain degree, created globalisation" (Mohan et al. 2000 p. 21; pp. 19ff). But the operating assumptions of neoliberalism – that fewer trade barriers and tariffs, more global competition, greater liberalization of local economies, greater export specialization, and elimination of domestic subsidies, will eventually narrow the gulf between the north and the south – have so far proven to be wide of the mark.[28] As long as the global economic playing field remains uneven, free competition is never truly free, nor, importantly, fair. In the context of this structural inequality, neoliberal economic principles cannot meet the basic human and developmental needs of the world's poorest sector. When the agricultural and industrial sectors in developing countries are not ready to compete in a global open market, forcing developing countries to open their borders to foreign competition renders local industries and farmers vulnerable to the more established industries and heavily subsidized farm products from developed countries. Rather than combating poverty, neoliberalism in the context of inequality results in job losses and productivity declines (Stiglitz 2002, p. 17; Kiely 1998, p. 33). As George F. DeMartino writes: "In the face of growing inequalities, the economic growth that neoliberalism promises may fail to deliver the improvement in economic welfare with which it is typically associated, and may interfere with the achievement of important political and economic rights and opportunities"

[26] Other examples of this disparity: export earnings have increased in developed countries, but declined in many underdeveloped ones. The top fifth of the world's richest countries account for 82 percent of total global exports, the bottom fifth barely more than 1 percent (UNDP 2000, pp. 30–1). On the domestic front, inequality has risen in countries like China and Chile which have recently liberalized their economies (UNDP 1996, p. 59, box 2.7).

[27] See DeMartino (2000) for one in-depth account.

[28] For some discussions of these assumptions and their failures see L. Miller (1994) and DeMartino (2000). See also essays in Kiely and Marfleet (1998).

(DeMartino 2000, p. 11). Not surprisingly, we are thus witnessing a growing public opposition, over the past few years, against economic globalization and its supporting global agencies.[29]

But much of this popular opposition has been presented as an outright rejection of globalization, and as such, to my mind, oversimplifies and misses the crux of the problem. What is at issue is not the process of globalization as such, but the *terms* of globalization, in particular the neoliberal ideology underpinning and driving it. After all, greater economic interdependency per se (e.g., more trade, intellectual exchanges, etc.), if properly regulated, could benefit individuals in developing countries. But, more to the point, it is not even clear if economic globalization is a process that poor countries may opt out of (if that is even possible) without suffering even greater economic costs.[30] As the Oxfam report, *Rigged Rules and Double Standards*, tells us, it is not trade per se that is the problem for development, but the *rigged rules* of trade.[31] While developing countries are asked to open their domestic markets to foreign competition in the name of free trade (and its alleged benefits), they are at the same time denied access to markets in the developed world due to high tariffs and stiff competition from heavily subsidized products (especially in sectors such as agriculture) in developed countries. Oxfam notes that these tariffs and subsidies cost poor countries $100 billion a year, twice what they get in foreign aid. Trade which allows goods to flow only in one direction is hardly free trade. The implications of this one-sided trade are immense. It is reported that were Africa, east Asia, south Asia and Latin America each to increase their share of world exports merely by 1 percent, the gain in the income of countries in these continents would take 128 million people out of poverty.[32]

What is needed, in other words, is not an outright renunciation of global economic interdependency, but better global principles and institutions to regulate this interdependency, and to distribute the burdens and benefits of globalization more equitably. The current failings of

[29] See the mass protests in Seattle, Washington, Windsor, and Prague during meetings of global agencies and world leaders associated with globalization. To be sure not all protestors were motivated by global concerns. Labor unions in some developed countries object to globalization on the ground that freer trade will transfer jobs to countries with poor labor standards and low wages. But the protest is nonetheless against economic globalization even if inspired by domestic and parochial concerns.
[30] In fact, many third-world observers have questioned the strategy and even the sincerity of the anti-globalization demonstrations. In their view, more trade is not necessarily bad. What is objectionable is *unfair* trade rather than free trade as such. See Kitching (2001) for one discussion.
[31] See Oxfam (2002).   [32] See Oxfam (2002).

globalization are due more to the lack of proper governance of economic integration than the fact of integration itself. We need to challenge the neoliberal ideology currently guiding the globalization process, an ideology which we have tended to take for granted, and consider possible alternatives. To claim that we have either to accept *neoliberal* globalization or the worse fate of economic isolation, a claim often made by defenders of neoliberal globalism, is to present a false dilemma. There is the third option of globalization on different, more egalitarian, terms.

So, more now than ever, we need standards by which to assess the global economic structure given its increasingly profound and pervasive effects on the world's population. As the global context comes more to resemble a single economic scheme, the more urgently we need to subject it to the considerations of justice.

I think something like the above was underscored by David Hume when he wrote that if "several distinct societies maintain a kind of intercourse for mutual convenience and advantage, the boundary of justice still grows larger, in proportion to the largeness of men's view, and the force of their mutual connexions" (Hume 1977 [1751], sec. III, part I, 153). As our economic practices take on a global scope, so too should our moral considerations and considerations of justice. Economic globalization must be followed by normative globalization, so to speak. As the marketplace becomes one without borders, so should justice be without borders.

In short, globalization, the greater economic "mutual connexion," has made the question of global justice all the more pertinent. But it is important not to misunderstand the relationship between justice and institutions. The fact of shared institutional arrangements makes justice consideration necessary; but the existence of such arrangements is *not* a prerequisite for justice. In other words, while a shared social scheme is a sufficient condition for justice, it is not a necessary one. On the contrary, that our actions or omissions have moral implications for others is a sufficient condition for others to make demands of justice on us (e.g., Jones 1999a, pp. 10–11). Broadly following Kant, considerations of justice come into being the moment our actions have implications for each other. As Kant writes: "The concept of Right, insofar as it is related to an obligation corresponding to it (i.e., the moral concept of Right), has to do, *first*, only with the external and indeed practical relation of one person to another, *insofar as their actions, as facts, can have (direct or indirect) influence on each other*" (Kant 1993 [1797], p. 56, my stress; also pp. 62ff). To put it differently, so long as others are vulnerable to our actions or omissions, we have certain duties of justice towards them.[33] The fact that we share "the earth's surface" in common (Kant 1991 [1795], p. 106) is sufficient for making justice considerations relevant. The requirements of justice are prior to institutional arrangements, and justice can call on us to establish common institutions where none existed if doing so is necessary to facilitate its ends.

Some philosophers have argued the reverse, or so their arguments imply, claiming that a shared institutional scheme is a necessary condition for justice, and so absent such a scheme, the circumstances of justice do not obtain (e.g., Walzer 1983, 1995). Extending this line of reasoning to the global context, they go on to argue that because the world does not admit of a common social cooperative scheme, the notion of global justice is, therefore, vacuous. Let me make two quick comments here. First, as this section has tried to show, the advent of globalization has rendered this argument obsolete. Charles Beitz, over two decades ago, observed that "the world is not made up of self-sufficient states. States participate in complex international economic, political and cultural relationships that suggest the existence of a global scheme of cooperation" (Beitz 1999a, pp. 143–4). His observation holds even more truth today in this era of economic globalization.

Second, and more fundamentally, the argument's starting premise, that justice depends on the prior existence of a social scheme, mistakenly inverts the relationship between justice and institutions. Justice aims to guide and regulate our existing institutions, and can call on us to create new ones if necessary. That is, justice constrains and informs our institutional arrangements, not the other way around. To tie justice to existing institutional schemes would be to misconstrue and pervert the purpose of justice; it would be to treat justice as a mirror of society, when in fact we should want justice to be society's critic, to borrow Ronald Dworkin's powerful imagery (Dworkin 1984). In a time in which individuals' economic decisions and policies are felt worldwide it has become all the more crucial for there to be some governing principles to fairly regulate our basic global structure. The fact of globalization underscores the importance of adopting a justice-based approach to global poverty – the shared global economic space we are all moving towards, like our

---

[33] If we accept the democratic principle that individuals who are vulnerable with respect to each other's decisions should have some say in the making of these decisions, then the fact that some of our decisions and practices have significant implications for individuals outside the borders of our country means that the idea of democracy cannot be confined to the nation state. David Held thus proposes the idea of cosmopolitan democracy, where decisions over matters with global implications (e.g., emissions of greenhouse gases) are to be decided (in some way or another) globally (e.g., Held 1993). I discuss the problem of nationalism and global democracy elsewhere (Tan, forthcoming). On protecting the vulnerable, see Goodin (1985).

domestic economic sphere, needs to be regulated by certain distributive principles.

The peoples of the earth have thus entered in varying degrees into a universal community, and it has developed to the point where a violation of rights in *one* part of the world is felt *everywhere*. The idea of a cosmopolitan right is therefore not fantastic and overstrained; it is a necessary complement to the unwritten code of political and international right, transforming it into a universal right of humanity (Kant 1991, pp. 107–8).

If these words were applicable when Kant wrote his famous 1795 essay, "Perpetual Peace," they are all the more so today.

Individuals versus states

We have seen why we need a theory of global *justice*, and not simply a doctrine of humanitarian assistance, if we are serious about alleviating global poverty. And the fact of globalization has made this institutional focus of justice all the more poignant.

But why should this call for a *cosmopolitan* theory of justice? The cosmopolitan view in its most basic form, to recall, holds that the individual is the ultimate unit of moral worth, and entitled to equal consideration regardless of contingencies like nationality and citizenship. But why should global justice be conceived from this egalitarian *individualist* perspective? Why not have an account of global justice that regards nations or, more precisely, states (though I will use these two terms interchangeably here) as the basic moral units?[34] Why not take international justice to cover literally inter*national* justice, rather than justice between individuals?[35] That is, why not base international justice on a "morality of states" (Beitz 1999a, part II), rather than on a morality of individuals as the cosmopolitan view demands?

The "morality of states" doctrine has indeed dominated international relations theory for much of its modern history – the ideal of state sovereignty and its corollary principle of nonintervention were historically premised on this ideal of the moral primacy of states. On this view, states are regarded as moral agents in themselves and are the basic moral

[34] I do not mean to imply that the distinction between states and nations is insignificant – far from it. My aim here is to show why a theory of global justice has to take the individual as the *basic* unit of moral concern as opposed to collectivities like states or nations.

[35] Thus some theorists have said – to draw out the contrast between a "morality of state" account and an individualist one – that we may understand an inter*national* theory of justice to be concerned mainly with distribution between nations or states; whereas a *global* theory of justice, properly understood, regards the world as a single unit and is concerned with distribution between individuals (e.g., Van Parijs 1995, pp. 227–8).

subjects for the purpose of global justice. But the "morality of states" doctrine, thus understood, does not withstand close scrutiny. It appears to suggest that global justice is simply domestic justice writ large, except that states or nations are now the basic moral agents instead of individuals. But such a (Hegelian) metaphysical conception of the state (or of a collectivity at any level of organization) as a moral person magnified, while once dominant in international relations theory, is quickly becoming outmoded. As Beitz argues, "[u]nless some independent sense can be given to the idea of the state as a moral agent, this view [that states are moral subjects in themselves] cannot be very persuasive" (Beitz 1999a [1979] p. 76; also Kymlicka 1989, pp. 241–4). A cosmopolitan approach, which takes individuals to be morally ultimate in both domestic and global contexts, seems more plausible and consistent with our modern sensibilities about the moral relationship between individuals and collectivities. We are moved by global injustices in the first place because of the pain and suffering inflicted on *individuals* rather than by the suffering of some abstract collectivity like the state. Thus, a theory of international justice that treats states as basic in this way shoulders considerable metaphysical burdens of proof.

There is, however, a different way of understanding the "morality of states" doctrine that need not invoke contentious metaphysical claims about the moral status of institutions like states. One could agree with the basic cosmopolitan idea that the individual is basic, yet think that, for individual well-being to be best realized, international relations should treat states *as if* they are the basic moral units. According to this revised "morality of states" view, an individualist focus is unnecessary for the purpose of distributive justice. Once distributive equality is ensured between states, equality between individuals (globally and within states) will follow. Perhaps we could call this position "methodological statism." No implausible group metaphysics is implied in this view. Individuals are what ultimately matters, morally speaking; it is just that as a method, as a strategy, for meeting the needs and interests of individuals, treating states as the basic units of concern is the best way to proceed.

But the belief that equality between *individuals* can follow upon equality between *states* is too optimistic. Domestic distribution can be ordered quite independently of how well a country as a whole is faring. Increases in the GNPs of developing countries during the past decade have not been necessarily accompanied by equal improvement in standards of living for all citizens of these countries; in fact, in many cases, economic growth has been accompanied by increased domestic inequality. It is also generally the case that women and children tend to be among the poorest social groups in underdeveloped countries, and it is surely not plausible to say that the reason for this is solely global inequality, and nothing at all to do with domestic social arrangements and wealth distribution practices. Methodological statism, in short, does not often achieve its stated goal of improving individual lives.

I do not deny that global maldistribution is much to be blamed for domestic maldistribution; my point here is that eradicating inequality between states without paying attention to *individual* well-being is not sufficient. It is myopic to think that the problems of global injustices that impact on individuals can be settled by focusing solely on justice between *states*. A "morality of states" approach does not go far enough if we are interested in improving individual lives. A complete theory of global justice must also transcend national boundaries, and provide a standard by which the domestic political and economic arrangements within states may be assessed. Taking states to be the basic units in international justice precludes this possibility, for by treating states as the basic moral subjects it puts their domestic institutions outside the scope of global justice.[36]

But the more important reason for adopting an individualist rather than a statist focus is that in treating states as the basic units of consideration, we risk providing the wrong answer to the all-important and familiar question "Equality with respect to what?" If states are *treated as* the basic distributive subjects, one might be too easily tempted to conclude quickly that what we need to equalize is per capita GNP. After all, GNP is common to all states, and hence a good indicator of how well each state as an entity is faring relative to others. In fact, until recently, development economists were fundamentally focused on raising the per capita GNP of poor countries (see Sen 1999). But, as has become clear, this focus on raising per capita GNP is highly one-sided and does not give us a clear enough picture of how human beings are in fact faring within countries. The development economist, Mahbub Ul-Haq, has dubbed this the "missing people" syndrome in development planning (Ul-Haq 1995, pp. 4–6).

A focus on individuals, which is central to the cosmopolitan idea, on the other hand, would remind us that what is basic to human well-being is not just a country's aggregate income, but its people's level of education, its literacy rate, its degree of gender equality, its infant mortality rate, the life

---

[36] It might be objected at this point that cosmopolitan justice is too demanding because it can impose conditions on domestic distributive schemes as well. Nonliberals could, perhaps, find cosmopolitan constraints on their domestic matters hard to accept. But my argument will be that these conditions are nonetheless consistent with and required by a liberal moral framework. I will discuss this matter in chapter 4. See also Tan (2000, chaps. 2 and 6).

expectancy of its population, its healthcare standards, and so on. These individual-based indices give us a better overall picture of comparative human development than the state-centered one based on increases in GNP (cf. Sen 1999, e.g., pp. 3, 5–6, 14, 290–1; Ul-Haq 1995, pp. 4–6).[37] Focusing on states as the basic subjects thus obscures the sorts of things we should seek to equalize if we are truly concerned about individual well-being. Retaining an individualistic as opposed to state-centric focus better directs us to the kinds of goods and services and programs that really do matter to individuals.

It is due to such a state-centric approach, I would conjecture, that structural adjustment programs of the IMF have failed miserably in terms of human development. IMF structural adjustments aim to bolster a country's faltering economy, but largely neglect the social and economic costs of these programs to certain groups of *individuals*, penalizing more often than not the most needy individuals (e.g., those who rely on government subsidies for food, fuel, etc.).[38] A cosmopolitan focus will keep the well-being of individuals firmly in our sight, and not overlook the human and social dimension to development, and hence be less prone to making such costly mistakes. We will be able to maintain a better perspective on the ends and means of development – that of individual well-being – if we do not "take as our basic objective just the maximisation of income or wealth" of nations taken as aggregate wholes (see Sen 1999, p. 14).

It is important that the individualist approach to justice should not be misunderstood. A cosmopolitan global justice differs from the state-centric one (both the metaphysical and methodological versions) in that it does not treat states as (if they are) the ultimate units of concern. The "morality of states" view (in both forms) thinks that an explicitly state-centered focus is sufficient. The cosmopolitan view, in contrast, insists that we need to maintain an individualistic focus. But this does not mean that cosmopolitans have to deny the moral worth or standing of states, nor does it mean that they always must reject all state-based claims to equality. On the contrary, the cosmopolitan view can accept that states can be useful channels for distributing certain goods and resources to individuals, and that membership in a state can itself be an important individual good, as we shall see (part III). But unlike the state-centric approach, the cosmopolitan approach does not claim that looking at how

[37] By "individual-based" I do not mean that these are goods that are never produced and enjoyed socially or even nationally. I mean simply that these are goods that are crucial for an individual person's well-being.

[38] It has been reported that women and children, as well as the urban and rural poor, are most adversely affected by the IMF programs (e.g., Cornia et al. 1987; Zack-Williams 2000, p. 66).

states fare with respect to each other is all that is required for global justice, and that the needs of individuals will be naturally taken care of in this way. The cosmopolitan view is not that states are irrelevant, but that they should not be seen as the primary subjects for the purpose of global justice. A literally inter*national* theory of justice does not go far enough.

Conclusion

I have tried to show that if we are serious about tackling the problem of global poverty, we need to develop a cosmopolitan conception of global justice. The scale and nature of global poverty demand not just that we look at how countries operate and interact within our current global (economic) structure, but that we reexamine that very structure, and the norms and principles that underwrite it. And if we are concerned ultimately with how individuals are faring in our world, the individualist focus of a cosmopolitan approach can better tell us the sorts of resources and goods that should be the concern of global justice, and also remind us that we need to look both at intranational and international distributive arrangements. I have, of course, not offered here a particular concep-tion of cosmopolitan global justice. My goal here has been to show that we have compelling and urgent moral reasons to take seriously the cos-mopolitan idea of justice. In the next chapter, I will survey some of the more important approaches to cosmopolitan justice.

3   Conceptions of cosmopolitan justice: a survey

As mentioned, the cosmopolitan idea of justice takes individuals to be entitled to equal moral consideration regardless of contingencies like their nationality or citizenship, among other factors. But there are different conceptions of this idea of justice, that is, different understandings of what it means to treat individuals with equal consideration, and I wish to quickly survey some of the more prominent ones in the contemporary literature. This critical survey of the literature will provide us with some useful background material for the rest of the work. Importantly, laying out the different conceptions of cosmopolitan justice will also allow me to identify and clarify the conception that I will adopt and against which we can fix ideas for the chapters to come. The comparative study here will be intentionally general, highlighting only the broad differences in approaches and goals of these theories. But this, I hope, will serve to satisfy my goal of showing how these different theories of cosmopolitan justice connect with the different ways of thinking about justice in current political philosophy.

I first discuss some well-known cosmopolitan approaches to the problem of global poverty: a utilitarian approach (e.g., Singer 1972), a rights-based approach (Shue 1996), and a duty-based approach (O'Neill 1986, 1991). I will suggest that neither the utilitarian nor the duty-based approach necessarily gives us a theory of global justice that is distinct from a rights-based theory of justice. Utilitarianism, to be acceptable, has to work into its theoretical edifice some account of rights; and a duty-based theory, while useful as a reminder to us to take duties seriously, does not offer a conceptual alternative to a rights-based theory.

One of the most influential contemporary rights-based theories of justice is that of John Rawls (1971). It is thus not surprising that the important systematic attempts at developing a theory of global justice are in fact attempts at extending Rawls's theory of justice to the global context. So after surveying the different broad approaches, I review how Rawls's theory, originally conceived for domestic society, has been developed (by others) into a cosmopolitan theory of justice. I will propose that Rawls's theory provides an appropriate starting point for thinking about global justice.

Utilitarian and deontological approaches

At a fundamental level, cosmopolitans can disagree over the ethical starting points of cosmopolitan justice. The debate between utilitarian and deontological ethical theories is one common case of such a disagreement. Utilitarianism is a consequentialist moral theory in that it takes the good of an act or a rule to be right or wrong by reference to the consequences of so acting or complying with such a rule. Specifically, act utilitarianism holds that the right act is that which brings about the greatest amount of good for the greatest number of people, and the good to be maximized is understood to be happiness, normally defined in terms of a net gain of pleasure over pain. Deontological theories, on the other hand, while not entirely dismissive of consequences, do not define the right solely in terms of the good.[1] Rather, the rightness or wrongness of an act is to be determined by reference to some defined set of actions or duties, the conformity with which need not necessarily maximize the good. To contrast deontological theories with utilitarian theories, we may call, following Onora O'Neill, the former action-based theories and the latter consequence-based theories (O'Neill 2000, chap. 1). Given the deep differences between these conceptions of right actions, it might seem on first glance that, depending on whether one adopts a utilitarian or a deontologist starting position, one would be led to a distinctive theory of global justice.

A famous utilitarian approach to global inequality is found in Peter Singer's "Famine, Affluence and Morality" (1972). Singer's defense of famine relief in particular, and humanitarian assistance in general, begins from the premise that "if it is in our power to prevent something bad from happening, without thereby sacrificing anything of comparable moral importance, we ought morally to do it" (Singer 1972, p. 407). Given the great disparity in wealth and well-being in the world's population, Singer concludes that well-off citizens in affluent countries ought to assist the poor and needy of the world up to the point of marginal utility, that is, up to the point where the agent has been reduced "to very near the material circumstances of" the recipients of assistance (1972, p. 411). Singer recognizes that this recommendation, although morally correct, may be

[1] As Rawls notes, "All ethical doctrines worth our attention take consequences into account in judging rightness. One which did not would simply be irrational, crazy" (Rawls 1971, p. 30).

too demanding for the average citizen in affluent countries. He thus proposes a more modest version of the principle, which says that we ought to contribute to humanitarian relief only up to the point where we would have to sacrifice "something morally significant" (1972, p. 411). Yet even this modest principle goes far beyond our current norm and practice of humanitarian assistance, and will still call for considerable sacrifices on the part of the rich, as Singer himself notes.

But rather than being the source of its strength, this moral austerity of utilitarianism (and consequentialism in general) is generally regarded by Singer's critics as its chief weakness. That utilitarianism requires individuals to act always in the name of maximizing the good seems to leave out any conceptual space for heroic and saintly acts, and this, instead of commending it to us as a worthy moral theory, is more often seen to be its *reductio ad absurdum*. A moral theory that leaves no space for supererogatory acts of these sorts flies in the face of commonsense morality. Thus James S. Fishkin faults Singer for failing to recognize (and place) reasonable limits on the moral duties that can be expected of individuals (Fishkin 1982, chap. 9). Even Singer's modest principle of humanitarianism, says Fishkin, requires individual sacrifices that go beyond the call of duty given the scale of global poverty and the great maldistribution of the world's wealth (1982, p. 72).

On a related point, and this is its most serious flaw in the eyes of those who take human rights seriously, utilitarianism fails to recognize "the distinction between persons," and hence can in principle require "the violation of the liberty of the few . . . [for] the greater good shared by many" (Rawls 1971, p. 27). That is, utilitarianism can permit, and even require, the sacrifice of the human rights of some, if this sacrifice in fact brings about a net gain in pleasure for all. And this seems to blatantly violate what most of us would regard as basic to any plausible theory of global justice.

Utilitarianism, to be plausible, must therefore be refined so as to be able to accommodate and make space for what Samuel Scheffler has called "agent-centred prerogatives" that would allow individuals to act in ways that do not necessarily maximize overall good, and "agent-centred restrictions" that prohibit the performance of good-maximizing actions if these involve violations of individual rights (Scheffler 1982; 1988, pp. 4–6).[2] The purpose of an ethical theory is to provide, among other things, an account of how individuals may live the good life; an ethical theory that gives no room for the pursuit of individual good (because it

---

[2] He also calls these agent-centered permissions and agent-centered constraints, respectively.

always demands good-maximizing actions) seems to be pointless.[3] And given that "[r]ights are on their way to becoming the accepted international currency of moral, and especially political debate" (Sumner 1987, p. vii), an ethical theory that does not endorse some notion of individual rights (as constraints to good-maximizing actions) will have little appeal for most people. These concerns are largely acknowledged by utilitarians themselves.

One way (among others) utilitarians can attempt to accommodate agent-centered prerogatives and agent-centered restrictions is by adopting an institutional approach. On the institutional approach, utilitarian principles do not apply directly to personal interaction and conduct, but to institutions and their rules. As Charles Jones points out, instead of saying that individuals ought always to act so as to maximize overall good, an institutional approach requires only that we put in place certain institutionalized rules and principles that, when complied with, would in the long run maximize overall good (C. Jones 1999a, pp. 36–7). And because we accept that agent-centered prerogatives are morally significant, we will work into our institutional schemes sufficient space for such personal pursuits. So within the constraints of these institutional rules, people will have room to exercise their agent-centered prerogatives. Indeed, it could be argued that a social or institutional scheme that does not allow for personal pursuits is, in the long run, contrary to the general good (e.g., Railton 1993; Scheffler 1988, chap. 11).

Applying this "institutionalized" utilitarian reasoning to global poverty, the conclusion now would not be that individuals ought to contribute up to the point where they are nearly reduced to the material level of those they are helping, or even to the point where they have to sacrifice something of moral significance (if we wish to stick to the modest principle), but that they ought to establish and support global institutional schemes that can coordinate and apportion such duties in a way that appropriately balances good-maximization and agent-centered prerogatives (e.g., C. Jones 1999a, pp. 38–9). An implicit premise here, of course, is that the rich can support and comply with these institutional rules without having to renounce their prerogative to pursue their personal projects

---

[3] Singer, in his later thoughts on this subject, acknowledges the tension between private morality (as required by utilitarian principles) and public morality (as determined by what the public in general can reasonably accept). He thus allows for some personal discretion concerning how one ought to contribute to assistance: "No figure should be advocated as a rigid minimum or maximum," although those earning more than average income in affluent countries ought to set 10 per cent of the income as the minimum expected contribution (Singer 1979, pp. 180–1). But other than setting an admittedly "arbitrary" bench-mark (1979, p. 181), Singer does not provide principled guidance on how to accommodate such agent-centered prerogatives consistent with utilitarian reasoning.

and ideas of the good, and hence institutionalization can avoid the problem of "overdemandingness" (Jones 1999a). And given the increasing absolute global wealth on the one side, and increasing global inequality on the other, this is not an unreasonable assumption.[4]

Similarly, utilitarians can plausibly build into their institutional scheme some notion of human rights, thereby securing the appropriate agent-centered restrictions. The reasoning here could be that respecting the "side constraints" (to borrow Nozick's term) imposed by individual rights provides the best "indirect" strategy for maximizing the good (e.g., Sumner 1987). Bentham's famous proclamation that rights are "nonsense upon stilts" should be remembered as an attack specifically on the notion of *natural* rights (e.g., rights as God-given or transcendental in some similar way, and thus foundational), not as an attack on the concept of rights per se, and is entirely consistent with modern-day utilitarian attempts to construct a theory of rights at a nonfoundational level.[5] Thus utilitarians can accept a rights-focused theory of global justice, even though rights (for them) are not foundational to, but derivative of, utilitarian reasoning.[6]

---

[4] Recall the figures in chapter 2.

[5] This remark by Bentham is commonly appealed to as evidence that the tradition of human rights clearly cannot be accepted by utilitarians. But this claim commits a category mistake: it confuses the justification of rights with the existence of rights. Few contemporary (secular) human rights defenders support the natural rights doctrine; when they speak of rights, they have in mind the sorts of liberties Bentham and Mill defended (though not just restricted to these).

[6] Sumner's indirect strategy consequentialism is entirely consistent with an institutional approach (though it is, of course, not restricted to it). The difference between rule consequentialism (the traditional way of saving consequentialism from the above objections) and indirect consequentialism is that rule consequentialism takes the right action to be that which conforms to certain rules, independently of the expected outcome in a particular instance. Indirect strategy, however, still takes the right act to be that of maximizing the good (Sumner 1987, pp. 185-6). It is just that it adopts an indirect approach to good maximization (e.g., by respecting individual rights) rather than a direct one (that would involve, say, a rights violation) because "[y]ou are . . . likely to do better [given human tendency to err in judgments, complications on the ground, etc.] if you pre-commit yourself to observe some relatively simple rules even when doing so seems, on the best evidence available to you, to disserve your basic goal" (1987, pp. 195-7). The important difference between these two approaches is that while rule consequentialism will call an act that respects the appropriate (utility-maximizing) rule a *right* one even though in that particular instance it results in more harm than good, an indirect strategist will say in such a case that the act is *wrong* from the point of view of good maximization, but nonetheless the right thing to do for *that* particular agent (given her moral dispositions, precommitments, etc.). Indirect strategists thus avoid the charge faced by rule consequentialism that it is "an unstable compromise" (Scanlon 1982, p. 103). Unlike rule consequentialism, which would be hard pressed to explain why a particular instance of rule following is the right action even if it inflicts great pain, indirect strategy readily admits that it is wrong but nonetheless the *best* course of action for the agent in question.

Whether such attempts at institutionalizing utilitarianism are, in the end, consistent with the core of utilitarian reasoning is a much debated point in contemporary moral philosophy.[7] But I will leave this issue to one side, for even if it is true that utilitarianism can deflect some of the charges against it by adopting an institutional approach, yet once utilitarianism requires institutions to accommodate agent-centered restrictions and prerogatives, it is no longer obvious how utilitarianism, conceived as a *theory of justice*, is distinct from a deontological theory of justice. A utilitarian can as well defend Rawls's two principles of justice as can a Kantian (albeit for different reasons), as Rawls himself notes in *Political Liberalism* (1996, pp. 170 and 211n).[8] On a utilitarian view, individual rights can be as morally forceful and inviolable (within the limits we normally accept), even if they are not foundational, as they would be in, say, a Kantian approach. From the point of view of global justice, then, utilitarianism is distinctive only at the level of (meta)ethical justification – it need not necessarily give us a unique set of principles of justice, but only a distinctive way of justifying these principles. This point is consistent with Kymlicka's observation that "[m]odern utilitarianism, despite its radical heritage, no longer defines a distinctive political position" (Kymlicka 1990a, p. 47).

One may think that, under indirect consequentialism, "rights" are not absolute but defeasible, as Sumner acknowledges – although the threshold for such violations will be set very high if the strategy is properly internalized (1987, p. 196) – and so cannot really qualify as rights properly speaking. But, in fact, it is not clear if deontologists themselves should want to take as absolutist a stance such as that expressed in the slogan "let justice be done even if the heavens fall." Rawls himself notes that individual liberties may have to be suspended in times of emergency for the purpose of public security: "[c]itizens may affirm the law [which holds that sufficient evidence for conviction is that weapons are found in the defendant's property] as the lesser of two evils, resigning themselves to the fact that while they may be held guilty for things they have not done, the risks to liberty on any other course would be worse" (Rawls 1971, p. 242). As noted earlier, Rawls writes that it would be "crazy" to say that consequences are never relevant in moral deliberation (1971, p. 30).

[7] Charles Jones has rightly argued that the "overdemandingness" of utilitarianism can be tempered by channeling our duties through institutions. But, in the end, he rejects utilitarianism as a basis for global justice because he thinks it cannot provide a satisfactory justification for human rights (1999a, pp. 48–9). My discussion above implies that this prognosis is hasty. Moreover, following Rawls's lead, I will say that rejecting out of hand different ethical perspectives that could potentially converge on our preferred model of justice (a rights-based one in this case) undermines the quest for an overlapping consensus with respect to justice (Rawls 1996, pp. 154ff).

[8] What Rawls objects to are utilitarian *principles of justice* – that is principles that say our social institutions should aim at maximizing "the net balance of satisfaction" for all individuals in society taken as a whole (1971, p. 22). In *Political Liberalism*, he took pains to stress that there is no reason why utilitarian *ethical* reasoning could not be part of an overlapping consensus affirming the idea of justice as fairness. Of course, this point is different from his stipulation that utilitarianism, or Kantianism, or any comprehensive moral theory for that matter, should not be offered publicly as *the* justification for justice as fairness (e.g., 1996, p. 162).

In sum, presented as an individual action-guiding principle, the utilitarian approach to global poverty faces the standard worries – that it is too demanding and does not account for the separation of persons (i.e., has no concept of rights). One way of circumventing these worries is for utilitarians to adopt an institutional focus. Utilitarian principles now are seen to apply to the question of institutional design rather than that of individual conduct. Here, the institutional rules could try to make room for agent-centered prerogatives and restrictions (i.e., the permissiveness of individual pursuits and the respect for individual rights) on the grounds that such prerogatives and constraints provide the best strategy for achieving the best results. But once utilitarianism becomes a theory of justice that permits these prerogatives and respects these restrictions, it is no longer distinguishable from deontological (or rights-based) theories of justice.

Basic rights

As we noted above, human rights have become the main moral "currency" in both domestic and international political discourse (Sumner 1987). We normally take social and political arrangements to be just or unjust depending necessarily (though not sufficiently) on how they promote and protect certain rights.[9] Most contemporary cosmopolitan conceptions of justice would thus defend some notion of rights, if not at the foundational level, then at some other level of their theoretical edifice.

A theory of justice that takes rights to be indispensable can be said to be deontological, as opposed to utilitarian, in that it does not take the justness of institutions to be solely dependent on whether they maximize happiness for society taken as an aggregate whole. But, as noted above, this does not mean that such a theory of justice can be affirmed only by those beginning from a deontological ethical framework, let alone only by those affirming the doctrine of natural rights. I pointed out that modern-day utilitarians acknowledge the moral relevance of rights, and accept that for utilitarianism to remain a plausible moral theory, utilitarianism must be shown to be conceptually capable of incorporating a robust notion of rights into its theoretical edifice. As said earlier, whether this can be done successfully or not is a separate question (which we would have to confront were our project here that of evaluating different ethical theories); what is of relevance here is that a rights-affirming theory of justice need not have appeal only to those who endorse non-consequentialist ethical theories.

[9] As Rawls puts it, "[h]uman rights set a necessary, though not sufficient, standard for the decency of domestic political and social institutions" (1999a, p. 80).

Thus different "comprehensive moral doctrines" (to borrow Rawls's phrase) can converge on an account of justice with rights at its core, albeit for different reasons. Given the range of ways of affirming the moral force of rights, cosmopolitans can proceed to develop a rights-based account of justice without having to engage in the distracting and possibly futile debate over the metaphysical foundations of rights (Donnelly 1989, pp. 22–3). Indeed some theorists say that there is in fact a global "overlapping consensus" regarding, at least, certain basic human rights, and point to the various international declarations and covenants on rights as evidence of this claim.[10] The idea of rights can therefore serve as a suitable starting point for working out a theory of global justice.[11]

Rights can be understood as legitimate entitlements and claims that people have against relevant others (Raz 1986, p. 166; Sumner 1987; Shue 1996, p. 14; Donnelly 1989, pp. 9–10; Ignatieff 2001). Because rights are claims against others, they generate correlative duties (on pertinent others) to avoid violating these claims, to protect these claims, and to assist those already deprived of these claims (Shue 1996, pp. 52–3, 59–60; Nickel 1993). As the description of duties above indicates, the popular distinction between negative and positive rights – i.e., rights that require only *negative* duties of forbearance, and rights that require *positive* action on the part of others – is incoherent, as Henry Shue points out. All rights, properly understood, entail the three corresponding duties of non-violation, protection, and assistance (Shue 1996, pp. 52–3), and these duties involve both forbearance and positive actions.[12]

---

[10] For a global overlapping consensus on rights see Rawls (1999a). For the latter point, see Donnelly (1989, p. 23). Rawls's list of rights is, however, too thin, some critics have argued. I will return to this point in chapter 4.

[11] It is of course true that, beyond certain basic rights, there remains much global disagreement over the universality of other rights that lie in what Daniel A. Bell (1996) refers to as "the grey area" of human rights – including many listed in the "Universal Declaration," like the rights to free expression and association, and the right to democratic participation, on the one side; and the right to development, and to social and economic equality, on the other side. Taking the existing global consensus on rights as fixed once and for all is, therefore, *not* going to be very progressive; the idea, rather, is to take this as a provisional fixed point from which to develop a more inclusive account of basic rights. In a sense, the aim of this work is to show how a commitment to the basic right to subsistence (the agreed fixed point) leads to a commitment to the right to a certain level of social and economic equality (the more contentious claim).

[12] Shue's aim is to show that the distinction between civil and political rights as pertaining only to negative rights, and social and economic rights as pertaining to positive rights, is mistaken because civil and political rights generate positive duties as well. So if we take civil and political rights seriously (as liberals do), including accepting (even if implicitly) that we have positive duties towards these rights, then the traditional view that economic and social rights are too demanding *because* they impose positive duties is ill-founded.

Shue's rights-based approach to global justice is one well-known alternative to a utilitarian approach. Shue identifies two basic rights: the right to security and the right to subsistence. These rights are *basic* because their enjoyment is necessary for the enjoyment of other rights. Basic rights thus constitute people's "minimum reasonable demand upon the rest of humanity" (1996, pp. 18ff). Whatever else one wants, and whatever other rights one might be entitled to, one needs first to achieve a basic level of subsistence, and to enjoy a certain level of security. Without either subsistence and security, all other rights and pursuits are practically unrealizable.

Concerning the basic right to subsistence, Shue concedes that there will be some disagreement as to when exactly subsistence is fully met. But he rightly points out that it is a brute fact of our world that many people are plainly not meeting their most basic subsistence needs. A sincere commitment to the basic right of subsistence will thus call on us not only to refrain from depriving others of their subsistence, but also to protect them from such deprivations, and to assist them when they are deprived. While Shue's main focus was on the foreign policies of nations (specifically of the US), he also noted that the protection and promotion of subsistence rights can also demand certain global institutional reforms as well as new cooperative schemes to facilitate the duties corresponding to these rights. As he notes, "That a right involves a rationally justified demand for social guarantees against standard threats means, in effect, that relevant other people have a duty to create, if they do not exist, or, if they do, to preserve effective institutions for the enjoyment of what people have rights to enjoy" (Shue 1996, p. 17, pp. 59–60).

The basic right to subsistence can, therefore, serve as the basic standard against which we may assess the distributive aspects of our global institutions: these are just to the extent that they are able to protect and promote the right of individuals to basic subsistence. On this basis, Shue objects to John Rawls's theory of justice on account of the ranking of its two principles. Recall that, for Rawls, the first principle concerning political and civil rights is lexically prior to the second principle that covers social and economic rights.[13] Shue thinks that this ranking incorrectly privileges political justice and does not provide a "floor" below which people may not fall (Shue 1996, pp. 127–9). But this is a criticism that Rawls can avoid. Reasoning about ideal justice takes place in a context in which it is assumed that people's basic needs are already met, and the principal issue is how resources and goods are to be distributed among people above this threshold of decent subsistence. As Rawls makes it

---

[13] Rawls's two principles will be described below.

clearer in *Political Liberalism*, the basic right to subsistence must be pre-supposed in the first principle: "the first principle covering the equal basic rights and liberties may easily be preceded by a lexically prior principle requiring that citizens' basic needs be met, at least insofar as their being met is necessary for citizens to understand and to be able fruitfully to exercise those rights and liberties. Certainly any such principle must be assumed in applying the first principle" (1996 [1993], p. 7).[14] That is, for principles of justice to be worth contemplating in the first place, people must first have their most basic physical needs satisfied. Shue's basic right to subsistence is presupposed in Rawls's theory; indeed one may say that it constitutes one of the unstated circumstances of justice.

Where Rawls falls short, so I shall later claim, is not in the way he has ranked his principles (for, as said, the ranking does not itself deny the importance of basic subsistence rights), but in his denial that the second principle (i.e., the distributive principle) applies in the global context. The important question remains, in spite of Rawls's endorsement of basic subsistence rights in his theory, as to whether the global moral objective should be just that of meeting basic needs, or whether it should also promote equality between persons. But before examining how a rights approach may move beyond subsistence to equality, let me turn to an advertised alternative to a rights approach: that which takes duty rather than rights to be fundamental to justice.

Duties versus rights

Some cosmopolitans oppose a rights-based approach to global justice, preferring instead a more explicitly duty-based one.[15] In international politics, this preference for duties over rights is reflected in the proposal of some countries for a "Universal Declaration of Human Responsibili-ties" to complement the "Universal Declaration of Human Rights." One of the arguments for this proposal is that a one-sided emphasis on rights has caused us to downplay the fact that rights come with corresponding obligations, including certain economic and social ones. So as a political or strategic complement to the politics of rights, a declaration of respon-sibilities has the important function of reminding us of our various duties vis-à-vis these rights, and of the need to specify, allocate, and enforce these duties. Moreover, such a declaration can help repair the rift between

---

[14] This background acceptance of Shue's theory of basic rights is openly acknowledged in *The Law of Peoples*, where Rawls notes that "the rational exercise of all liberties . . . implies having general all purpose economic means" as covered by the basic rights to subsistence (1999a, p. 65 n1).

[15] I use "duty" and "obligation" interchangeably here.

"liberal" rights-supporting countries and "nonliberal" rights-suspicious countries. A language of rights supplemented by a strong vocabulary of duties can assuage the common suspicion that rights are mere political tools serving the interests of certain dominant (liberal) countries.

But it is also sometimes argued that a duty-based approach offers a different, and indeed superior, conceptual perspective on global justice. According to Onora O'Neill, rights theories are conceptually incomplete because while rights must have certain corresponding duties, not all rights correspond to an assigned duty-bearer and a clearly specified duty. Unlike the right not to be, say, physically harmed, which has both an assigned duty-bearer and a clearly specified duty (i.e., *all* others have the duty *not to physically harm* another), the right to assistance, generally, does not correspond to duties that are as clearly defined and assigned. To say that the poor of the world have a right to some relief does not tell us *who* has the obligation to provide this relief, and the *nature and extent* of this obligation. It does not help to say that all others have a duty to provide assistance – we still need to know against which *particular* individuals and/or institutions the claim to assistance can be made and enforced. Without a clearly assigned agent who is to bear responsibility for a right that another has, that right cannot in effect be claimed.

Such rights are what O'Neill calls "manifesto rights" (adopting Feinberg's term); they are "empty rights" in that they generate only *imperfect* obligations on the part of others.[16] Unlike perfect obligations, for example the obligation not to physically assault another, in which who the agent is, what her exact responsibility is, and to whom she owes this responsibility are clearly defined, obligations are imperfect when no particular agent has been identified, when there is considerable latitude on how an agent may discharge the obligation, and when it is unspecified for whom the act is to be performed. While perfect obligations are assigned and specified, and hence claimable and in principle enforceable, "[i]mperfect obligations can be enforced only when they are institutionalized in ways that specify *for whom* the obligation is to be performed" (O'Neill 1989, p. 191).[17] So unless we first assign and specify the duties correlative to manifesto rights, these rights cannot be claimed; the

---

[16] Joel Feinberg speaks about a "special 'manifesto sense' of 'right', in which a right need not be correlated with another's duty." But his purpose is not to disparage the idea of rights, but to show how an unfulfilled need gives one a rightful claim even if there is *no one in particular* against whom to make that claim (Feinberg 1980, p. 153).

[17] In the literature, imperfect duties are duties that fail to meet *any one* of the following criteria: (a) a specific claimant (to whom it is owed); (b) has a specified content (what is to be done); and (c) is demandable and morally enforceable (how it can be done). See O'Neill (1989, pp. 224–5). I discuss imperfect and perfect duties, and the implications of this Kantian distinction for global justice, in Tan (1997).

"*enforcement* [of these rights] cannot be discussed or take place until obligations are identified and allocated" (1989, p. 296, emphasis mine). In short, on a purely rights-based approach, certain rights, especially the sort of concern to us here, "drop out of sight." As O'Neill puts it:

unless the obligation to provide food to each claimant is actually allocated to specified agents and agencies, this "right" will provide meagre pickings. The hungry *know* that they have a problem. What would change their prospects would be to know that it was others' problem too, and that specified others have an obligation to provide them with food. Unless obligations to feed the hungry are a matter of allocated justice rather than indeterminate beneficence, a so-called "right to food", and the other "rights" of the poor, will only be "manifesto" rights (1986, p. 101).

Unlike a rights approach, a duty-based approach, O'Neill argues, will draw the attention of advocates of justice to the imperfect duties corresponding to manifesto rights, and remind them of the need to institutionalize these duties, in order to assign, specify, and enforce them (1989, p. 199). Concerning global distributive justice, a duty-based approach will press on us, concerned moral agents, the importance of fostering and establishing the appropriate global institutional scheme by which to specify and allocate our duties of justice to the poor, and through which, subsequently, their rights to subsistence can be meaningfully claimed.

O'Neill raises important points about the relationship between a meaningful right and an enforceable duty, and her emphasis on institutionalizing the duties of justice so as to make them assignable, specific, and demandable is an extremely important one. But O'Neill's characterization of the rights-based approach as theoretically inadequate seems to run together a strategic question with a conceptual one (see Pogge 1992c).[18] As acknowledged by both sides of the debate, there are duties corresponding to rights. But that certain duties are vague and unassigned does not alone tell us that their corresponding rights are empty or meaningless. On the contrary, these "manifesto" rights, should we take rights seriously, will generate the more *immediate* obligation on us to assign and specify their correlative duties. The assignment and enforcement of duties (corresponding to rights) is a strategic question, and the fact that the concept of rights does not immediately give us an answer to this question does not mean that it is conceptually inadequate. Unless O'Neill thinks that such an assignment of imperfect duties is a practical impossibility (which she will not, given her own claims about allocating and assigning such duties), it is not clear why this initial nonspecificity of duties counts as

[18] Here I expand on arguments made previously in Tan (1995).

an argument against a rights-based approach to justice.[19] In other words, the problem of imperfect duties corresponding to some basic rights does not show that the concept of rights is inadequate to the task of global justice; it only shows that advocates of rights have to be aware that there are important practical steps that need to be taken in order to facilitate the performance of duties corresponding to these rights.

In fact, a rights approach can provide us with a *justificatory* basis for making "perfect," so to speak, our imperfect duties. Rights generate corresponding obligations, including, as mentioned, the immediate obligation to establish some means by which these obligations can be assigned and enforced. So a rights approach is not only consistent with the claim that some duties have to be assigned before their corresponding rights can be claimed; more significantly, it also provides a moral argument for assigning these duties. Taking rights seriously would require taking their corresponding duties seriously, and this can include making institutional arrangements to render these duties more precise and specific, and hence claimable. The neglect of duties is not due to an overemphasis on the concept of rights, but the practical failure of not taking rights commitments seriously enough.

Ironically, it is the duty-based account that seems unable of its own accord to give us a reason why we care about "perfecting" our imperfect duties. What would be the moral motivation for this in the first place? For O'Neill, the answer rests, in the end, on the Kantian duty to protect and promote individual moral agency. But if this is right, it seems that O'Neill's duty-based approach has to rely on an account of individual moral primacy that is rather consistent with the doctrine of individual rights (C. Jones 1999a, p. 107).

In short, O'Neill's "maverick Kantianism," which seeks to return to the Kantian roots of deontological ethics by focusing on duties, does not provide a conceptual alternative to a rights-based approach. A focus on duties serves an important strategic and practical purpose, and O'Neill is right to criticize rights-defenders for extolling rights without often

---

[19] An underlying problem seems to be that O'Neill takes the right to assistance to generate only *charitable acts* until assigned and specified: "A world in which rights discourse is thought the appropriate idiom for ethical deliberation is one in which a powerful theoretical wedge is driven between questions of justice and matters of help and benefit. Justice is seen as consisting of assignable, claimable and enforceable rights, which only the claimant can waive. Beneficence is seen as unassignable, unclaimable and unenforceable" (O'Neill 1986, p. 102). But this seems false: although *charity* is unassignable and unenforceable, it does not follow that *all* that is unassigned and unenforceable is charity. The imperfect duties corresponding to various rights are not charitable acts but duties, even if it means that we need to first assign and specify them before they can be fully enforced.

clearly identifying the duty-bearers corresponding to these rights.[20] A duty-based approach, however, does not do any distinct conceptual work. Rights and duties are different sides of the same coin on a deontological perspective. While both provide different ways of describing and interpreting our understanding of justice, and to this extent we should not overlook duties (as unfortunately tends to be the case in practice), they do not offer different conceptual groundings for cosmopolitan justice.[21]

Basic rights and equality

The account of basic rights as described above may not go far enough for purposes of cosmopolitan justice as I am defending it here. Recall that the account of cosmopolitan justice that I am working with takes an interest in distributive equality and not just in ensuring that individuals are able to meet basic needs.

One way of extending a basic rights approach to cover a theory of distributive justice is to show that so long as there are great inequalities between people, the basic rights of the poor (or at the very least the worst-off) cannot be fully met for a variety of reasons. Fulfillment of basic needs is relational in that what people may actually purchase with their money (to meet their needs) is dependent on its purchasing strength, which in turn depends on how much money other people have. It is common knowledge that many people do without adequate nourishment, clothing, housing, and healthcare, not because of an absolute shortage of resources globally, but because of a severe maldistribution of these resources. Inequality in the distribution of resources undermines what Amartya Sen calls a person's entitlements to these basic needs (e.g., the money with which to purchase food, healthcare). So while poverty and equality are distinct concepts, there is a strong link between the two in that much global poverty can be attributed to pervasive inequality in resource distribution (Sen 1981, p. 15; also Dreze and Sen 1989, pp. 3–4). Also great inequalities allow for exploitation of the poor, including the forcing of unfair trade terms on them, thereby threatening their basic right to subsistence (Beitz 2001; cf. Scanlon 1997). Equality can thus be a normative concern derived from the more basic moral concern with ensuring that people are able to meet their basic needs. On this

---

[20] See for example, her discussion on women's rights and obligations (O'Neill 2000, chap. 6).

[21] The above critique of O'Neill does not cover the entire ground of her "maverick Kantianism," but focuses on the points where she thinks duties and rights approaches differ. For a more thorough study of O'Neill's theory of global justice, see Jones (1999a, chap. 4).

"derivative" approach to equality, equality matters because it affects how people fare at the minimum level (Beitz 2001, pp. 101–3).

Another approach takes distributive justice to be a fundamental or "direct" concern (Beitz 2001). This can be done by showing that the basic rights individuals have include the right to equal consideration, and that this right to equal consideration entails among other things a direct concern with distributive equality between persons. Egalitarian liberals like Dworkin have presented arguments for distributive equality along this line. Some cosmopolitans, as we will see below, have attempted to extend the traditional reasoning of egalitarian liberals beyond the borders of the state to include the world as a whole.

Direct and derivative arguments for equality are not mutually exclusive, and indeed both classes of arguments have often been associated with Rawls's defense of distributive equality.[22] I will discuss more fully (chapter 6) how a concern for basic rights can translate into a concern for distributive equality. But the relevant point here is that while a rights-based approach can naturally take into account distributive equality, a utilitarian approach risks ignoring how the good that is to be maximized is distributed among individuals. To recall Rawls's famous remarks, "[t]he striking feature of the utilitarian view of justice is that it does not matter, except indirectly, how this sum of satisfaction is distributed among individuals any more than it matters, except indirectly, how one man distributes his satisfaction over time. The correct distribution in either case is that which yields the maximum fulfillment" (1971, p. 26). Thus, "the most natural way of arriving at Utilitarianism (although not, of course, the only way of doing so) is to adopt for society as a whole the principle of rational choice for one man" (1971, pp. 26–7). Deontological theories, on the contrary, take individuals to have certain inviolable claims and hence take the separation of persons seriously. They can thus better ground distributive principles than can utilitarian theories of justice.

Rawls's *A Theory of Justice* is generally considered to be the most complete and systematic account of a rights-based justice in contemporary philosophy. It is not surprising, therefore, that the important attempts at developing a systematic theory of global justice have been attempts at "globalizing" Rawls's theory of justice.[23] The methodology common

---

[22] See, for example, Elizabeth Anderson's point that Rawls's difference principle is often seen to reflect a direct concern with equality (what Anderson calls "luck egalitarianism"), although, according to Anderson, it is more accurately seen to reflect an indirect concern for equality (what she calls "democratic equality"). In his later writings, Rawls makes it clear that he supports the "democratic equality" reading of his difference principle (2001, p. 43). See also J. Cohen (1989).

[23] Two of the most influential attempts are Beitz (1999a [1979]) and Pogge (1989, part III).

to many of these attempts is to show that on Rawls's own reasoning, he should endorse a cosmopolitan conception of justice, and not confine his theory to a single society conceived "as a closed system isolated from other societies" (Rawls 1971, p. 8).[24] In what follows, I recount and comment on some of the early important attempts at "globalizing" Rawls.

Globalizing Rawls

The method and conclusions of Rawls's *A Theory of Justice* are well known, so some brief points by way of background should suffice. Rawls begins from the very intuitive idea that a person's race, gender, talents, wealth, and other natural and social particularities are "arbitrary from a moral point of view" (1971, p. 15) and their effects on her life chances ought to be nullified in a just social arrangement. To this end, he introduces the original position, "a device of representation," where representatives of rational but reasonable individuals deliberate on the appropriate principles of justice behind a "veil of ignorance." That is, they are asked to imagine that they do not know their actual status and station in society, their natural talents and conceptions of the good and other contingent facts about themselves, and have to decide under this condition of imagined ignorance on the principles against which to regulate their society (1971, pp. 17ff). In this hypothetical scenario as constructed, no party could insist on terms biased in her favor according to her own social standing or other contingencies about her.

Rawls concludes that from this initial condition of fairness, individuals will agree on the following two principles of justice, lexically ranked: (1) each person is to have an equal right to the most extensive basic liberty compatible with a similar liberty for others, and (2) social and economic inequalities are acceptable only if they are (a) attached to offices and positions open to all under conditions of fair equality of opportunity, and (b) to the greatest benefit of the socially least advantaged persons (Rawls 1971, p. 302).

One of the hallmarks of Rawls's important work is the bringing together of liberty and equality in a mutually consistent manner. The second principle ensures "a liberalism for the least advantaged, a liberalism that pays moral tribute to the socialist critique," as Amy Gutmann puts it, by

---

[24] Rawls notes that this is only a working assumption, and whether his theory of justice can be globalized is to be decided only after its general structure has been worked out (1971, p. 8; also 1996, pp. 11–12). But even in *A Theory of Justice*, Rawls briefly suggested that his principles do not apply *fully* to the global context (1971, pp. 377–9). He has since developed detailed arguments for this view (1993 and 1999a), and I will discuss these arguments in the next chapter. For an excellent overview of Rawls, see Freeman (2003).

limiting the sorts of inequalities that are to be tolerated in society.[25] The first part of this principle specifies the importance of equality of opportunity in more than just the formal sense, and the second part, known as the difference principle, allows for inequality in our basic structure only to the extent that such inequality benefits the worst-off individuals in society.

Yet in his brief discussion on international relations in the same work, Rawls does not think the two principles apply equally to the global context. Rawls imagines a second original position being convened; this time, however, instead of individuals being represented behind the veil of ignorance, it is *states* that are represented. While these representatives know certain general facts about the international context, they "know nothing about the particular circumstances of their own society, its power and strength in comparison with other nations" (1971, p. 378). The international principles that result from this second (global) original position are restricted to the "familiar" issues, like those of self-determination, and just war and justice in war. It is unclear at this point whether the first principle applies fully at all, and the second principle is evidently left out altogether.[26]

But Rawlsians have argued, contra Rawls, that, on his own reasoning, Rawls must adopt a more global perspective on his own principles. For example, Thomas Pogge says that "[n]ationality is just one further deep contingency (like genetic endowment, race, gender, and social class), one more potential basis of institutional inequalities that are inescapable and present from birth. Within Rawls's conception, there is no reason to treat this case differently from the others" (1989, p. 247; 1988a). So rather than adopting Rawls's two-stage procedure that seems to take nationality to be a given with moral standing, we should adopt a single global original position in which *individuals* of the world are represented, and in which "the relevant closed system" is "the world at large" (Pogge 1989).

Under this revised Rawlsian scenario, Pogge argues that Rawls's two principles of justice apply between individuals *across* societies and not just within a single society. This result accords better with Rawls's professed individualism, "that only *persons* are to be viewed as the ultimate units of

---

[25] Quoted in Lukes (1995, p. 52n).

[26] Rawls is mostly concerned here with the issue of conscientious objection and hence the arguments regarding international justice are sketchy. His more detailed study on international justice was presented only later. Concerning the early argument, Pogge notes a slight ambiguity in Rawls's global original position: in one instance, it is states that are represented (1971, pp. 378f); in another it is "peoples" (1971, p. 378). See Pogge (1989) for discussion on the implications of this shift for the principles of global justice.

(equal) moral concern" (1989).[27] On Rawls's own conception of justice, then, the justness of our global institutions is to be assessed with reference to the least advantaged individuals – our global scheme is just if it maximizes the situation of the worst-off individuals compared to other feasible schemes.

The early attempts at globalizing Rawls were thus largely attempts to show that there exists a global basic structure in the relevant way, that "the world is a closed social scheme," in order for Rawls's own reasoning to apply to it. In his landmark *Political Theory and International Relations*, Charles Beitz took Rawls's claim that considerations of justice apply among individuals sharing a cooperative scheme for mutual advantage to mean that an existing cooperative scheme is a necessary condition for justice, and agreed partly with this view. While he thought that a principle regulating the arbitrary distribution of natural resources is in order even in the absence of a global basic structure (1999a, pp. 136–43), he accepted that the difference principle could not apply in such a case (1999a, p. 143). He thus saw the central task of developing a Rawlsian global justice to be that of demonstrating the fact of a mutually advantageous global cooperative scheme.

Beitz argued that it was a mistake to think that states are self-sufficient and isolated units as Rawls had assumed. He pointed to the increasing international trade and investment, mobility of capital and labor, global markets and goods, and global agencies and rules regulating such practices as evidence to the contrary (1999a, pp. 143–53). Borders are rapidly becoming more and more permeable, and interaction is the norm; thus the assumption that states are isolated and self-contained units did not hold. Instead the global plane meets Rawls's condition for a shared cooperative social scheme for mutual advantage. The world, on Rawls's own terms, ought to be taken as a single social scheme to which his principles of justice also apply.

Beitz's early attempt to globalize Rawls thus aimed to preserve the structure of Rawlsian justice (as he had interpreted it), rejecting instead the assumption that societies are isolated and self-sufficient. But some have questioned whether from the basic claim about interaction between states that it follows that the world resembles a cooperative scheme in the

---

[27] Rawls writes: "We want to account for the social values, for the intrinsic good of institutional, community, and associative activities, by a conception of justice that in its theoretical basis is individualistic. For reasons of clarity, among others, we do not want to rely on an undefined concept of community, or to suppose that society is an organic whole with a life of its own distinct from and superior to that of all its members in their relations with one another" (Rawls 1971, p. 264; in Pogge 1989, p. 247). We will later see that Rawls did not intend this idea of the individual to apply globally.

appropriate sense for Rawls's principles to apply to it. Brian Barry, for example, thinks that it is not true that the world resembles a cooperative scheme. According to Barry, a cooperative scheme, properly speaking, entails more than just interaction (through trade and commerce). But more to the point, even if there is a global cooperative scheme, it is not one that is mutually advantageous. The global balance of power and wealth is such that some countries are doing far better than others in our current global system. If we insist that justice has to be mutually advantageous, says Barry, then there can be no basis for global justice: redistribution of wealth and resources cannot "plausibly be said to be advantageous to rich as well as poor countries" (Barry 1982, p. 232). For instance, "aid to the needy is going to flow from, say, the United States to Bangladesh rather than vice versa. The conditions for reciprocity – that all parties stand prospectively to benefit from the scheme [i.e., a global distributive scheme] – simply do not exist" (1982, p. 233). So justice understood as cooperation for mutual advantage does not provide an adequate argument for why citizens of rich countries should endorse global distributive principles (much of which burden they are the ones to bear).

Barry is not rejecting the idea of global justice; to the contrary, Barry himself holds that it is a test point for a liberal theory of justice that it has global application – a liberal theory of justice that has no global scope is, on the face of it, unacceptable (e.g., Barry 1974; 1982; 1989). Barry's claim here is that the idea of justice as a cooperative venture for mutual advantage – which he associates with Rawls – cannot ground even the modest global principles Rawls had hinted at in *A Theory of Justice*, let alone the more robust account Beitz wants (Barry 1989, p. 189). Therefore, the idea of justice as mutual advantage is objectionable.[28] So while Barry would agree with Beitz's general conclusions, he thinks that one cannot reach those conclusions from a Rawlsian perspective.

Barry is right to say that justice as mutual advantage, as he has interpreted it, cannot ground global distributive justice, and is therefore fundamentally flawed as a conception of justice. But he is mistaken in attributing that idea of mutual advantage to Rawls. By mutual advantage, Rawls does not simply mean a Pareto optimal arrangement in which individuals' given interests are mutually maximized; rather he means by it a mutually beneficial cooperative scheme based on *reasonable terms* (1971, e.g., pp. 102–3). In his more recent work, Rawls clarifies this point by

[28] More accurately, Barry says that Rawls vacillates between justice as mutual advantage and justice as impartiality (Barry 1989). Barry's preferred theory is that of justice as impartiality.

explicitly dissociating himself from the idea of mutual advantage (as Barry understands it), and contrasting it with the idea of reciprocity, defined as a relationship in which individuals benefit most "with respect to a bench-mark of equality" (1996, pp. 16–17), i.e., a relationship whose terms each can reasonably accept. Justice, for Rawls, is reciprocity (which brings in the ideas of both the reasonable and the rational) and not mutual advan-tage (which brings in only the idea of the rational).[29]

But Barry nonetheless has a point (even though it might not apply to Rawls) worth retaining: if considerations of global justice apply, they must apply regardless of the existing global cooperative arrangement. We misconstrue the aim of justice if we allow justice to be limited by our preexisting institutions. Constraining the applicability of justice to what-ever social arrangements we currently happen to have "would arbitrarily favor the status quo" (Beitz 1983, p. 595), which is plainly contrary to the aim of justice. As I mentioned in an earlier chapter, so long as others are vulnerable to our actions (or omissions), they fall within the scope of our just concern, whether or not our existing institutions facilitate such a concern.[30]

In light of Barry's objection, Beitz in his later writings acknowledges that his earlier argument "misses the point" even if its conclusions still hold. On a more consistent Kantian (and by extension Rawlsian) rea-soning, Beitz argues, "the argument for construing the original position globally need not depend on any claim about the existence or intensity of international social cooperation." The fact that individuals are "self-authenticating sources of valid claims" is a sufficient reason for construct-ing an encompassing global original position (Beitz 1983, p. 595; Rawls 1980; also Beitz 1999a, pp. 202–4). Of course, if the requisite global institutional scheme for realizing the ends of justice is not feasible (for whatever reason), then global justice is a moot point. But the present lack or absence of appropriate institutions does not itself tell us that these institutions are not feasible (Beitz 1983, p. 595).

---

[29] See also Beitz (1999a, pp. 202–3); Pogge (1989, pp. 263–5).
[30] In the afterword to the new edition of *Political Theory and International Relations*, Beitz says that if a society could avoid the global economy – which in fact most societies cannot – then justice consideration need not apply to it (Beitz 1999a, pp. 202–5). I think this is consistent with my above claims. The point is that we have the duty to create a just global structure that this society may avail itself of, should it desire. People have a just claim to a just basic structure; but how and whether they make use of the opportunities presented to them in this context is their own responsibility. Justice does not require that people be compelled to take full advantage of the options available to them in a just society, nor does it require that they be compensated should they not wish to make use of these opportunities. What justice demands is that these opportunities are made available through the basic structure.

It is a common enough mistake to interpret Rawls to be taking justice to be dependent on there being some preexisting cooperative scheme. This misconstrues Rawls's own understanding of justice, as I mentioned in chapter 2. As Rawls himself puts it plainly: "From the standpoint of justice as fairness, a fundamental natural duty is the duty of justice. This duty requires us to support and to comply with just institutions that exist and apply to us. It also constrains us to further just arrangements *not yet established*, at least when this can be done without too much cost to ourselves" (1971, p. 115, my emphasis). If Rawls himself opposes the application of his theory to the global context, it is not because the relevant institutions are lacking (for if this was the only reason, the natural duty of justice would require the implementation of the relevant institutions where possible), but for other reasons that he has made clearer in his later writings, and which we will consider in the next chapter.

A Rawlsian approach to global justice, then, would apply the difference principle to the global basic structure as a whole, not in the sense of confining its applicability within that structure as given, but by determining the *kind* of structure we should have that would maximize the situation of the worst-off representative individuals. To illustrate this point: the difference principle will not simply say that we maximize the situation of the worst-off individuals within the context of our current system. It would not say, for example, that we should allow MNCs free rein because, given the current context, to force MNCs to withdraw from poor countries (e.g., through the imposition of universal labor standards) will actually worsen the lot of many citizens in developing countries. Rather the difference principle operates at a much higher level of generality. It assesses not how we do business within a given global scheme but that very scheme itself.[31] It will ask if we can envision an *alternative global scheme* that would maximize the well-being of the worst-off individual. So Rawlsian justice would require a reformed global order in which MNCs, to retain the above examples, no longer have such immense power over the lives of people.

For the purpose of this work, I will adopt the Rawlsian model as our cosmopolitan conception of justice. Endorsing the general arguments of theorists like Beitz and Pogge, I hold that a just global distributive scheme would be one which meets his second principle of justice – equality of opportunity and the regulation of global equality by the difference

---

[31] As Rawls writes: "To say that inequalities in income and wealth are to be arranged for the greatest benefit of the least advantaged simply means that we are to compare schemes of cooperation by seeing how well off the least advantaged are under each scheme, and then to select the scheme under which the least advantaged are better off than they are under any other scheme" (2001, pp. 59–60).

principle. That is, it would be one that would keep the plight of the worst-off individuals (globally situated) firmly in its sight.

The Rawlsian model of justice is not without its challengers. Some might ask whether Rawls's account of primary goods is sufficient, if we do not need to add to or modify that list. For example, Martha Nussbaum and Amartya Sen have argued that Rawls's index of primary goods is not sensitive to differences in the "basic capacities" of persons to make use of their primary goods, and that his narrow focus on primary goods constitutes what Sen calls a "fetishism" (Sen 1992, 1979; Nussbaum 2000a). This is an important challenge, but it does not detract from the structure of Rawls's theory, and we can still use Rawls's list of goods as provisional, to be added to or modified if need be.[32] It could also be asked, more generally, if Rawls's difference principle is the best way of regulating inequality. But my goal is not to offer defenses on behalf of Rawls's basic theory of justice, but to see if a cosmopolitan extension of that theory can withstand the objections of nationalism and patriotism commonly leveled against the cosmopolitan ideal. Given that Rawls has presented the most systematic and arguably the most influential account of justice in contemporary philosophy, it is worth taking Rawls as our starting point, and exploring the extent to which his theory can be "globalised." My question is: if the difference principle is a suitable distributive principle for the domestic context, are there reasons for not applying it to the global context? More specifically, do the demands of nationalism and patriotism present special problems for globalizing Rawls's account of distributive justice?

In this regard, it is an important point that Rawls himself has recently given arguments against attempts to globalize his distributive principle (Rawls 1993; 1999a). Indeed, he explicitly rejects the cosmopolitan idea of global justice as envisaged by Rawlsians like Beitz and Pogge. So before defending a cosmopolitan version of Rawls's egalitarian liberalism against the challenges of nationalism and patriotism, it is essential that I examine Rawls's own objections to the cosmopolitan ideal.

---

[32] See Rawls's response that the notion of capacities is already implicit in his overall framework of justice, and that "an index of primary goods" is in fact "flexible" enough to be sensitive to differences in people's capacities (Rawls 2001, pp. 168ff).

4   Liberalism and cosmopolitan justice

Taking their inspiration from John Rawls's *A Theory of Justice*, liberals like Charles Beitz and Thomas Pogge have argued that Rawls's arguments for social and economic equality should apply also to the global context (Rawls 1971; Beitz 1999a [1979]; Pogge 1989; 1988a). Just as Rawls considers a person's race, gender, talents, wealth, and other natural and social particularities to be "arbitrary from a moral point of view" (Rawls 1971, p. 15), so too, they argue, are factors like a person's nationality and citizenship morally arbitrary. And as the effects of these contingencies on a person's life chances in the domestic sphere are to be nullified by certain distributive principles of justice, so too should the effects of global contingencies be mitigated by certain global distributive principles. Thus, Rawls's principles of justice – including the second principle governing social and economic equality – should apply between individuals *across* societies and not just within the borders of a single society.[1]

But in his extended commentary on international relations, Rawls explicitly rejects the concept of global distributive justice. In this chapter, I wish to evaluate Rawls's reasons for rejecting the idea of global distributive justice. An important contrast between Rawls's Law of Peoples and the views of liberals like Beitz and Pogge, as we will see, is that the former is avowedly noncosmopolitan. I will argue, however, that a *liberal* Law of Peoples ought to endorse the cosmopolitan ideal.

Rawls's Law of Peoples

To see better where the dispute between Rawls and the proponents of cosmopolitan justice lies, let me provide a very quick overview of Rawls's

---

[1] To recall, the two principles are: (1) each person is to have an equal right to the most extensive basic liberty compatible with a similar liberty for others; (2) social and economic inequalities are to be arranged so that they are both (a) to the greatest benefit of the least advantaged, consistent with the just savings principles, and (b) attached to offices and positions open to all under conditions of fair equality of opportunity. Rawls (1971, p. 302). Principle 2(a) is labelled the difference principle.

international project. The fundamental aim of *The Law of Peoples* is to examine how the content of a theory of international justice "might be developed out of a liberal idea of justice similar to, but more general than, the idea [of] *justice as fairness*" (1999a, p. 3).[2] This "globalizing" project proceeds in three stages. The first stage extends "the social contract idea to the society of liberal peoples" (1999a, pp. 4–5). This first stage allows us to identify the international principles that would be agreed to by representatives of liberal societies at a global original position.[3] Among the principles affirmed here is the duty of humanitarian assistance (1999a, p. 37).[4]

The second stage, which concerns one of the central themes of *The Law of Peoples*, aims to show how and why representatives of certain *nonliberal* but well-ordered societies would also endorse the same set of principles. These are nonliberal societies in that they do not endorse the standard range of liberal democratic rights, like the freedoms of expression and association, religious equality, the right to equal political participation, and so on. That is, individuals in nonliberal societies are "not regarded

[2] One issue I will leave aside in this discussion is Rawls's assumption that peoples are more or less coextensive with states as these are currently demarcated, as his remarks on pp. 38–9 suggest. But, for the purpose of consistency, I will use "peoples" or "societies" (interchangeably as Rawls does) instead of "states." To be sure, Rawls took pains to dissociate peoples from states; but his main intention here is to distinguish peoples from "political states as traditionally conceived" (1999a, p. 25) in the realist tradition, i.e., as political entities motivated primarily by self-interests and power, and not to question existing political boundaries and the legitimacy of existing states (1999a, p. 39, also pp. 25–8).

[3] The original position, as we may recall, is "a device of representation" where representatives of rational but reasonable individuals deliberate on the appropriate principles of justice for the basic structure of their society. To ensure that this hypothetical deliberation is fair and equal, parties to the original position go behind a "veil of ignorance." That is, they are asked to imagine that they do not know their actual status and stations in society, their talents and conceptions of the good; nor the wealth and the extent of their territory and its population in the case of the global original position (1999a, pp. 32–3). In this way, no party can insist on terms biased in her favor according to her own social standing. See also Rawls (1971, pp. 17ff). An important difference in the global original position is that the parties to the deliberation are representatives of *peoples* rather than of individuals. The significance of this anti-individualist shift will be discussed in due course.

[4] The eight principles (abridged) are:
1) Peoples are free and independent.
2) Peoples are to observe treaties.
3) Peoples are equal and are parties to the agreements binding on them.
4) Peoples have a duty of non-intervention.
5) Peoples have the right of self-defense, but not the right to wage war other than for self-defense.
6) Peoples are to honor human rights.
7) Peoples are to observe justice in war.
8) Peoples have a duty to assist peoples lacking the resources to sustain just regimes.
These principles are not exhaustive and more may be added (Rawls 1999a, p. 37).

as free and equal citizens, nor as separate individuals deserving equal representation" (1999a, p. 71; see pp. 71–5). Yet these societies honor *basic* human rights (e.g., right to life and security, and subsistence) and are respectful of other peoples (1999a, pp. 64–7) as required by the Law of Peoples. Consequently, these nonliberal "decent peoples," as Rawls calls them, qualify as "societies in good standing," and are, therefore, to be tolerated by liberal societies. This means that liberal societies are "to recognize these nonliberal societies as equal participating members in good standing of the Society of Peoples," and not just to "refrain from exercising political sanctions – military, economic, or diplomatic – to make a people change its ways" (1999a, p. 59). Nonliberal peoples are tolerated as a matter of liberal principle, and not merely accommodated on account of practicality.

This last point is important. The Law of Peoples wants to achieve a global stability with respect to justice, and not stability as a modus vivendi, i.e., stability as a balance of forces (1999a, pp. 12–13, 44–5). The two-stage procedure described above is thus crucial to Rawls's project because it attempts to show that the global principles proposed by liberal peoples are also principles that can be independently adopted by decent nonliberal peoples, and that it is not the case that liberal peoples have tailored their global principles specifically in view of accommodating nonliberal peoples or existing global institutional arrangements. Whether Rawls succeeds in meeting his stated goal is a question we will take up below.

These two stages complete the ideal theory part of the Law of Peoples. The aim of ideal theory is to identify the principles that should govern the relationship between societies with the requisite political and economic conditions to be well ordered and to comply with the Law of Peoples. In this ideal condition, the goals of justice and stability *for the right reason* between societies can be achieved.

But how about societies without the economic resources to support well-ordered institutions, or societies that blatantly refuse to comply with the principles of the Law of Peoples? These difficulties, stemming from "the highly nonideal conditions of our world with its great injustices and widespread social evils" (1999a, p. 89), are the concern of the third stage of Rawls's project. The nonideal theory aspect of the Law of Peoples thus addresses (i) the problem of noncompliance, as when "outlaw" societies "refuse to comply with a reasonable Law of Peoples" (1999a, p. 90), and (ii) the problem of unfavorable conditions, where "burdened" societies lack the basic resources to become well ordered. A complete Law of Peoples has to confront these nonideal cases, and offer guidance on how well-ordered peoples may defend themselves against outlaw regimes and help bring on reform within these regimes in the long run (1999a, pp. 92–3); and how they may assist burdened societies and help bring them "into the Society of well-ordered Peoples" (1999a, p. 106).

From his discussions concerning burdened societies and his proposal of a duty of assistance, it is clear that Rawls does not advocate an isolationist foreign policy which holds the fate of these societies to be a matter of indifference for liberal and decent peoples. He maintains that better-off societies have a duty of assistance towards burdened societies in order to help them achieve the requisite level of economic and social development to become well ordered. This duty of assistance would also follow from the principle affirming basic human rights which, as Rawls makes very clear, include the right to subsistence. Because the duty of assistance has as its goal the meeting of individuals' basic needs as well as their collective capacity for sustaining decent institutions, I will refer to this duty as a humanitarian duty. Yet Rawls also stresses that this duty of humanitarian assistance is distinct from, and does not entail, a duty of distributive justice. So while a duty of humanitarian assistance is required by the Law of Peoples as part of its nonideal theory, a distributive principle has no place at all here.

A point of clarification is important here. I am not claiming that Rawls has no account of global justice as such – the principles in his Law of Peoples are explicitly principles of justice; the Law of Peoples is a theory of justice for the society of peoples. Nor should the Law of Peoples be taken to be in support of the status quo – if by "status quo" we mean literally the current state of affairs. The duty of assistance that is required by the Law of Peoples, if taken to heart, will bring about a radical change in our present world in which a fifth of the world's population live in absolute poverty, in which 1.2 billion people lack access to clean water, and in which 17 million people die each year from curable diseases. The requirement that liberal and decent peoples help burdened societies achieve the required level of development to sustain well-ordered institutions, a developmental level that could in practice be quite considerable, and the requirement that liberal and decent peoples protect basic rights, which include protecting individuals' access to subsistence, are radical departures from how the well-off presently perceive their global responsibilities towards the needy. What is lacking in Rawls's account of global justice is the commitment to *distributive* justice. That is, there are no ongoing distributive principles regulating the inequalities between the rich and the poor of the world beyond the duty of the better-off to ensure that the badly-off are able to meet a certain threshold level of basic needs. Thus one can rightly recognize the progressiveness of Rawls's global theory compared to the current state of affairs and still fairly ask if Rawls's theory goes far enough. That is, one might wonder if an ideally just world would not only require that the basic needs of persons be met and that peoples be enabled to support their own decent institutions, but also require that the gap between the rich and the poor not be too wide even if the goals of meeting basic needs and supporting decent institutions have been attained. In short, the issue in the present discussion is whether there should be distributive principles to regulate global relations, as many cosmopolitans think, or whether Rawls is right that there is no place for distributive principles in the global setting. For ease of expression, I will use "duties of justice" to refer specifically to "duties of distributive justice," and "justice" to mean specifically "distributive justice."

Humanitarian duty and duty of justice

Why does Rawls reject the concept of global distributive justice? He gives us two main arguments, as I see it. The first is that since a duty of humanitarian assistance is already required by the Law of Peoples as part of nonideal theory, global principles of distributive justice would be redundant. The other is that global distributive principles, moreover, would have unacceptable results. I will explain and assess these arguments in turn.

Consider the redundancy argument. In our nonideal world, with its gross injustices, vast inequality and abject poverty, the Law of Peoples, as we have seen, recognizes that "well-ordered peoples have a *duty* to assist burdened societies," to bring them into the society of well-ordered peoples (1999a, p. 106). Yet, the argument goes, these "goals of attaining liberal or decent institutions, securing human rights, and meeting basic needs . . . are [sufficiently] covered by the duty of assistance" (1999a, p. 116). Thus, a global distributive principle serves no additional purpose in this regard.

But this argument obscures an important difference between duties of *humanity* and duties of *justice*, a difference that is more than semantic. If we accept that rich countries have *only* a duty of humanity to poorer countries, we are also accepting that the *existing* baseline resource and wealth distribution is a just one, and that the global basic institutions organized around and legitimizing the prevailing allocation of wealth and resources are acceptable. Duties to assist each other, on this account, are duties that take place within a just institutional framework. In other words, duties of humanity speak to how states should interact with one another, and while certain institutional mechanisms may be required to facilitate some of this interaction, the global basic structure (e.g., the norms governing the allocation and ownership of resources and wealth), within which such interactions occur, is taken as a given. By contrast, duties of justice speak directly to the basic structure; justice is concerned with the *baseline* distribution of wealth and resources, and the basic institutions and principles that legitimize and rationalize this distribution. To put it perspicuously, while duties of humanity aim to *re*distribute wealth, duties of justice aim to identify what counts as a *just distribution* in the first place. The aim of justice, properly speaking, is not to transfer wealth as such (i.e., by taking it from its *rightful* owners and reallocating it to others), but, rather, to establish the criteria of rightful ownership, to redefine "what justly belongs to a country" (Barry 1982, p. 248; also Pogge, 1989, pp. 16–17, 68–70). Duties of justice, then, would call on us to reconceive our present global basic structure, whereas duties of humanity take this to be more or less sound, and only exhort countries to do more *within* this given framework. One could say with Brian Barry that justice is prior to humanity in that "[w]e cannot sensibly talk about humanity unless we have a baseline set by justice. To talk about what I ought, as a matter of humanity, to do with what is mine makes no sense until we have established what is mine in the first place" (Barry 1982, p. 249).

Hence the long-term aims of humanity and justice are quite distinct, not just in their objective or duration, as Rawls notes, but also in their scope and focus. The former calls for greater humanitarianism between countries *within an existing institutional framework*, whereas the latter calls for a critical evaluation *of* that framework. This is an important difference. As many egalitarians have long argued, a fundamental cause of global poverty and inequality lies with our global arrangements and institutions, and so to seriously tackle global poverty would require reforming these institutions and arrangements.[5]

Moreover, this difference in focus has important and more immediate consequences for foreign policy. If foreign aid is considered a matter of humanitarian aid, it could be subject to conditions imposed by donor countries (it is *their* resources they are giving up, after all, on this view). But if we treat foreign aid as a matter of justice, it would not be vulnerable to such exhortation in principle, for any resource transfer is, on this view, strictly speaking, not a *re*distribution in the sense of taking something from its rightful owner and giving it to the more needy, but a correction of an initial unjust distribution. Thus treating global inequality as a matter of humanity, as Barry points out, obscures the basic point, "that if some share of resources is justly owed to a country, then it is (even before it has been actually transferred) as much that country's as it is now normally

---

[5] I will not argue for this point here, but see, for some examples, Nielsen (1991, pp. 229–32); O'Neill (1986); Pogge (1999, pp. 27–34); and Shue (1996, afterword).

thought that what a country normally produces belongs to that country" (Barry 1982, p. 248).[6]

So it makes an immense difference whether wealth redistribution between countries is conceived as a matter of humanitarian assistance or justice. Far from being superfluous, treating duties between countries as a matter of justice highlights for us the proper locus of our concern (i.e., institutions and their underlying norms) and reminds us that the crucial issue is ultimately the question of rightful ownership rather than that of humanitarian contribution. Even if we are to confine ourselves to the nonideal case of burdened societies, it makes an important normative difference whether we think we are assisting only out of humanitarian concern, or whether we are assisting because we recognize the fact of prevailing injustices in our global arrangement.

None of the above denies that humanitarian assistance is important as well. But as long as humanitarianism takes place within the present global arrangement, it serves only to treat the symptoms of injustice rather than tackle the underlying cause of it. Humanitarian assistance applies as long as there are burdened societies, but principles of justice would push us to assess the framework within which such assistance is being rendered. Thus, although humanitarianism can demand the creation of new institutions if necessary for the promotion of humanitarian ends, it begins from different assumptions about the nature of the problem and is motivated by very different goals. Justice is concerned with structural equality of some form, whereas humanitarianism is concerned primarily with the meeting of basic needs (even if structural changes are called for to this end).

It is a familiar fact that Rawls's domestic egalitarianism is directed at the basic *institutions* of society; his second principle provides liberals with a basis against which to assess and critique these institutions, and to reject institutional arrangements which perpetuate and legitimize inequality of opportunity between citizens. So it seems that to be consistent with his basic philosophical ideals, Rawls too should hold up the basic structure of the Society of Peoples against his principles of justice, instead of taking that as a given.

---

[6] Of course this does not mean that we are never in a position to withhold that which rightly belongs to another – recall Plato's example of not returning a dagger to its rightful owner who has gone mad (*The Republic* 331c). Barry notes that it is as acceptable to withhold resources justly owed to a country that is violating basic human rights, or spending vast quantities of money on arms, as it is "to refuse to pay debts to it or to freeze its assets" (Barry 1982, p. 248). And certainly such disincentives could be used as a tool for human rights reform, if properly applied. The crucial point here is that treating inequality as a matter of *justice* shifts the burden of proof away from "recipient" countries and onto the "donor" country. Instead of asking recipient countries why they should receive, the right question to ask is why so-called "donor" countries should not give.

So Rawls is clearly aware of the important differences between human-itarian duties and duties of justice. His supposition seems, then, to be that the global distribution of resources and wealth is not an issue of justice. A global distribution of wealth that does not meet the egalitar-ian requirement of his difference principle is acceptable so long as assis-tance is provided to help "burdened" societies. But why does Rawls think this?

An examination of Rawls's second argument for rejecting global dis-tributive principles may shed some light on this question. Rawls's belief here is that global distributive principles, unlike domestic distributive principles, would have unacceptable results. As he tells us, a duty of humanitarian assistance is a "principle of *transition* . . . [it] holds [only] until all societies have achieved just liberal or decent basic institutions. [It is] defined by a target beyond which [it] no longer hold[s]" (1999a, p. 118). That is, the duty of assistance is satisfied once all societies have attained the basic developmental level sufficient for establishing and maintaining decent institutions. By contrast, distributive "principles do not have a defined goal, aim, or cut-off point, beyond which aid may cease" (1999a, p. 106). So while a duty of humanity would work towards improving the situation of societies "burdened" by unfavorable circum-stances, such assistance is not required as part of ideal theory in which all societies are assumed to have attained the basic developmental level re-quisite for a decent society. A principle of distributive justice, on the other hand, is an integral part of ideal theory, and so would apply as long as there are inequalities between societies, even "after the duty of assistance is fully satisfied" (1999a, p. 117).

But, and here is the crux of the argument, this would have unaccept-able results, argues Rawls, for we would then not be able to discriminate between societies which through foresight and prudence have increased their wealth, and societies which through neglect and imprudence have squandered theirs (1999a, p. 117); or, societies which have managed to curb their population growth and are therefore better able to optimize their resources, and societies which have neglected to control their pop-ulation and hence are worse-off as a result (1999a, pp. 117–18). A global egalitarian principle would insist, in both of these cases, that resources be transferred from the wealthier societies to the poorer ones, even though both may have started with an equal amount of wealth and resources. And this is unacceptable for it would mean penalizing some societies for their sound domestic policies in order to compensate other societies for their careless policies.

In short, while a duty of assistance is in force only within nonideal theory and will cease once no societies are so burdened as to be unable to establish well-ordered institutions, a distributive principle falls under ideal theory and will continue to apply as long as inequality between societies persists. And it is this fact – that distributive principles would insist on redistribution as long as there is inequality between peoples *no matter what the cause of this inequality* – that Rawls takes exception to.

Implicit in Rawls's argument here, it seems to me, is the distinction between inequality as a result of choice and inequality due to circumstance. Just as a domestic distributive scheme ought not to compensate individuals for their poor choices by taking from those who have made good choices, neither ought a global scheme to compensate societies for their poor governance by penalizing other societies for their good governance. The aim of distributive justice is to counter the effects of unchosen inequality of circumstances on persons, and not to compensate them for their (poor) choices.[7] But, and this seems to be Rawls's worry, a global distributive principle would be insensitive to the choice/circumstance distinction; it would treat citizens of well-managed economies *unfairly* by transferring their gains to citizens of poorly managed economies continuously as long as global inequality remains. The choices a people makes about its domestic arrangements would not be respected if the gains or losses due to these choices were annulled by a distributive principle between peoples.

One crucial premise of this argument is that the reasons for a country's failure to adopt sound social and economic policies are largely internal, and hence *freely* adopted by governments of worse-off countries. Rawls draws attention to various domestic factors that determine a society's economic and social performance, including its political culture and virtues (including here a respect for basic human rights), its civic society, "its members' probity and industriousness," and its population policy (1999a, pp. 108–11). Yet this premise, which Thomas Pogge has labeled "explanatory nationalism," is highly questionable as a matter of empirical fact (Pogge 1998, pp. 497–502). Explanatory nationalism "present[s] poverty as a set of national phenomena explicable mainly as a result of bad domestic policies and institutions that stifle (or fail to stimulate) national economic growth and engender national economic injustice" (Pogge 1998, p. 497). But, as Pogge notes, this explanation "leave[s] open important questions, such as why national factors (institutions, officials, policies, culture, natural environment, level of technical and economic development) have *these* effects rather than others" by ignoring the causal effects of global factors (e.g., trade practices, consumption patterns of affluent countries, international law, etc.) on a nation's domestic policies and their outcomes (1998, pp. 498–9).

---

[7] See Kymlicka (1990a, pp. 73–6).

Distributive arrangements between societies need not be insensitive to choice, then, if the distributive goal is to offset the effects of these (unchosen) global factors and not the effects of (chosen) national policies on a people's well-being. A less well-off society that is the beneficiary of a global distributive principle need not be seen as a society that is being unfairly subsidized for the domestic choices it has made, but is rather being compensated for the effects of global factors not of its choosing on its options. Or, to put it more accurately, it is getting its fair share as would be defined under a fair global context. A global egalitarian order, so understood, could still in principle allow room for inequalities due to differences in national pursuits (within the limits I will note below). What is required is that the background context in which societies pursue their diverse ends is a fair one, and this would require its regulation by some distributive ideal. Just as egalitarian justice in the domestic context need not be insensitive to individual choice, but is concerned only with the fairness of the basic structure within which individuals make their choices and interact (Rawls 1996, p. 266), so global egalitarian justice is concerned with the fairness of the global context and need not require resource transfer across the board without giving due recognition to domestic decisions and choices.

To illustrate, assume that the ideal of a global difference principle is approximately realized by a global taxation scheme of some sort. That is, under this taxation scheme, the worst-off person is best-off compared to alternative schemes. Such a taxation program would require ongoing transfers from the better-off to the worst-off. But this arrangement need not militate against the effects of domestic national choices, for within the rules of this scheme societies are to take responsibility for how they use and deploy their justly allocated resources and wealth. Within this fair global structure, some societies will do better economically than others due to their domestic policies, and such resulting inequalities are not objectionable from the point of view of justice. Considerations of justice aim to secure equal opportunity and fair background conditions for persons and societies in the pursuit of their ends, but it does not necessarily require that everyone and every society take full advantage of the opportunities presented to them, nor does it compensate those who fail to make successful use of the opportunities available to them. There is space, then, under a global distributive scheme for diversity in national pursuits, and for nations to take responsibilities for their domestic goals. The aim of justice is to secure a fair background context within which rules individuals and their associations can make choices and take responsibility for them. Global distributive justice and national self-determination, the latter being the underlying premise in Rawls's argument, are not incompatible goals. Justice holds that persons have a right to a global basic arrangement of a certain sort – in the Rawlsian spirit, this would be a global arrangement in which the worst-off persons are best off. But justice does not require that individuals and their societies take full advantage of this basic arrangement to maximize their gains. Within the terms of a just global scheme, there is room for peoples to collectively determine their domestic priorities and the sort of societies that they want to live in; but this is distinct from the question as to the terms of the global scheme that peoples *are entitled to* as a matter of justice.

This debunking of the myth of explanatory nationalism is important, I think. For the average person in developed countries, explanatory nationalism provides the central objection against global justice: if some countries are doing well because of their careful policies and sacrifices and others are doing badly because of their careless policies and unwillingness to make economic sacrifices, why should citizens in better-off countries be obliged to assist the worse-off? To insist on redistribution under this scenario offends against a very basic moral intuition most people have, that humans, as rational agents, are to take responsibility for their choices and ends. But if the preceding arguments are right in that not all global inequalities can be blamed on poor domestic (i.e., national) choices, but are in large part (or at least in part) due to global factors outside the control of most poor countries, and if it is recognized that the aim of global justice is not to compensate peoples for their bad choices but to mitigate the unfairness in global conditions under which choices are made, then the idea of global justice need not be morally offensive. What is unjust, and what distributive justice aims to mitigate, is the background condition within which self-determination is exercised, not the outcome as such of self-determination. The basic idea that individuals are to take responsibility for their actions, a common view among citizens in liberal societies, is not violated by global distributive principles once the source of global injustice and the scope of justice are made clear.

So, Rawls's worry about the unacceptability of a global distributive principle need not hold, if we reject the explanatory nationalism thesis underlying it. But even if we were to accept the thesis of explanatory nationalism, that most inequalities can be traced to domestic decisions, it does not follow that global distributive principles would violate the choice/circumstance distinction, as liberals understand this distinction. As Charles Beitz points out, the domestic equivalent to the case of citizens faring poorly due to the bad policies of their own governments is not that of an individual having to bear the consequences of *her own* bad choices, but, rather, more like that of children who have to suffer for the poor choices of their parents. And, in such a case, we would not "say

that the offspring are responsible for their own condition . . . [and] considerations about responsibility do not diminish the weight of the ethical
concern about the well-being of the offspring" (Beitz 1999c, p. 527).[8]
Similarly, *individual* citizens of poor countries need not have freely consented to their countries' policies and social choices – indeed, they likely
would not have had the option if they belong to hierarchical and non-
democratic societies, or if these were policies implemented before their
time (as the case might well be, given the intergenerational implications
of social policies like population control). Thus their disadvantages are
due more to circumstance than choice, albeit circumstances of the *society*
that they happen to find themselves in, and distributive principles that
aim to compensate individuals for these disadvantages cannot be said to
offend against the choice/circumstance distinction if we take individuals
to be the basic moral subjects. If justice is *individual* choice-sensitive and
circumstance-insensitive, then one cannot accept that global distributive
principles neglect this distinction.

Another problem, then, with Rawls's second argument is that while
the choice–circumstance distinction, that is basic to liberal reasoning,
is applied *individualistically* in the domestic case, it is applied commu-
nally (to a people as one entity) in the global context. Citizens of disadvantaged countries are *collectively* held accountable for their country's
unsound domestic policies, even when a majority of them had no part in
the making of these policies. And this is clearly inconsistent with Rawls's
own moral individualism.[9] On Rawls's own reasoning, a person born into
a society with poor population control and economic policies cannot be
said to deserve her fate any more than another born into more favorable
circumstances deserves hers. These are mere accidents of birth, and are
as morally arbitrary as is being born into wealth or poverty in the domestic
context.

We may put the above point in a somewhat different way: while Rawls's
moral individualism sets firm limits on the extent to which collective decisions may affect individual well-being in his domestic conception of justice, there seem to be no similar limitations in his international theory.
"Each person possesses an inviolability founded on justice that even the
welfare of society as a whole cannot override," Rawls has famously written

---

[8] For a similar line of argument, see Caney (2002, pp. 116–17).
[9] Recall: "We want to account for the social values, for the intrinsic good of institutional,
community, and associative activities, by a conception of justice that in its theoretical
basis is individualistic. For reasons of clarity among others, we do not want to rely on an
undefined concept of community, or to suppose that society is an organic whole with a
life of its own distinct from and superior to that of all its members in their relations with
one another" (Rawls 1971, p. 264).

(Rawls 1971, p. 3). Collective national decisions are regulated and con-strained by principles of justice that take the individual to be the basic reference point in the domestic context; yet in moving to the international context, the same restriction no longer applies.

It is of course true that questions of inefficiency and waste do arise when channeling resources to poorly planned economies (so we may have to think carefully how we are to tackle these problems efficiently and with minimum waste); but this does not undermine what justice as a matter of principle demands. Distributive principles are still in force; how they are to be best realized is a separate question, a question of policy and political judgment, and it is only at this level that a country's domestic policy becomes a relevant factor of consideration.

Here a critic might point out that in Rawls's theory (if not in all defensi-ble conceptions of justice), efficiency is one of the factors (even if it is not among the most fundamental) to be taken into consideration when delib-erating about justice. So my claim that we can separate efficiency from principle is mistaken, one might object. But this objection would commit a category mistake by conflating two different accounts of efficiency. A complete presentation of a theory of justice has to first (a) *identify* a set of principles that fulfills, inter alia, some stipulated efficiency criterion (e.g., that it does not stunt individual incentive or ambition or stifle economic progress); then, it has to (b) ask how we can most efficiently *realize* these principles. The former poses a *conceptual* question, the latter, a *strategic* one. Both these efficiency considerations are, of course, highly relevant to the pursuit of justice; but while the former bears *directly* on what our principles should look like and how we should conceive of them, the lat-ter does not. My comment about efficiency and principle above concerns the latter understanding of efficiency. Unless one wishes to assert that corrupt third-world governments and wastage in cross-border resource transfers are inevitable facts of our world, there is no reason why such contingent and alterable facts alone should compel us to reconceive what justice requires.

Cosmopolitan justice and political liberalism

The aim of my above argument is not to show that Rawls's Law of Peoples is objectionable because it is not sufficiently individualistic – that would be no objection, for one of Rawls's propositions is that the basic units of the Law of Peoples are peoples or societies, and not individuals. My point, rather, is that the choice/circumstance distinction I take to be implicit in Rawls's argument (that global distributive principles would have unac-ceptable results) makes sense only when applied individualistically, but not when it is applied to a society as a whole. At any rate, Rawls explicitly retracts the individualism that informs his domestic theory of justice. As he contrasts the Law of Peoples with what he calls the cosmopolitan view, "The ultimate concern of a cosmopolitan view is the well-being of individuals and not the justice of societies . . . What is important to the Law of Peoples is the justice and stability for the right reasons of liberal and decent societies" (1999a, pp. 119–20).

Rawls's rejection of cosmopolitanism, to my mind, reveals a fundamental shift in his political philosophy. Starting from purportedly liberal individualistic grounds, Rawls arrives at an international theory that is more aligned with those of "communitarians," like David Miller and Michael Walzer, who have very different philosophical starting points.[10] Compare, for example, Rawls's opposition to global distributive justice with Miller's: "To respect the self-determination of other nations also involves treating them as responsible for decisions they may make about resource use, economic growth, environmental protection, and so forth" (D. Miller 1995, p. 108). That is, Rawls now seems to think that, for the purposes of international theory, it is acceptable to hold that individuals' conceptions of the good are socially defined and constitutive of their identities, that there is a common good conception of justice and that, as he puts it explicitly, "persons belong first to estates, corporations, and associations" – that is, groups (1999a, p. 73). This position can be described as "communitarian" in that, for some societies, the "broader interests of political life" can have precedence over individual interests (1999a).

Why does Rawls reject the cosmopolitan ideal in his international theory? After all, the cosmopolitan view seems to be more consistent with his famous phrase that individuals are "self-originating sources of valid claims" (Rawls 1980, p. 543). And, as mentioned, Rawls's own followers have long argued that the cosmopolitan view follows naturally from Rawls's own fundamental commitments.[11] There is thus an interesting normative shift in Rawls in his move from a domestic theory of justice to an international theory. The normative individualism fundamental to his domestic theory is replaced by a "communitarianism" of a sort that takes societies or peoples to be the basic subjects of justice.

Rawls's reason for this shift from what we may call his *domestic individualism* to his *international communitarianism* is that a Law of Peoples

---

[10] D. Miller (1995, chaps. 3 and 4); Michael Walzer (1980, 1983); MacIntyre (1984).

[11] Thus Pogge: "Taken seriously, Rawls's conception of justice will make the life prospects of the globally least advantaged the primary standard for assessing our social institutions" (1988a, p. 233); and Beitz: "It seems obvious that an international difference principle applies to persons in the sense that it is the globally least advantaged representative person (or group of persons) whose position is to be maximized" (Beitz 1999a, p. 152).

founded on the ideal of individuals as free and equal would make the basis
of that Law "too narrow."[12] In other words, to insist on an international
theory of justice premised on the cosmopolitan ideal that individuals are
ultimate, is to propose a conception of justice that nonliberal societies
could *reasonably* object to. It would amount in effect "to saying that all
persons are to have the equal liberal rights of citizens in a constitutional
democracy . . . that only a liberal democratic society can be acceptable"
(1999a, pp. 82–3). And this, Rawls says, "would fail to express due toleration for other acceptable ways (if such as there are, as I assume) of
ordering society" (1999a, p. 59). It is for this reason that Rawls rejects the
proposal that there be a single global original position procedure where
individuals are represented, and opts instead for a two-stage procedure in
which only representatives of societies are convened at the second global
stage. A global original position would have to assume that all individuals
"have the equal liberal rights of citizens in a constitutional democracy"
(1999a, pp. 82–3, 30–5), and this we should not do.

This toleration for nonliberal ways of organizing society, Rawls argues,
stems from a principle basic to political liberalism, that "a liberal society is
to respect its citizens' comprehensive doctrines – religious, philosophical,
and moral – provided that these doctrines are pursued in ways compatible
with a reasonable political conception of justice and its public reason"
(1999a, p. 59). Thus, likewise, liberal societies are to tolerate nonliberal
societies so long as these are decent, i.e., capable of conforming to the
principles of the Law of Peoples. And, as mentioned, one of the central
aims of *The Law of Peoples* is to show how and why certain nonliberal
peoples can nonetheless endorse the principles of the Law of Peoples, and
why they are therefore reasonable societies or societies in good standing
and to be tolerated by liberal peoples.

The idea of public reason central to Rawls's political liberalism is
therefore extended to the international context in the following way: "in
proposing a principle to regulate the mutual relations between peoples, a
[liberal] people or their representatives must think not only that it is reasonable for them to propose it, but also that it is reasonable for other peoples to accept it" (1999a, p. 57).[13] So while it would not be unreasonable,

---

[12] The phrase in quotes is from the essay, "The Law of Peoples" (Rawls 1993, p. 65). David
Dyzenhaus has argued that this rejection of "individualist liberalism" is already evident
in Rawls's move from the comprehensive liberalism of *A Theory of Justice* to the political
liberalism defended in *Political Liberalism* (Dyzenhaus 1998, p. 280). If this is right, our
criticism of Rawls's Law of Peoples amounts ultimately to a criticism of Rawls's political
liberalism. I pursue this point in Tan (2000).

[13] *The Law of Peoples* includes a reprint of Rawls's latest account on the idea of public
reason, "The Idea of Public Reason Revisited," previously published in the *University
of Chicago Law Review* 64 (1997). For an instructive discussion on public reason, see
Freeman (2004).

but indeed "is a consequence of liberalism and decency" (1999a, p. 81) to criticize, and even intervene against in grave cases, violations of *basic* human rights in outlaw societies, it would be unreasonable to demand that all societies adopt liberal democratic institutions.[14]

This idea that the liberal concept of toleration extends also to *nonliberal* societies – in spite of their restrictions on important liberal freedoms like freedom of association, expression, right to democratic participation and so on – is a point of much contention in Rawls's international theory.[15] But I will leave this matter aside for the moment, and focus primarily on the implications of Rawls's account of toleration for *distributive* justice. Is it true that "political liberalism would fail to express due toleration for other acceptable ways . . . of ordering society" (Rawls 1999a, p. 59), if it insisted on some liberal conception of distributive justice (e.g., Rawls's own second principle) as part of an international theory?

In his first presentation of the Law of Peoples in an essay of the same name, Rawls writes that nonliberal societies would reject any liberal distributive principles between societies because they reject liberalism. In his own words: "For their part, the hierarchical societies reject *all* liberal principles of domestic justice. We cannot suppose that they will find such principles [e.g., the difference principle] acceptable in dealing with other peoples" (1993, p. 75). That is, because nonliberal peoples reject liberal principles for their own societies, they will also reject liberal principles, including liberal distributive principles, for the global sphere.

But this argument is too quickly made, it seems to me. It is not clear why the rejection of liberal principles has to be an all-or-nothing affair. Just because nonliberal societies reject (as they likely would) liberal principles pertaining to the full range of liberal civil and political rights, it does not follow at all that they will also reject liberal principles pertaining to economic and social rights. There is no reason why a society which does not accept as relevant, say, the ideals of free association and expression, cannot nonetheless endorse global principles that will distribute resources more equally *between* societies.[16] Adopting principles of justice to regulate

---

[14] For a constructive interpretation and defense of Rawls's position, see Reidy (2004) and Wenar (2002).

[15] For more on toleration and the Law of Peoples, see Teson (1995) and Hoffmann (1995). I discuss this also in Tan (1998 and 2000, Chaps. 2 and 4). For articles that explicitly focus on cosmopolitanism and the idea of toleration in the Law of Peoples, see Caney (2002) and Kuper (2000).

[16] This is the case in the real world: nonliberal developing countries want more financial assistance from the developed world (economic equality) while resisting pressures from the developed world that they liberalize their political institutions. A global distributive scheme on a Rawlsian concept would be readily adopted by these nonliberal countries. If there should be difficulties here, it would be that Rawlsian principles do not go far enough.

distribution between peoples, unlike the ideals of civil and political rights, need not have any direct liberalizing implication for the domestic politics of nonliberal peoples. To put it simply, nonliberal societies can accept, as principles governing the relations between societies, liberal principles of *economic* justice even as they reject liberal principles of *political* justice.[17]

Indeed given his own claim that "a people sincerely affirming a nonliberal idea of justice may still reasonably think its society should be treated equally in a reasonably just Law of Peoples" (1999a, p. 70), Rawls has to agree that it is consistent for nonliberal peoples to endorse liberal *egalitarian* ideals to regulate relations between societies even as they reject the same ideal for their own domestic institutions. As Simon Caney puts it, ideals of global equality and the principle of "not imposing [e.g. liberal] values on people that they can reject" are not really incompatible on Rawls's own terms (Caney 2001, p. 129).

As a matter of fact, given that in the real world it is nonliberal societies that tend to be the less well-off ones, and hence would be the main beneficiaries of global distributive justice, it seems all the more likely that, in reality, nonliberal peoples would wholeheartedly embrace such a distributive ideal between societies.[18] In short, the worry that imposing a liberal conception of distributive justice for the purpose of regulating the relations between societies would be an imposition on nonliberal societies – and hence a violation of the liberal principle of toleration – is unfounded both conceptually and empirically.

But while the above argument will take us beyond the duty of humanitarianism to a duty of distributive justice *between* societies, it still does not go far enough for cosmopolitans. It only accounts for equality between societies, but it could *in principle* be indifferent to inequality *within* society (if it is the case that domestic inequality has no negative effects on equality between societies). Hence it is possible, within this conception of international justice, that resources and wealth equally distributed between societies are not in turn redistributed equally between persons within hierarchical societies. Given its focus on the individual, cosmopolitan justice requires more than distributive equality between societies; it also calls for distributive equality within societies. Adapting Rawls's difference principle, for instance, a cosmopolitan view would hold that our social

---

[17] These labels are Beitz's (1999c, p. 515).

[18] This observation was made by Pogge (1994, p. 218). I do not imply here that nonliberal states may pick and choose aspects of liberal theory that they find useful and discard aspects that they find troublesome. My point here is that nonliberal states, in general, will not find liberal distributive principles (to regulate relations between countries) to be burdensome and unreasonable, as Rawls thinks. That nonliberal states are also expected to endorse basic civil and political liberties is a position I argued for in Tan (1998).

institutions are to maximize the life prospects of the globally worst-off *individuals* no matter where they reside.

This means that a cosmopolitan theory of global justice has to go beyond regulating the relationship between societies, and has to impose certain egalitarian demands within societies as well. Yet the Law of Peoples objects to this on the ground that it would undermine liberalism's principle of toleration by requiring that all societies conform to liberal egalitarian standards (by adopting, for instance, Rawls's second principle, or some other distributive principle premised on the equal moral worth of individuals).

But can *egalitarian* liberals consistently accept nonegalitarian ways of ordering societies? As mentioned, Rawls argues that liberalism has to be accepting of well-ordered though nonliberal modes of ordering society. This, he says, is analogous to the political liberal ideal of tolerating nonliberal but reasonable philosophical, moral or religious comprehensive views within a democratic liberal society. The Law of Peoples, he says, extends this conception of toleration to the international plane. But it seems to me that the analogy between the domestic and the international spheres does not hold: while political liberalism tolerates nonliberal philosophical, moral and religious outlooks, it does not, and cannot, tolerate challenges to liberal political ideals. As Rawls himself points out, "comprehensive doctrines that cannot support . . . a democratic society are not reasonable" (1999a, pp. 172–3; see also pp. 178–9).[19] That is to say, the scope of liberal toleration does not and cannot extend to alternatives to liberalism itself. A political philosophy, for reasons of consistency, must take a stance against competing political philosophies. Ronald Dworkin puts this point across neatly: any political theory must "claim truth for itself, and therefore must claim the falsity of any theory that contradicts it. It must itself occupy . . . all the logical space that its content requires."[20] To hold the counterintuitive view that liberalism must also tolerate nonliberal politics calls to mind Robert Frost's well-known caricature of the liberal as a person who is unable to take sides in her own quarrel.[21]

If it is correct that the scope of liberal toleration does not extend to nonliberal ways of ordering politics, it is hard to see why it should do so when we move to the global context. To be consistent with its own fundamental commitments, a *liberal* Law of Peoples has to take a stance against nonliberal hierarchical societies. While hierarchical societies may find such critical judgments on their domestic institutions an imposition, this is not an *unreasonable* imposition from the liberal point of view. A Law

---

[19] See also Rawls (1996, pp. 152–3).   [20] Dworkin (1985, p. 361).
[21] My argument here is indebted to Dyzenhaus (1996).

of Peoples that claims to be "an extension of a *liberal* conception of justice for a domestic regime to a Society of Peoples" (Rawls 1999a, p. 9, my stress) has to remain steadfast in its commitment to liberalism. The shift from domestic individualism to international communitarianism cannot be justified within a liberal individualist framework.

Justice and global institutions

It might be said here that the absence of an enforceable international law is the central reason why Rawls thinks liberal principles cannot be extended globally. Naturally, the objection cannot mean merely that there is a *current* lack of the appropriate institutions, for this would be contradictory to the Rawlsian idea of justice, and hence an argument that Rawls himself would not accept.[22] For Rawls, justice informs and constrains our institutions, not the other way around. For instance, concerning the case of outlaw societies, Rawls writes: "The Society of Peoples needs to develop *new* institutions and practices under the Law of Peoples to constrain outlaw states when they appear" (1999a, p. 48, my emphasis). To limit the Law of Peoples against existing institutional schemes is to render it "political in the wrong way," thus contradicting Rawls's expressed goal of achieving stability with respect to justice (1999a, pp. 44–5).[23] Given Rawls's stated goal and his idea of justice (that it is not merely a political compromise), the suggestion that it is the absence of institutional enforcement mechanisms that has compelled him not to extend liberal principles globally amounts, in fact, to an objection to, rather than a defense of, Rawls's Law of Peoples.[24]

The above objection, however, could be interpreted to mean that there are simply *no feasible* global institutions, short of enacting a world state, that can support cosmopolitan distributive principles; and the untenability and undesirability of a world state has been famously pointed out by Kant (Kant 1991 [1795], p. 113).[25] To be sure, if it is true that the principles of cosmopolitan justice can be realized only by certain forms of institutional arrangements that are either unattainable in the real world, or undesirable even if attainable (or both), then we will have to seriously reevaluate the cosmopolitan idea.

But this claim, that either we establish a world state or we reject cosmopolitan distributive principles, presents a false dilemma. Various

---

[22] As we saw in chapter 3, Rawls holds that it is a natural duty to "further just arrangements not yet established" if justice requires it (Rawls 1971, p. 115).

[23] See also Rawls (1996, pp. 146–8).

[24] For one such objection, see Hoffmann (1995, p. 54).

[25] Rawls supports Kant's view in Rawls (1999a, pp. 35–6).

plausible institutional means of regulating global distribution have been proposed that do not invoke the idea of a world government.[26] At the very least, these alternative (nonstatist) means of implementing and regulating global principles should be given due consideration, before we may rule them out as unpracticable. Rawls himself believes that alternative means of enforcing the principles of his Law of Peoples are available. He thinks that global institutions other than a world state, "such as the United Nations ideally conceived" (1999a, p. 36), can have the requisite authority and capacity to express and enforce these principles.[27] The feasibility of establishing new global institutions for implementing and enforcing principles of global justice (i.e., the principles of his Law of Peoples) is not ruled out by Rawls. More crucially, at no point in his rejection of global distributive justice does Rawls tie that idea to the concept of a world government. He rejects global distributive justice not because he thinks that this idea is inevitably dependent on some account of a world state, but for the reasons considered earlier.[28]

In short, to put too much weight on the problem of enforceable international law obscures (by pushing a step back) the real dispute between Rawls and the cosmopolitans.[29] The fundamental reason why Rawls thinks that the cosmopolitan idea is unacceptable is the fact of reasonable pluralism.[30] In Rawls's view, justice among peoples should differ from justice within a state, not *ultimately* because of the absence of enforceable international law, as one might suggest, but because he thinks the scope of

---

[26] See, for example, Pogge's proposal for a Global Resource Tax (GRT) and his outline as to how this could be put into effect without a world state (Pogge 1994). Other long-term means of redistributing wealth globally that have been seriously advanced in global forums, again without the presupposition of a world state, include the Tobin Tax (that will both tax and discourage short-term international financial speculation); and the recently proposed "bit tax" (to be imposed on internet transmission). See also George DeMartino (2000, chap. 7).

[27] See also Young (2000, p. 268).

[28] The cosmopolitan theorists with whom Rawls is dealing have themselves explicitly rejected the idea of a world state (see, e.g., Pogge 1988b). The problem of a world state is thus not relevant to the dispute between Rawls and these cosmopolitans. It is important, in this regard, not to commit the mistake of associating cosmopolitanism with world statism. See Beitz (1999a, pp. 182–3; pp. 199–200); also Wenar (2002, p. 59). I return to this point in chapter 5.

[29] This is not to say that the issue of international law is not an important one in its own right; on the contrary, a complete defense of cosmopolitan justice has to certainly confront this issue. My point here, to repeat, is that this is not central to the dispute between Rawls and the cosmopolitans.

[30] To see more clearly why the question of enforceable international law is not the fundamental issue, we may ask this question: would Rawls propose a *fully* liberal theory of international justice should it be possible for liberal states to effectively enforce liberal principles globally, everything else being equal? The answer would still be in the negative, given Rawls's (more fundamental) concern about reasonable pluralism.

reasonable pluralism ought to be broadened in the global context. And I have tried to show above why this relaxing of the criteria of reasonableness is objectionable from a liberal point of view.

Conclusion

Given existing institutional lack, and entrenched habits and customs, it is true that liberals are sometimes limited in how they can go about supporting reforms globally and within hierarchical societies. And, for the sake of peace, liberal societies may sometimes be forced to mute their global commitments. A *liberal* Law of Peoples may, therefore, sometimes (or even often) be compelled to accommodate nonliberal states for practical reasons and limitations. What is important, though, is that it should treat this as an accommodation for the purpose of a modus vivendi, a non-ideal scenario, rather than as a matter of toleration as required by ideal theory, as argued for by Rawls.[31] And this is not merely an academic quibble: the aim of an ideal theory of justice is to provide us with a standard to aspire to. As Rawls himself has put it in *A Theory of Justice*, ideal theory "presents a conception of a just society that we are to achieve if we can" (1971, p. 246). A Law of Peoples that regards hierarchical decent societies as societies in good standing in the society of peoples, and that tolerates great inequality between states as part of its ideal theory, sets our sights too low. Approximating justice in our far-from-perfect world is, no doubt, an enormous challenge. But to set for ourselves a lesser goal because of this is too easily to give up our hope for a just world.

[31] Hoffmann (1995, p. 54). See also Nagel (1999, p. 41).

Part II

Nationalism

5 Nationalism and cosmopolitanism

I have suggested that liberalism is committed to a cosmopolitan under-standing of distributive justice. That is, liberals ought to take distributive principles to apply to all individuals of the world equally regardless of their nationality and other contingent facts about them. In short, lib-erals ought also to be cosmopolitan liberals. I will refer to this as the "traditional view," meaning by this label not that there is a strong histor-ical connection between liberalism and cosmopolitanism (because this is not necessarily the case), but that the universalism commonly associated with liberal justice is widely seen to entail the cosmopolitan ideal.[1]

But in recent years, the traditional view has come under challenge from within liberalism itself. A growing number of liberal theorists argue that implicit in liberalism is a theory of nationalism. The resurgence of nationalist movements in different parts of the world in recent years and the renewed challenges of multiculturalism and migration within liberal democracies have prompted a burgeoning interest among liberal theo-rists in the idea of nationalism.[2] One outcome of this confrontation with nationalism is the growing consensus among contemporary liberal theo-rists that liberalism and nationalism, far from being contradictory ideals as once commonly thought, are not only compatible but indeed mutually reinforcing ideals. As nationalism needs liberalism to tame it and to set moral constraints on it, so liberalism needs nationalism in order to achieve its ends. As liberal nationalists argue, it is within the context of a national culture that "the core liberal values" of individual autonomy, social jus-tice and democracy are best realized (Kymlicka 2001a, pp. 224–9; also D. Miller 1995; Nielsen 1999; and Tamir 1992). A theory of nationalism, therefore, undergirds (even if unacknowledged) most liberal theories of justice, thus prompting Yael Tamir's observation that "most liberals are liberal nationalists" (Tamir 1992, p. 139).

[1] See, for example, Beitz, Pogge, Nussbaum, O'Neill, and Shue.
[2] See Kymlicka and Christine Straehle (in Kymlicka 2001a, chap. 11) for a helpful survey of the relatively recent explosion of interest in nationalism in contemporary political philosophy.

What these liberal nationalists argue is that much of the liberal theorizing on justice has simply assumed the existence of a single national
community *within* which liberal principles of justice are to apply (Tamir
1992, pp. 119–20; Kymlicka 1995, chap. 5; cf. Rawls 1971, p. 4), and so
it has become more of an open question as to whether these principles
do in fact apply outside the context of the nation. The liberal ideal, that
the individual is entitled to equal respect and concern, is thus exposed to
be more parochial than it was once thought to be: it is meant primarily
to apply to individuals qua fellow nationals, and not necessarily to *all*
individuals as such.

If it is correct that implicit to liberalism is a doctrine about nationality, then my claim that liberals ought also to be cosmopolitans seems
to face a problem. This is because it is often thought that nationalism
and cosmopolitanism are diametrically opposed ideals. Consequently, if
one is a liberal nationalist, one cannot also be a cosmopolitan liberal.
So if it is true that implicit and integral to liberal political philosophy
is a theory of nationalism, then the attempt to derive cosmopolitan justice from liberalism is apparently doomed to failure. With the increasing
prominence and acceptance of the doctrine of liberal nationalism in the
current philosophical literature, it is not surprising that there has been,
lately, a noticeable skepticism or agnosticism, even among liberals, concerning the cosmopolitan aspiration to liberal justice.[3]

The cosmopolitan liberal confronted by this challenge has two possible options by way of defending cosmopolitanism. One is by denying
the doctrine of liberal nationalism. That is, the incompatibility between
cosmopolitanism and nationalism is accepted and the central task for
cosmopolitans is, on this view, to deny the doctrine of liberal nationalism
(e.g., Barry 1999; Brock 2002; Lichtenberg 1998; Moellendorf 2002,
pp. 51–4). Another option open to cosmopolitans, however, does not
deny liberal nationalism, but instead rejects the alleged incompatibility
between cosmopolitanism and nationalism. That is, cosmopolitan liberalism is defended, on this approach, by showing how it can be reconciled
with the demands of liberal nationalism. I want in this chapter to explore
this second way of defending cosmopolitanism.

The conciliatory approach seems to me to be a more fruitful defense of
cosmopolitan justice. First, given the growing support for liberal nationalism, a defense of cosmopolitanism that depends on the rejection of
liberal nationalism risks alienating many liberals whom the cosmopolitan
should want on her side. (Cosmopolitans should not want to be fend-
ing off nonliberals on one flank and liberals on another; the former is

---

[3] Thus some (professed) liberal nationalists have explicitly denied the cosmopolitan idea.
See D. Miller (1995, 2000) and Walzer (1983, 1995).

challenge enough.) Second, and more importantly, as I have noted in
chapter 1, a cosmopolitan theory that cannot accommodate certain forms
of associative ties that characterize the lives of individuals, including the
ties of nationality, is prima facie implausible. Such an account of cosmopolitanism would be morally rigoristic, and would be likely rejected
as a *reductio ad absurdum*. The traditional view, that liberals should be
cosmopolitans, gains more plausibility if it does not rule out nationalism
in toto, particularly liberal forms of nationalism.

In what follows, I will argue that the alleged tension between cosmopolitanism and liberal nationalism is only apparent. Once the goals and content of cosmopolitan global justice, on the one hand, and the parameters
of *liberal* nationalism, on the other, are properly defined and identified,
the perceived conflict between liberal nationalism and cosmopolitanism
disappears. After sorting out the conceptual terrain of cosmopolitan justice and liberal nationalism, I will consider some common nationalistic
objections against cosmopolitan justice, and I will try to show that to the
extent that these arguments do tell against cosmopolitan global justice,
they cannot be *liberal* nationalist arguments.

Given that my goal is to show that cosmopolitans need not reject liberal
nationalism, I shall largely grant the liberal nationalist position.[4] However, to the extent that one commonly raised objection against liberal
nationalism is that it violates the universality so commonly associated
with liberalism, including its acclaimed (by many liberals) commitment
to global equality, my conclusion, if successful, will have the bonus of
defending liberal nationalism against this common objection.

To start, I provide a brief outline of liberal nationalism, noting in particular two of its features that have been commonly thought to render it
antithetical to cosmopolitanism. This will be largely a descriptive task and
there is no pretense that all possible objections against the specific liberal nationalist position I shall put forward have been taken into account
beyond any doubt. I intend only to present and clarify one plausible and
reasonable account of liberal nationalism that also happens to pose the
greatest challenge for cosmopolitan justice compared to other plausible
accounts.

Liberal nationalism

Liberal nationalism is a form of nationalism in that it affirms the general nationalist thesis that all states, including liberal ones, should promote and inculcate a sense of shared nationality among their respective

---

[4] For important arguments in defense of nationalism, see Kymlicka (1995, 2001a);
D. Miller (1995, 2000); and Tamir (1992).

citizens.[5] This sense of common belonging is thought by nationalists to be necessary for grounding a common citizenship among individuals in the modern state, a problem that is especially poignant in the context of the liberal democratic state where individuals seek diverse and sometimes incompatible ends. The nation, as understood here, is the "historic community," to adopt Walzer's phrase (1980), that underlies the state and that makes it realizable. Yet liberal nationalism is a *liberal* form of nationalism because liberal principles set constraints on the kinds of nationalist goals that may be legitimately pursued and the strategies that may be deployed to further these goals.

Liberal nationalists do not make the error commonly charged against them, namely, that they assume that states are homogeneous nation states. On the contrary, liberal nationalists recognize that states are rarely unified around a common national membership, and it is precisely this recognition of the lack of congruity between state and nation that motivates the nationalists' main thesis that states do and/or ought to take a more active role in inculcating a sense of shared nationality among its citizens.

What state-level nation-building might mean, morally speaking, for minority nationalities within the state is understood differently by different liberal nationalists. Some theorists recognize that in the case of multinational countries, the aspiration for a uniform citizenship irrespective of the diversity in nationality may be a futile one in addition to being an unjust imposition, and they recommend instead some form of differentiated citizenship along these national cultural lines. This may require granting minority nationalities certain group rights, including some form of self-government rights for minority nationalities, to offset the potential injustices of majority state nation-building (Kymlicka 2001a, chap. 5; 1995). Others are less receptive of minority rights on account of the belief that fostering a viable and cohesive nation state precludes such concessions to minorities (D. Miller 1998, p. 269). The problem of minorities is one central problem for nationalism that I will return to at various points in this and the next chapter as our discussion progresses. State nation-building presents potential problems for domestic justice (the problem of minorities) and for cosmopolitan justice (the problem of nonmembers). A complete defense of liberal nationalism will, therefore, have to address both these dimensions of justice. My question concerns the latter, namely, whether liberal nationalism can be compatible with the requirements of cosmopolitan justice. Because I am focusing on state nation-building,

---

[5] Kymlicka notes four areas in which nation-building strategies are evident in most states: public education, immigration and naturalization, public employment, and settlement of population and domestic boundary-drawing (Kymlicka 2001a, pp. 23–7).

I will take "nation" to mean the ideal of the nation state unless otherwise noted, and "nationalism" to mean specifically state-level nationalism, again unless otherwise noted.

Some liberal nationalists have tried to reconcile cosmopolitanism and liberal nationalism by defining liberal nationalism as *civic* nationalism in contrast with *ethnic* nationalism (Barry 1999, pp. 53–60). Civic nationalism is supposedly organized around political ideals rather than around a culture; it "envisages the nation as a community of equal rights-bearing citizens" united only in their common allegiance to shared political ideals and practices (Ignatieff 1993, pp. 6–7). Thus, unlike ethnic nationalism, which begins from the basic premise that "an individual's deepest attachments are inherited [through one's culture], not chosen" (1993, pp. 7–8), civic nationalism is allegedly neutral about culture, and hence is, in principle, inclusive and universalistic rather than exclusive and parochial (Barry 1999, pp. 53–5). The idea of civic nationalism is obviously tempting for liberals. After all, it is a nationalism that is based on (liberal) principles, and thereby not exclusive but inclusive of all persons willing to embrace these principles. It is a form of nationalism that is seemingly based on rationally defensible principles rather than on unchosen, narrow and seemingly exclusive factors such as ethnicity and culture.

Thus Brian Barry argues that once we limit liberal nationalism to civic nationalism, the incompatibility between liberal nationalism and cosmopolitanism largely disappears. He writes:

There is no reason for civic nationalism to be opposed to this [global] redistribution. On the contrary, anyone who wishes to see the spread of civic nationalism must recognize that it has material preconditions. Transferring resources from rich countries to poor ones does nothing to injure civic nationalism in the rich ones (almost all of them were the same in that respect when they were half as rich) but offers at least the chance to the poor countries of creating civic nations of their own (Barry, 1999, pp. 58–60, quotation at p. 60).

In short, because the principles and ideals of civic nationalism are universal, and indeed cosmopolitan, ideals, liberal nationalism *understood as* civic nationalism is a form of nationalism that "has no principled position on boundaries" (1999, p. 56), and is hence conceptually consistent with cosmopolitanism.

But this attempt to reconcile liberal nationalism and cosmopolitanism, by distinguishing liberal nationalism from nonliberal nationalism in terms of civic versus ethnic nationalism, succeeds only by "misunderstanding" nationalism (Kymlicka 2001a, chap. 12). As Will Kymlicka has argued, all forms of nationalism, liberal or nonliberal, necessarily have a cultural component that is reflected and reinforced in the public and social institutions of a nation and the shared language(s) under which these institutions operate (Kymlicka 2001a). What distinguishes liberal nationalism from nonliberal nationalism is not the issue of cultural neutrality, but the content, scope, and inclusiveness of the national *culture* that is being fostered and promoted (Kymlicka 2001a, pp. 258–61). A liberal state would promote a "thin" national culture, which Kymlicka calls a "societal culture," that is characterized by a shared language and a set of public institutions covering different areas of social life, including the law, education, and the economy, rather than a "thick" ethno-culture that is characterized by (say) shared religious beliefs, family customs, and personal lifestyles.

The civic/ethnic nationalism divide thus plays into the long-taken-for-granted myth of state ethnocultural neutrality. But once this myth is exposed as such, we see that even our paradigmatic cases of so-called ethnoculturally neutral states, like the United States, are not really neutral in this way, but have (historically and currently) taken active steps to foster and preserve their respective "societal cultures" (Kymlicka 2001a, pp. 244–5; cf. Walzer 1994). The civic/ethnic nationalism distinction, thus, not only does not help to demarcate liberal from nonliberal nationalisms, but is in fact an altogether inaccurate and misleading distinction on account of its false understanding of the nature of nationalism. To try to reconcile liberal nationalism and cosmopolitanism by defining liberal nationalism as civic nationalism too conveniently side-steps the issue by defining away the realities of nationalism.

Besides the fact that state neutrality with respect to culture is a non-starter, many liberal nationalists have also offered positive arguments for why liberals should also be actively promoting a particular national cultural identity: why, that is, liberals must also be liberal nationalists. One main line of argument, as briefly noted above, is that it is within the context of a national culture that the core liberal values of individual autonomy and self-identity, social justice, and democracy are best realized (Kymlicka 2001a, pp. 224–9; also Gutmann 1996; Tamir 1992; D. Miller 1995; Nielsen 1999).

Simply put, membership in a national culture provides individuals with "the context of choice" within which to form, pursue and revise their conceptions of the good life (Kymlicka 1989, 1995; Tamir 1992, chap. 1), as well as the basis of self-identity (Nielsen 1999, pp. 452ff). Moreover, common nationality provides the crucial bond for what David Miller has called a "community of obligation" (Miller 1995, pp. 83–4) through which separate and unrelated individuals can come to see themselves as mutually indebted and morally engaged to begin with, providing thus the requisite grounding and motivation for social justice commitments among citizens. Finally, common nationality ensures a certain degree of trust and mutual respect among fellow citizens that is necessary for a functioning deliberative democracy. Mutual respect, with its attendant ideal of reciprocity, ensures that individuals will only forward arguments that "others, as free and equal citizens might also reasonably be expected reasonably to endorse" (Rawls 1999a, p. 140); and mutual trust insures that they will abide by democratic results that are not in their favor, with the understanding that should results be in their favor next time, others would likewise concede (Kymlicka 2001a, chaps. 10 and 11; D. Miller 1995, pp. 96–8). Also, and very importantly, democratic politics is, in Kymlicka's neat phrase, "politics in the vernacular" in that "debating political issues" is best done in people's own national tongue (2001a, p. 213).[6]

So, many liberal nationalists are nationalists with respect to culture, and hence the attempt to reconcile liberal nationalism with cosmopolitanism by rendering the concept of liberal nationalism culturally vacant is not a reconciliation strategy that they can accept.

In addition to the cultural content of nationalism, there is another feature of nationalism that is often thought to be contradictory to the cosmopolitan ideal. This has to do with the institutional implications of national self-determination. Self-determination, in its most fundamental interpretation, is a claim for a public political sphere in which a nation's cultural identity can be expressed, reflected and fostered. Such a sphere is crucial because, as Yael Tamir writes, "[i]n order to preserve their *national* identity, *individuals* must be given the opportunity to express this identity, both privately and publicly . . . The existence of a shared public space is a necessary condition for ensuring the preservation of a nation as a vital and active community" (Tamir 1992, p. 73, italics in original). Nationality is a *publicly* shared identity characterized by a common language that must be allowed expression in a public sphere if it is to be sustained and promoted. "[A]ny language which is not a public language becomes so marginalised that it is likely to survive only amongst a small elite, or in ritualised form, not as a living and developing language underlying a flourishing culture" (Kymlicka 1995, p. 78). A "private" nationality, like a private language, would be no nationality at all.

While national self-determination is, arguably, most *ideally* realized through independent statehood, sovereign statehood is not a possibility for every nation, nor is it necessary. Alternative political arrangements

---

[6] Indeed, in so far as we treat the ideals of autonomy, justice, and democracy as the quintessential cosmopolitan ideals, cosmopolitans, on this argument, should also be liberal nationalists (Nielsen 1999; also Kymlicka 2001a, chap. 10).

other than sovereign statehood – such as a confederative democracy in the case of multinational states – can, in principle, adequately secure a public sphere centered around the relevant institutions that could reflect and promote a minority national culture within a multinational state (e.g., Tamir 1992, pp. 74–7; cf. D. Miller 1995, p. 81). The crucial point here is that central to the idea of nationalism is the securing and maintaining of a relatively autonomous set of public and nationalized *institutions*, in one appropriate form of political arrangement or another, so that a given national culture may be publicly expressed and fostered.[7]

In sum, liberal nationalism is a form of nationalism with a *cultural* content which, as with all brands of nationalism, commands the establishment of certain *nationalized institutions* for the purpose of promoting and securing a cultural identity in the name of self-determination. It is for these reasons that nationalism is often alleged to be *by definition* anti-cosmopolitan. First, the establishment and maintenance of nationalized institutions seem to go against a common understanding of cosmopolitanism as an argument for specific kinds of global and transnational institutions that would eventually supersede national institutions in significance. Second, the cultural content of nationalism seems to be incompatible with a common understanding of cosmopolitanism as a doctrine that is neutral about, and indeed suspicious of, individual attachments to particular cultures.

As is clear from the above, the "culturally based" nationalism is not endorsed by all professed liberal nationalists (e.g., it is not endorsed by those who argue for civic nationalism), and I do not pretend to have given a full defense of this view of liberal nationalism even though I have suggested its greater plausibility. But a culturally based nationalism, in addition to being the dominant account of nationalism among many important liberal nationalists writing today, is also, more to my purpose, the form of liberal nationalism that presents the greatest challenge for cosmopolitanism. (As we saw, liberal nationalists who adopt civic nationalism see no problem of consistency at all between liberal nationalism

---

[7] To this end, all states, including liberal ones, are in the business of nation-building. What distinguishes liberal states from nonliberal ones is "not *whether* states engage in nation-building, but rather what *kind* of nation-building" (Kymlicka 2001b, p. 262). Kymlicka points out nine (interrelated but distinct) features of nation-building that could distinguish liberal from nonliberal nationalisms. These are, very briefly, (i) the level of coercion used in fostering the national identity, (ii) the breadth of the "public space" within which the national identity must be expressed, (iii) the degree of dissent and public discussion permitted regarding a national identity, (iv) the criteria of nationality (i.e., is it based on race [illiberal] or common language [more liberal]?), (v) the thickness or thinness of its national identity, (vi) the relative weight given to nationality compared with other ends in life, (vii) the plurality of the national identity, (viii) the possibility of dual nationalities and identities, and (ix) its treatment of national minorities (Kymlicka 2001b, pp. 257–62).

and cosmopolitanism.) By taking the culturally based liberal nationalism described above to be representative of liberal nationalism, I am therefore setting the bar higher for a successful reconciliation of liberal nationalism and cosmopolitanism, rather than begging the question in my favor. My arguments, if successful, will in any case apply a fortiori to forms of liberal nationalism that stress cultural neutrality. So, for the purpose of the present discussion, I will endorse the account of liberal nationalism that takes cultural belonging seriously, and I hope to show how this idea of nationalism can nonetheless be consistent with cosmopolitan distributive justice.

Variants of cosmopolitanism

As we have seen, cosmopolitan global justice is often thought to be inherently anti-nationalistic with respect to its views on national institutions and culture. Yet, so I shall argue, once we identify the different strands of cosmopolitanism, and disentangle them from each other, we can see that the cosmopolitan idea of distributive justice does not depend on, nor entail, either of these anti-nationalistic claims. In particular, we can sort out two different sets of cosmopolitan distinctions. On the one hand, we can distinguish between (a) cosmopolitanism as a *moral* claim as opposed to cosmopolitanism as an *institutional* claim; and, on the other, (b) cosmopolitanism as a claim about *justice* as opposed to cosmopolitanism as a claim about *culture*. While cosmopolitanism as an institutional claim and as a claim about culture is indeed at odds with the idea of nationalism, cosmopolitanism understood as a moral claim and as a claim about justice is not necessarily at odds with nationalism. The cosmopolitan idea of global justice, as we shall see, entails only these latter variants of cosmopolitanism.

Moral and institutional cosmopolitanism

It is often charged that cosmopolitanism is inherently anti-nationalistic because it calls for the creation of a world state (or some similar global institutional form) and, consequently, the cultivation of world citizenship. This is how one prominent critic of cosmopolitanism, Danielo Zolo, understands the cosmopolitan position – consequently, Zolo goes on to reject the cosmopolitan ideal by showing that the idea of a world state is a non-starter (Zolo 1997). Nationalism, in contrast, enjoins the right to national self-determination, which may take the form of sovereign statehood or, if not feasible, other forms of autonomous political arrangements such as a multinational federalism (Tamir 1992, p. 9). In either case, national self-determination calls for the establishment and strengthening of certain major public institutions (e.g., in education, immigration/naturalization policies, official language policies, etc.) at the national level, in order to bring about (relatively) autonomous political institutions that "members might see as 'their own,'" and a public sphere in which the national culture may be expressed (Tamir 1992). Thus cosmopolitanism understood as "world statism" is obviously in some tension with nationalism. Each makes opposing institutional demands – one aiming to concentrate and locate political sovereignty in a centralized world body, the other to keep sovereignty decentralized and dispersed at the national level.

But few contemporary cosmopolitans, *pace* Zolo, actually support the idea of a world state and the subsequent outright rejection of national self-determination.[8] Adapting Charles Beitz's terminology, I shall call the above interpretation of cosmopolitanism *institutional* cosmopolitanism, and contrast it with *moral* cosmopolitanism (Beitz 1999b, p. 287).[9] Unlike institutional cosmopolitanism, which calls for the establishment of a world state, moral cosmopolitanism makes no necessary *institutional* demands or recommendations. Moral cosmopolitanism simply says that the individual is the ultimate unit of moral worth and concern, and that how we ought to act or what kinds of institutions we ought to establish "should be based on an impartial consideration of the claims of each person who would be affected" by our choices (Beitz 1999b). In other words, moral cosmopolitanism is not concerned *directly* with the question of how global *institutions* are to be ordered, but with the *justificatory basis* of these institutions. And nothing in this interpretation of cosmopolitanism necessitates the idea of a world state. On the contrary, a moral cosmopolitan can as well defend national self-determination if she believes that the ideal of equal and impartial concern for individuals is best realized by respecting their claims to national sovereignty. So there is no necessary conflict between moral cosmopolitanism and the idea of national self-determination.

It is plain that the cosmopolitan conception of distributive justice depends fundamentally on the cosmopolitan moral view – that individuals are the ultimate units of moral worth and are entitled to equal and impartial concern regardless of their nationality. But it is far from evident that this idea of justice must also depend on institutional cosmopolitanism (i.e., a world government). We can think of different *feasible* global institutional arrangements for redistributing wealth and resources globally

---

[8] Kant can be read as a moral cosmopolitan who is not an institutional cosmopolitan.

[9] Pogge makes a similar distinction in terms of moral and legal cosmopolitanism (Pogge 1992b).

without recourse to the punitive and administrative powers of a world state. Proposals like the Tobin Tax (that would tax short-term capital flows and currency speculation), or Thomas Pogge's global resource tax (that would tax countries for extracting natural resources) are global distributive schemes that are not tied to the idea of a world state (Pogge 1994).[10]

So, once we distinguish moral cosmopolitanism from institutional cosmopolitanism, and see that cosmopolitan global justice is premised on moral cosmopolitanism but not on institutional cosmopolitanism, the worry that cosmopolitan justice and nationalism make conflicting *institutional* claims is shown to be unfounded.

Some might insist that the goals of moral cosmopolitanism are realizable only through institutional cosmopolitanism, that it is only through the institutionalizing of a world state and its accompanying idea of global citizenship can the well-being of *all* individuals be effectively accorded equal moral concern. If this is correct, the cosmopolitan vision is practically, if not conceptually, incompatible with nationalism.

But this claim would be too hastily made. As said, we can imagine certain global distributive arrangements that could realize the ends of moral cosmopolitanism without the benefit (or, more precisely, the drawbacks) of a global state. Indeed, as we can recall, many liberals have argued that certain moral cosmopolitan goals are *best* achieved in the context of the national community, rather than in the context of a global state (e.g., Kymlicka 2001a, pp. 212–16; Nielsen 1999, pp. 461ff). As Amy Gutmann points out, the aims of cosmopolitanism are better achieved through cultivating a strong sense of democratic citizenship than through a global transplanting of the nation-state system: "Democratic citizens have institutional means at their disposals that solitary individuals, or citizens of the world, do not. Some of those institutional means are international in scope . . . but even those tend to depend on the cooperation of sovereign societies for effective action" (Gutmann 1996, p. 71). Global democracy, thus, is best achieved not through some account of democratic global citizenship, but through the strengthening of local and nationally based democratic citizenship (Thompson 1996).[11]

The claim that cosmopolitan justice has no specific institutional entailment does not contradict the general point that justice is concerned

---

[10] For an example of how economists see the Tobin Tax being implemented (alongside other global distributive reforms) without the benefit of a world state, see J. G. Smith (1999).

[11] Thus David Held, the well-known proponent of cosmopolitan democracy, does not advocate a democratic global state as such, but differentiated levels of global governance with different levels of democratic participation (Held 1993, 1995).

primarily with institutions. Cosmopolitan justice does not call for a world state, even though its principles are to regulate and determine the justness of institutions. It is open to the possibility that a range of institutional forms can serve the moral ideal that individuals are entitled to equal moral consideration.

Thus moral cosmopolitanism is not only in principle separable from institutional cosmopolitanism, but even in practice the evidence suggests that we can hope – in fact, better hope – to meet the ends of moral cosmopolitanism by not committing ourselves to a world government and the vague idea of global citizenship. If anything, the goals of moral cosmopolitanism are furthered, rather than thwarted, by liberal nationalism.

The above suggestions notwithstanding, I am not denying that certain practical difficulties are hard to overcome, and I certainly have not offered any precise or definitive views on how global justice may be implemented without a world state. Ultimately, my goal here is conceptual, but nonetheless not trivial from the practical point of view: we can become motivated to seriously study the difficult and technical questions of implementation, and to explore possible institutional mechanisms of global justice, only if we are convinced that global justice is possible, and/or even desirable all things considered – that is, that nothing about global justice conceptually ties it to a world state. Before we can be inspired to see how something may be actualized, we need first to know that it is possible.

Culture and justice

Another reason for the alleged incompatibility between cosmopolitan justice and nationalism is that cosmopolitanism is often thought to be primarily a doctrine about culture. Specifically, it is thought that cosmopolitanism is a thesis about the irrelevance of membership in a particular culture. On this cosmopolitan account, the truly free and autonomous individual is a free-wheeling and culturally unattached person who is able to transcend, and even renounce, her own cultural particularities, and to borrow, adapt and learn from a selection of different cultural options (e.g., Waldron 1992, p. 778). In contrast, the kind of nationalism that I am considering has a cultural content. That is, it begins from the basic idea that a given national culture is worth protecting and fostering; hence the importance of national self-determination. Whether or not cosmopolitanism about culture is defensible is a question I will leave aside. The point here is that cosmopolitanism so understood is clearly at odds with the cultural premise central to liberal nationalism.[12]

[12] But for one response to the cosmopolitan rejection of cultural membership, see Kymlicka (1995, pp. 85–6, 101–3).

But it is important to keep distinct "cosmopolitanism as a doctrine about culture," and "cosmopolitanism as a doctrine about justice" (Scheffler 2001, p. 111).[13] Unlike cosmopolitanism about culture, cosmopolitanism about justice says nothing about the (ir)relevance of cultural membership. Cosmopolitanism about justice holds that the baseline distribution of material goods and resources among individuals should be decided *independently* of the national and state boundaries within which individuals happen to be. Such contingencies ought not to affect one's legitimate entitlements, and the purpose of justice, accordingly, is precisely to mitigate the biased effects of such arbitrary factors on people's life chances. Nothing, positively or negatively, is asserted here about the moral significance of cultural membership for individuals.

Cosmopolitanism about culture, on the other hand, is not directly concerned with how material goods and resources are to be distributed, but is concerned with the question as to whether cultural membership is a *relevant good* to be distributed; and, as noted above, cosmopolitans about culture want to deny that it is. But there is no necessary correlation between this view of cosmopolitanism and cosmopolitan justice. It is logically possible for one to reject the cosmopolitan doctrine about culture (i.e., maintain that cultural membership is an important individual good) and at the same time affirm the cosmopolitan idea of justice (i.e., deny that the baseline distribution of material goods should be limited by membership considerations).[14]

The cosmopolitan conception of global distributive justice obviously affirms cosmopolitanism as a doctrine about justice. It holds that our principles of distribution ought to apply to all individuals globally, and not be restricted and shaped by national boundaries. But this idea of justice, as shown above, is independent of cosmopolitanism understood as a doctrine about culture. Cosmopolitan distributive justice, fundamentally understood, says nothing about the value or disvalue of membership in

---

[13] Although I am borrowing from Scheffler, I should note that he uses this distinction for a slightly different end, namely, to show that cosmopolitanism of either sort when understood in an "extreme" form cannot accommodate patriotic claims. His goal is to propose a "moderate" version of cosmopolitanism that can take special ties seriously. My aim, as it will be clear I hope, is to show that one can take cosmopolitanism about justice to be fundamental without endorsing extreme cosmopolitanism. The discussion on conational partiality in the last section of this book will elaborate on this point.

[14] Indeed, one can as well imagine the converse – a person may reject cosmopolitan justice but accept cultural cosmopolitanism. That is, this person will deny that cultural membership is an important individual good (i.e., be a cosmopolitan about culture), yet reject the idea that distributive principles should transcend social boundaries (i.e., reject cosmopolitan justice). For example, libertarians often do not think that culture is a matter of state concern but is something to be left to the marketplace to decide (so can be said to be cosmopolitans about culture); yet they are also likely to deny that one owes any positive duties of justice to people in the world (i.e., they reject cosmopolitan justice).

a national culture. Distributive justice is foremost concerned with how resources and wealth are to be fairly allocated, and can remain neutral about the separate issue of culture and individual freedom.

To be sure, as with institutional and moral cosmopolitanism, it might be the case that the ideals of cosmopolitan justice cannot be fully realized unless we also adopt the cosmopolitan view about culture. It might be argued, for instance, that believing that cultural membership is an important good would unavoidably force us to support other claims (e.g., that we have special obligations to fellow members of that culture) that are in opposition to the ideals of cosmopolitan global justice (e.g., Lichtenberg 1998; Parekh 1998). This is an important question, and I will return to it later (in part III). My claim in this section is just that there is no conceptual contradiction in endorsing cosmopolitanism about *justice* (which would be consistent with liberal nationalism) while rejecting cosmopolitanism about *culture* (which would be inconsistent with liberal nationalism).

Let me put the different forms of cosmopolitanism discussed above more perspicuously. Moral cosmopolitanism is a claim about the moral *starting point* of cosmopolitan justice, whereas institutional cosmopolitanism is a claim about its institutional *ending point*; and cosmopolitanism as a doctrine about justice speaks to the *scope* of justice, whereas cosmopolitanism as a doctrine about culture speaks to the *content* of justice. While these different variants of cosmopolitanism are clearly interrelated, it is important not to commit the category mistake of treating them as identical and inseparable aspects of cosmopolitanism.

So, although the cosmopolitan idea of global distributive justice certainly begins from a particular moral view about the universality of individuality and equality, it need not be forced into making institutional demands that are inconsistent with nationalism. Neither does it necessarily make any judgments about the content or the goods of justice in a way that denies the importance of cultural membership, even though it has to take a stance concerning the scope of justice. Once these different aspects of cosmopolitanism are sorted out and disentangled from one another, we can see that cosmopolitan global justice is not at odds with the nationalist ideals of self-determination and cultural belonging.

The limits of reconciliation

Thus, cosmopolitan global justice presupposes neither a world state nor the irrelevance of cultural membership. Understood precisely as *moral* cosmopolitanism, and as a claim about *justice* and not about culture, cosmopolitanism is not inherently incompatible with the basic tenets of nationalism. One can recognize the importance of membership in a national culture and the importance of national self-determining institutions, without having to reject the cosmopolitan conception of global justice.

Of course, cosmopolitan global justice does not pretend to be compatible with all forms of nationalism. Clearly, "chauvinistic nationalisms" (as labeled by some commentators), which claim that only one's own nation is worthy of self-determination and respect, violate the cosmopolitan principle that all individuals count equally. Similarly, what Margaret Canovan has called "Romantic Collectivist" forms of nationalism – that is, those that take the nation to be a moral entity in and of itself, and hence able to command individual sacrifices for the sake of some abstract national end – offend against the cosmopolitan view that the individual is the ultimate unit of moral concern, and so cannot be compatible with the cosmopolitan ideal (Canovan 1996a, pp. 6–9).

But *liberal* nationalism is essentially universalist and individualist in its scope and foundation (e.g., Kymlicka 2001a, chaps. 10 and 11; Tamir 1992, pp. 90–1).[15] Liberal nationalists accept that the right to national self-determination is a universal right of all nations, and that the reason why national self-determination is important is not because the nation itself enjoys a certain transcendental moral worth, but because of the value of nationality for individuals. As mentioned, liberal nationalists take membership in a national culture to be an important liberal good because culture provides individuals with the context of choice within which to form, pursue, and revise their conceptions of the good. The moral worth of individuals is that which is crucial here, rather than the worth of the nation independently of what individuals value. So the liberal paradigm of liberal nationalism ensures that it stays consistent with the universalist and individualist tenets of cosmopolitanism. A truly liberal nationalism, as Kai Nielsen says, must also be a *cosmopolitan nationalism* in the sense that it has to cohere with the quintessential cosmopolitan principles of normative individualism and ethical universalism (Nielsen 1999, pp. 448–50).

But it might be pointed out here that the idea of nationalism comes packaged with certain intrinsic features that render nationalism, even

---

[15] Even those "liberal" nationalists with a communitarian bent, like David Miller, accept the universality of the principle of nationality, and do not hold a "romantic-collectivist" account of the nation. See, respectively, D. Miller (1995, chaps. 4 and 2). Miller does restrict the right to national self-determination to only certain nations, not because he thinks the principle to be *non*universal, but because he thinks some groupings do not truly qualify as nations. And, as should be clear, this is fundamentally a question about whether certain groups properly qualify as distinct national groups, and not a question about the *universality* of national self-determination (D. Miller 1998, p. 272).

in its liberal incarnation, antithetical to the demands of cosmopolitan justice. I will consider two common arguments in the contemporary discourse on global justice. I will call them (a) the argument from national self-determination and (b) the argument from national affinity. I will contend that the features of nationalism invoked in these arguments, while indeed integral to nationalism, do not contradict cosmopolitan justice if they are kept within the bounds of *liberal* nationalism.

The nationalist objections

National self-determination

The self-determination objection challenges global distributive justice on two fronts. On one front, it says that the right of self-determination implies that nations have a sovereign right over resources within their borders, and hence any "outward" redistribution of such resources to other nations is at their discretion, contra the demands of global justice (D. Miller 1995, pp. 103–8). On the other, it says that self-determination means that nations are to take full responsibility for their own economic development, but global distributive principles contradict this ideal of responsibility by compensating, through redistributive channels, poor nations for their bad domestic decisions. As David Miller writes: "To respect the self-determination of other nations also involves treating them as responsible for decisions they may make about resource use, economic growth, environmental protection, and so forth" which should give us pause when advocating a more egalitarian global redistribution of wealth and resources (Miller 1995, p. 108). As we saw in the last chapter, a similar argument was made in Rawls's *The Law of Peoples* (1999a).

But both fronts of this argument are ill-advanced in the context of liberal nationalism. While nonliberal nationalists could invoke the self-determination argument to oppose outward distribution of resources within their borders, liberal nationalists may *not*. One of the goals of a liberal account of nationalism is to mark permissible forms and practices of nationalism from impermissible ones. Unlike chauvinistic nationalism, which recognizes no constraints on its nation-building methods, even if this means destroying other nations in the process, liberal nationalism accepts limits on how its nationalist goals may be pursued. Liberal principles set constraints on how a nation may exercise its right to self-determination, and one such constraint is that the nation does not use more than its fair share of the world's resources when exercising this right. From the liberal egalitarian point of view, the current global distribution of wealth and resources is far from just (e.g., Beitz 1999a, part III; Pogge 1989, part III). To insist, then, that self-determination implies that (well-endowed) nations may not be compelled to redistribute their resources globally is to permit the exercise of self-determination to overstep the bounds of liberal justice itself.

In other words, the "liberal" part of the liberal nationalist equation limits the ways in which national self-determination may be expressed. More precisely, if we begin from an egalitarian conception of liberalism and want to marry that understanding of liberalism to nationalism, then the liberal nationalism we get has to be an *egalitarian* liberal nationalism. And as egalitarian liberalism begins from the basic idea that there are no principled differences between individuals on the basis of contingencies, or what Rawls has called factors that are "arbitrary from a moral point of view" (Rawls 1971, p. 15), so too must egalitarian liberal nationalism discount morally arbitrary facts about persons when it comes to determining their just global entitlements. And one arbitrary factor here would be people's national membership.

It may seem odd that liberal nationalists, if they are egalitarian liberals, must consider nationality a morally irrelevant factor when determining the terms of global distributive justice. What does it mean to be a nationalist in this case? But this oddity dissipates once we are clear about the circumscribed place of nationality in liberal nationalist theories. The liberal framework of liberal nationalism sets limitations on how nationality may be invoked when deliberating about justice. This claim will be illustrated and reinforced, I believe, when we confront the national partiality argument below.

Concerning the other front of the self-determination argument, that national self-determination means that nations must take responsibility for their domestic policies and that global distributive justice contradicts this ideal of responsibility, we have already addressed one version of this argument in the previous chapter. The present argument, like the earlier, relies on the thesis Thomas Pogge calls "explanatory nationalism." And, as we saw, explanatory nationalism is an objectionable thesis because it falsely attributes national performance solely to domestic decisions, without recognizing that global conditions do have a crucial role in determining the state of a nation's economy (Pogge 1998, p. 497; also 1994). If the ideal of national self-determination means that nations are to take responsibility for their choices, the ideal of justice would require that the background conditions against which such choices are made be fair. As mentioned earlier, there is no inconsistency with saying that the global conditions against which nations exercise their right to self-determination be regulated by principles of justice and that nations are to take responsibility for their choices made within the rules of just institutions.

The aim of global justice is in part to redress, or help buffer weaker nations from, the detrimental effects of the decisions and policies of richer and more powerful nations. To say that global distributive justice would undermine self-determination (by failing to hold nations responsible for their own policies) simply overlooks this fact of the vulnerability of poor nations to the decisions of more powerful ones. As we do not say, in the domestic case, that every individual failure is due entirely to poor individual choice, likewise we cannot say that every national failure is due to a nation's failure to take full responsibility for its self-determination. To do so is to assume falsely, as liberals have warned us not to in the domestic setting, that the global background context is beyond rebuke, and that the results of decisions made within that context are thus fairly and freely made.

Thus the self-determination argument, as it applies to liberal nationalism, cannot be turned against the demands of global justice. Liberal nationalism, by definition, can support only a conception of self-determination that is situated within the bounds and understanding of liberal justice. This does not mean that no *liberal* national self-determination is ever legitimate in our vastly unequal world; but it does mean, importantly, that liberal nationalists have to be actively committed to global equality if they want to fully legitimize their exercise of self-determination. Indeed, rather than arguing against global justice, the principle of self-determination tells us that we should be concerned about bringing about a more egalitarian global structure in which the preconditions for self-determination do in fact obtain universally for all.

National affinity

The national affinity argument claims that justice depends on shared meanings and common understandings about the goods to be distributed. Yet these shared meanings and common understandings are not available outside the context of a national community (Walzer 1983; also D. Miller 1995, pp. 75, 105–6). As Walzer has famously put it, "The idea of distributive justice presupposes a bounded world within which distribution takes place" (Walzer 1983, p. 31). It is only within such a bounded world that individuals can agree on the kinds of goods that they need to share and distribute.

Although this objection need not obviously present itself as a point against reconciling cosmopolitanism and nationalism, but more obviously as a claim about the conditions of justice, it can be seen as a problem for reconciliation in the following way: if nationalists hold that national affinity is necessary for justice, then a cosmopolitan framework cannot satisfactorily accommodate nationalism without giving up on its aspiration for an idea of justice that transcends national membership. The argument, in other words, draws attention to the tension between a nation-centric idea of justice and a transnational idea of justice.

Yet it seems to me that this argument can be dismissed. Development economists have long argued that the notion of individual human capabilities, as defined by a combination of such factors as life expectancy, literacy rate, income, infant mortality rate, and so on, provides us with a common cross-societal standard against which to compare developmental levels and quality-of-life globally (e.g., Sen 1999, chap. 4; also Nussbaum 2000a, chap. 1). Such indicators are currently employed by the United Nations Human Development Program in its global quality-of-life assessment. A commitment to global egalitarianism can target these general indicators of human development without invoking any controversial presuppositions about the substantive ends and goals of human life across different societies.

There is, therefore, sufficient consensus and shared understanding for us to answer the question "equality of what?" when dealing with global inequality. It is hard to deny that there is a widespread, cross-cultural agreement that longer life span, literacy, health, real income, and so on are cherished goods, and that whatever else people need or desire in life, they need these basic goods (Nussbaum 2000a, chap. 1).[16]

But the argument from national affinity can be read as an argument about moral motivation. So understood, it is a claim about the need for a common belonging, in particular a moral community (the "bounded world") shared by individuals, before we can reasonably (and possibly) expect their compliance with the demands of justice. As Sandel writes, a distributive principle "must presuppose some prior moral tie among those whose assets it would deploy and those whose efforts it would enlist in a common endeavor" (Sandel 1992, p. 22). But unlike nations which are "historic communities" embodying a common history, language, culture and way of life, and hence embodying a viable moral community, the global society exhibits none of these shared common ideals, and hence,

---

[16] Indeed, if the national affinity argument allows (as it seems to presuppose) for agreement within multicultural countries over shared goods and meanings in spite of the great diversity within such groups, its conclusion that the global society is culturally too diverse and deeply divided to constitute a common moral community needs to be reassessed. If citizens of multicultural states can come to an agreement concerning shared goods, it is not too much of a stretch to think that perhaps individuals of the world too can have some shared understandings about basic goods. At the very least, this shows that national affinity does not present an insurmountable obstacle for cosmopolitan justice.

unlike the nation, cannot be a moral community (Walzer 1980, 1983). Thus Sandel worries that "[p]olitical associations more expansive than nations, and with fewer cultural traditions and historical memories to draw upon, may find the task of cultivating commonality more difficult still" (Sandel 1996, p. 339).

Liberal nationalists, as we can recall, do certainly endorse the claim that national affinity provides an important precondition for social justice. But this is very different from saying that nationality is the only available basis for social justice. Rawls writes that it is "the task of the statesman to struggle against the potential lack of affinity among different peoples . . . What encourages the statesman's work is that relations of affinity are not a fixed thing, but may continually grow stronger over time as peoples come to work together in cooperative institutions they have developed" (1999a, pp. 112–13). Rawls, it should be pointed out, recognizes this need for affinity between peoples not to ground global distributive schemes, but to ground humanitarian duties between peoples. Yet his point "that the narrow circle of mutually caring peoples in the world today may expand over time and must never be viewed as fixed" is an important one and can be adapted, I would argue, to ground more than just humanitarian duties but duties of justice as well.[17] The issue here is whether there is sufficient affinity and sense of common moral identity among individuals to motivate compliance with global principles; and Rawls's argument shows us that it would be premature to rule out this possibility just because it is not fully realized now.

Thus, although liberal nationalists have pointed to the importance of shared nationality for the purpose of grounding social justice, it is important to note that this reflects an expansionary rather than constricting moral aspiration and project. That is, the purpose of a common nationality, in the view of liberal nationalists, is to enable citizens to transcend the local and parochial bonds and ties of family, kin, and tribe, and to extend the scope of their moral universe to also encompass strangers (who are fellow citizens). Shared nationality, therefore, motivates citizens to tend to the needs of compatriots who are otherwise strangers by making them all fellow members of a shared "imagined community" (to borrow Benedict Anderson's famous phrase). This reason for cultivating a shared nationality operates as an equally compelling reason for "cultivating humanity," to borrow Nussbaum's inspiring phrase (Nussbaum 1997).

So, understood as an expansionary moral project, there is nothing in the liberal nationalist idea of affinity to suggest that our moral world has to cease suddenly at our national borders. Indeed, as Charles Jones asks, why

---

[17] I examined this point in chapter 4.

not capitalize on this "expansionary momentum" to expand the scope of our moral concern beyond conationals to include also foreigners (Jones 1999b, p. 160)? To the extent that liberal nationalism does succeed (and to a not inconsiderable extent) in enabling individuals to extend their moral spheres to include fellow strangers within a given state, there is no reason off-hand to think that this expansionary project cannot be pursued beyond the borders of the state. To assume that this development of our moral world has to be arrested at our national borders seems grossly arbitrary (Nussbaum 1996, pp. 14–15). To be sure, different forms of individual affinity must be identified and forged (other than those based on shared nationality) in the global context to support the possibility of a global moral community;[18] but one should not preempt such a possibility by assuming, off-hand, that national boundaries are morally impermeable, and that they fix once and for all the outermost limits of the scope of people's moral concern (e.g., Kymlicka 2002, pp. 269–70).

The argument from national affinity tells us that it is important that the liberal nation state cultivates some sort of shared nationality among its citizens for the purpose of promoting social justice. But this alone does not mean that considerations of social justice are important only within a national community, nor does it tell us that such considerations have no basis outside the national community. Indeed, the achievements of liberal nationalism in fostering shared sentiments and affinity could serve as the basis for extending people's commitments towards global justice (Kymlicka 2002, p. 270). The search for some form of global affinity to ground global justice may be an ongoing quest, but this is not the same as saying that such searches are in principle futile or irrelevant, as the affinity argument claims. If anything, nationalism shows us that it is possible for individuals to overcome the near and the familiar and to include strangers in our moral world as well. The trick is not to exhaust this expansionary quest at the national level, and "not to lose steam when [we] get to the borders of the nation" (Nussbaum 1996, p. 14).

Conclusion

I have tried to show that once the conceptual terrain of cosmopolitan justice and liberal nationalism is properly mapped out, the alleged contradiction between the cosmopolitan ideal and liberal nationalism disappears. I then argued that certain nationalist sentiments commonly thought to be

---

[18] There is reasonable hope that this can be done. See, for example, the substantial cross-regional and transnational resource redistribution that member nation states of the European Union support.

inherently anti-cosmopolitan are not so once we situate these nationalist sentiments within the context of *liberal* nationalism. I want to show, in the next chapter, that liberal nationalists not only can be committed cosmopolitan liberals (as argued for here) but that they ought, on their own understanding of nationalism, to take equality between nations very seriously. If this argument is successful, then not only may liberal nationalists support cosmopolitan justice but they have a commitment of justice (on account of their nationalist commitments) to bring about a more egalitarian world.

6   Equality among nations

I argued in the previous chapter that the commonly alleged incompatibility between liberal nationalism and cosmopolitanism disappears once we get clear the parameters of liberal nationalism and the scope of cosmopolitan global distributive justice. There is nothing inconsistent about endorsing liberal nationalism on the one hand, and holding, on the other, the cosmopolitan egalitarian idea that distributive principles should be impartial about nationality and are to be applied to the world taken as a single scheme.

But the fact of compatibility alone does not show that liberal nationalists must necessarily be committed to global justice. In this chapter, I want to establish the stronger claim that not only is liberal nationalism consistent with cosmopolitan justice but that liberal nationalists must also be *international egalitarians*. That is, liberals who take their nationalistic agenda seriously have an obligation to regulate inequalities between nations.[1]

This is a particularly important point, not just because it will demonstrate a strong convergence with respect to global justice between liberal nationalism and cosmopolitan justice, but also because it provides a response to some self-described "liberal" nationalists who deny that there is a commitment of justice to regulate inequality as such between nations. The influential nationalist theorist David Miller, for example, denies that international justice is to be understood in terms of principles of equality because "justice assumes the form of a principle of equality only in certain contexts, and here the relationship between citizens of a nation-state is especially important as a context in which substantial forms of equal treatment can be demanded as a matter of justice" (Miller 2000, p. 174). My main target in this chapter is, therefore, liberal nationalists like Miller, and I hope to argue, in effect, that the international context presents a setting within which considerations of equality between nations

---

[1] Because the nationalist view is that states ought to be nation-building states, equality between nations will in the first instance include equality between countries.

are relevant on account of the professed commitments of these liberal nationalists. To be sure, a limited concern for international equality need not take us all the way to cosmopolitanism, for the former is interested foremost in inequalities between nations rather than between individuals as such, whereas cosmopolitan justice, as I am defending it, has an individualist egalitarian commitment. Nonetheless, as pointed out in the previous chapters (chapters 4 and 5), inequality between countries affects how *individuals* within the worse-off countries fare. For instance, international inequality limits the resources poorer countries have to distribute internally among their respective citizens, and it constrains the domestic choices and policies of poorer countries by, for example, weakening their relative global bargaining position. These will affect the life chances of individuals in these countries. Thus equality between nations provides a crucial first step towards the cosmopolitan goal of equality between individuals. The aim of this chapter is to show that liberal nationalists must be committed to this first step. I will, therefore, deliberately use the term "international" equality or justice in this chapter, as opposed to the more inclusive "global" equality or justice, in light of this restricted goal.

The claim that liberal nationalists must also be egalitarian internationalists is not new. While some professed liberal nationalists, like Miller as noted above, deny that liberal nationalism has an international egalitarian commitment, other liberal nationalists have unequivocally stated that liberal nationalism is committed to international equality of some form. Yael Tamir, for instance, writes that "one of the most important implications of a theory of liberal nationalism" is that it supports some account of international distributive justice (Tamir 1992, p. 161; also Kymlicka 2001b, pp. 271–2; 2002, pp. 268–70; Nielsen 1999). But this position, to my mind, has not been adequately articulated and defended in the liberal nationalist literature. Indeed, where the international implications of liberal nationalism have received more detailed analysis, the attention has come from those nationalists who are critical of international egalitarianism, like D. Miller (2000, chap. 10; 1999a), or from egalitarian internationalists who are critical of liberal nationalism (e.g. Barry, Brock, Moellendorf, Lichtenberg, and Parekh). That is, where the connection between liberal nationalism and egalitarian internationalism has been examined in greater detail in the contemporary literature, it has been to establish the negative relationship between the two. I want, therefore, to show and defend in greater detail the opposite view: that liberal nationalists must be committed to international egalitarianism.

This relative neglect in the current liberal nationalist literature with respect to showing the positive connection between liberal nationalism and international justice is, of course, understandable. The central challenge for liberal nationalists has been to show the connection and compatibility between liberal justice and nationalism in the context of a single state – a considerable challenge as it is, given the common misperception that liberalism and nationalism are incompatible ideals. Reflections on the international implications of liberal nationalism, even if thought to be positive, tend to be offered as an afterthought, where possibilities are suggested but left undeveloped. By fleshing out these suggestions, I hope that the discussion in this chapter will contribute to this liberal nationalist aspiration as well as defending cosmopolitan justice.

The international egalitarianism that will be discussed here is, of course, not equality in actual holdings per capita for each nation, but equality with respect to the *international order* or *institutional scheme*. It is the background context against which nations interact that principles of international egalitarian justice regulate, not the distributive outcome of interaction itself. Using the Rawlsian model to anchor our discussion, we might say that a just egalitarian international order is one in which the worst-off benefits most compared to alternative international arrangements.

The gist of my argument is that the pursuit of *nationalist* goals in a nonegalitarian international order inevitably subverts liberal principles of justice; thus, the legitimacy of national pursuits necessitates a prior concern for the justness of the background global context within which such pursuits take place. My arguments for international equality will, therefore, focus on the "nationalist" component of liberal nationalism, rather than its "liberal" aspect as such. I want to show, not why liberals per se, but why liberal *nationalists* must also be international egalitarians. So, while liberals have good liberal reasons (as I have tried to show in chapters 2 and 4) to support cosmopolitan justice, my contention in this chapter is that liberal *nationalists* have additional reasons – reasons that derive from their principle of nationality – for doing so. If my arguments hold, then in as far as we accept that "all liberals are also liberal nationalists" (Tamir 1992, p. 139), we must also accept that liberals have more reasons than they think – reasons *apart from the standard liberal ones* – for supporting international justice. Because some liberal nationalists, as mentioned above, reject the common arguments in defense of international equality, it is not redundant to provide additional arguments founded on other (i.e., nationalist) claims to establish a conclusion in support of international egalitarianism. To the contrary, if I am right, then those liberal nationalists such as Miller, who reject the normative individualism normally invoked in liberal arguments in defense of international distributive justice, will see that there are other reasons consistent with their non-individualist philosophical framework for endorsing some form of international egalitarianism.

I will discuss two arguments to this effect. First, I argue that in as far as all liberal nationalists take the right to national self-determination to be a "reiterative right" (Nielsen 1999), i.e., a universal right of all nations, they must also, if they take this reiterative right seriously, ensure that the material preconditions for the realization of this right in fact obtain for all nations. This entails a *pro tanto* commitment to some form of economic equality between nations.

The second argument recalls the nationalist thesis noted earlier, that all states, including liberal ones, are nation-building states (chapter 5). As mentioned, it is an inescapable and legitimate fact that states must engage in the practice of promoting, fostering, and protecting a particular national identity and culture. Among the more important strategies that a liberal state must adopt to this end is that of regulating (i.e., restricting) immigration into the country (Kymlicka 2001b, pp. 271–2; Tamir 1992; also Walzer 1983, chaps. 2 and 3). Yet immigration restriction, on first glance, seems inconsistent with the liberal principle of equal opportunity, given the fact of global inequality in resource and wealth distribution (e.g., Carens 1987). Accordingly, liberal nationals find themselves in a bind: they have seemingly legitimate nationalist reasons for wanting to restrict immigration, but such restrictions, on the other hand, seem to offend against the requirements of liberal justice. A way out of this moral bind, as we will see, is to bring about a more egalitarian global order in which immigration restrictions need not violate equal opportunity. Thus liberal nationalists must be specially committed to international equality if they want to legitimize their nation-building policies.[2] As in the previous chapter, my aim here is not to offer an independent defense of liberal nationalism, but to show what those who are committed to liberal nationalism are further committed to, in light of their own avowed principles.

Self-determination and equality

The universality of self-determination

The right to national self-determination is integral to the idea of nationalism. As David Miller has put it, "[t]he assumption of nationhood and the

---

[2] There have been recent arguments that cosmopolitans should be liberal nationalists on the ground that the quintessential cosmopolitan ideals of individual autonomy, democracy, and social justice are best realized in the context of a liberal national community (Nielsen 1999; Kymlicka 2001a, chap. 10: see previous chapter). But, as I hope is evident, I am proceeding from the other side of the cosmopolitanism–nationalism equation: I want to show why liberal nationalists should also be cosmopolitans; that is, why liberal nationalists have to work in the direction of cosmopolitan justice.

quest for self-determination are merely two sides of the same coin" (1995, p. 83).[3] Rawls, too, recognizes the significance of self-determination for protecting the distinct identities of peoples. He writes that

> it is surely a good for individuals and associations to be attached to their particular culture and to take part in its common public and civic life. In this way belonging to a particular political society, and being at home in its civic and social world, gains expression and fulfillment. This is no small thing. It argues for preserving significant room for the idea of a people's self-determination and for some kind of loose or Confederative forms of a Society of Peoples (Rawls 1999a, p. 111).

As we saw in the previous chapter, the claim to self-determination is fundamentally understood as a claim to a public political sphere in which a nation's cultural identity can be expressed, reflected, and fostered. As mentioned in the previous chapter, national self-determination does not entail independent statehood. What is basic to the idea of self-determination is that nations have a claim to a certain degree of political autonomy (from limited self-government to actual statehood) so that they may secure a public sphere and the relevant set of public institutions that best reflect and sustain their particular cultural identities.

But fundamental to liberal nationalism, indeed a necessary (though not sufficient) feature of liberal nationalism, is that the principle of self-determination is a *universalizable* one. What this means is that, for liberal nationalists, self-determination is a right that all nations, under the appropriate conditions, are entitled to. An obvious implication of this universalizability condition is that a nation's exercise of its right to self-determination must not infringe another nation's similar right. This universalizability condition applies not just to nations outside a country's borders, but, as some liberals have argued in recent years, to minority nations within as well. Treating the principle of self-determination as a universalizable principle therefore imposes constraints on how a nation may exercise this right both in the domestic and international spheres.[4] Indeed it is this universality of self-determination, what Kymlicka calls the principle of reciprocity, that grounds the liberal defense of minority rights. Kai Nielsen thus calls the right of self-determination

---

[3] For more arguments for self-determination, see D. Miller (1995, pp. 83–90).

[4] There are other important conditions on how self-determination may be exercised, though these conditions are not set by the ideal of collective self-determination but by the normative individualist premises of liberal nationalism. For instance, an exercise of self-determination which suppresses the rights of individual members of the nation to question and challenge the traditional interpretation of nationality violates basic liberal rights and freedom, and so fails to meet liberal nationalist standards. I am concentrating here on arguments for self-determination that need not rely on the normative individualism common to standard liberal views so as to include those "liberal" nationalists (like David Miller) who reject normative individualism.

a "reiterative" right: if nationality is a good for some, then it must be a good for all under relevantly similar conditions (Nielsen 1999, p. 449).

National self-determination is important for liberal nationalists because, as mentioned earlier, it secures the cultural context within which individuals are able to exercise their choices; it also generates the sense of shared belonging and "common sympathies" that are thought to be necessary for the ends of social justice and the practice of deliberative democracy. In as far as liberals do take the value of autonomy, justice, and democracy to be universal ideals, *liberal* nationalists have to affirm the universality of self-determination. The universality of self-determination stems from the universal values that liberal nationalists see self-determination to promote.

This respect for the self-determination of all nations is one crucial distinguishing feature of liberal nationalism that sets it apart from patently illiberal forms of nationalism that see no inconsistency in claiming self-determination for themselves while denying it to others. Indeed, it seems that the universality of national self-determination is basic to any defensible account of nationalism. Few serious theorists of nationalism can advance a form of nationalism – what Margaret Canovan aptly calls "chauvinistic nationalism" – that takes self-determination to be a right applicable only to one's own nation, and hence a right that may be exercised at the expense of other nations' similar claim (Canovan 1996a, p. 6). Such a position would violate a central feature of any morally defensible claim – that it be based on a principle that can be universalized as a moral law for all rational beings. In short, at minimum, most serious accounts of nationalism take self-determination to be a universal principle, if nothing else about nationality is.

According to Tamir, the universalizability of national self-determination claims is sometimes overlooked by critics of nationalism because of how nationalist demands are often in fact made. Tamir notes that national self-determination can be advanced using either a particularist or universalist discourse. The first invokes the particularity of the nation, justifying its nationalist demands by reference to particular and special features of that nation. The second invokes a "universal dimension," justifying the nation's demands by reference to moral arguments that are generalizable and universalizable (Tamir 1996, p. 71). But many "real-world" nationalists, Tamir observes, prefer to adopt a particularist mode of justification, pointing to their nation's unique history, experience of injustice and so on, and will in fact deliberately downplay the universal aspects of their demands even where present. This is because particularist arguments are seen as politically expedient and beneficial in some contexts – they can, for example, more directly reinforce the right of a nation to a particular territory (such as a historical homeland) and not just any territory – and so tend to be stressed over universalist arguments even when these arguments are actually available. Hence, Tamir notes a certain paradox in nationalist practice, that instead of using a universal language of justification, nationalists often prefer a particularist one, thus obscuring the universalist principles that provide the necessary moral justification for their demands. That nationalists in practice tend to use a particularist mode of justification is one reason why the universal dimension of national self-determination can be overlooked. The preferred discourse that is used to politically promote morally defensible (because universalizable) forms of nationalism has ironically contributed to the skepticism about the universality of the principle of national self-determination.[5]

It is true that nationalist theorists do not necessarily agree on the social groupings to which the principle of self-determination may apply. They disagree over whether a given community counts as a nation, properly speaking, and, hence, whether it qualifies for national self-determination. David Miller and Michael Walzer, for instance, believe that some national communities, like certain indigenous groups in North America, are really subnational communities, and so do not display a sufficiently distinct identity to count as a nation (D. Miller 1995, 1998; Walzer 1992, 1995).[6] Hence, on their view, the right of self-determination does not apply to such groups.

This disagreement over the criterion of nationhood is obviously an important one and merits serious discussion. However, this is fundamentally a debate over whether certain groups properly qualify as distinct national groups, and is not a dispute over the *universality* of self-determination per se, which is the point being stressed here. So, important as this dispute is for our understanding and practice of nationalism, I will put it to one side here, for it does not bear on my main premise that all liberal nationalists (and most plausible theories of nationalism, one might add) take self-determination to be a universal principle.[7]

---

[5] None of this denies that chauvinistic forms of nationalism are also frequently practiced (see, for example, Serbian nationalism in recent times), morally indefensible as they are.

[6] Miller writes that in order for a group to qualify for national self-determination, it "should form a nation with an identity that is clearly separate from that of the larger nation from which they wish to disengage" and that the "group should be able to validate its claim to exercise authority over the territory it wishes to occupy" (D. Miller 1998, p. 272).

[7] According to Miller, the Catalans and the Kurds thus have "qualitatively different" claims to national self-determination given their respective relationships to the larger society in which they are situated. For Miller, Kurds are entitled to self-determination but not necessarily the Catalans (Miller 1996, p. 267). But this account of nationality seems to hold groups hostage to arbitrary historical factors: it seems to say that a cultural group

Equality

What else does a commitment to self-determination as a universal principle commit the liberal nationalist to? If there are certain necessary preconditions for self-determination, it seems to follow that if one accepts sincerely the universality of self-determination, one must also be committed to protecting or bringing about these preconditions. One cannot seriously endorse an end without accepting also the necessary means to that end.

One obvious set of preconditions are political and legal ones. These include institutionalizing decolonization, prohibitions against unwarranted interference, the right to territorial and communal integrity and so on. These political rights do not apply only to nation states, as is commonly interpreted, but are arguably also applicable in perhaps more limited ways to minority nations within states. Some central minority national rights include those of language rights, the right to regulate education and immigration, and even limited self-government. Indeed, as Antonio Cassese points out, the self-determination principle, when it was first proclaimed in 1917, was understood primarily as a national minority right. It was held "to apply both to [minority] nationalities in Europe (chiefly those under the Austro-Hungarian monarchy) and to colonial peoples" (Cassese 1986, p. 131). But I will focus my attention here on self-determination as the claim of nation states.

The political conditions of self-determination are widely recognized in contemporary international law and practice. The right of nation states to self-determination and noninterference is a basic norm of international law, and is affirmed and institutionalized in the various international declarations and covenants on individual rights and peoples' rights.[8] The ideal of self-determination understood as a legal and political right was, of course, the main drive behind the decolonization movements in much of the world during the latter half of the last century.

---

that needs self-determination most (because its identity has already been corroded) is not entitled to it; whereas those that need it less (because they constitute a distinct national community) have a greater claim to self-determination. For more discussion on this, see Kymlicka (2001a).

[8] Much work, of course, remains to be done. This includes not only the theoretical work of showing how universal human rights (commonly understood as the rights of individuals) could be consistent with the rights of peoples, but also the political work of bridging the gap between rhetoric and practice. There is also the issue of extending the political right of self-determination to minority nations within nation states, and not just to sovereign states, as these rights are commonly narrowly interpreted. It is well known that "peoples" and "nations" in the various UN and international documents are commonly interpreted to refer to "states," thus bypassing minority nations within states.

But other important preconditions of self-determination that have received less global attention are economic ones. The lack of material resources can negatively impact on a nation's capacity to preserve and express its national culture in a variety of ways. First, a lack of basic resources deprives needy nations of the social and economic resources that are needed to sustain functioning and well-ordered national institutions. At the fundamental level of human functioning, not being able to meet basic human needs simply undermines individuals' capability to live a minimally functioning human life, let alone be able to sustain and promote their national way of life.

Second, the lack of ample social and economic resources compromises a nation's ability to support the necessary institutional schemes (cultural programs, education, etc.) to preserve and promote its cultural heritage. Nation-building is an enterprise that requires not just the political freedom to do so, but the material resources with which to carry out such projects. In *The Law of Peoples*, Rawls recognizes that peoples facing what he calls unfavorable conditions – i.e., lacking basic resources and development needs – are unable to sustain well-functioning decent institutions, and so need the support of the Society of Peoples.

Thus, given the different ways economic deprivation can adversely affect a nation's realization of self-determination (i.e., its ability to express and sustain its culture in a particular political sphere), it is imperative that liberal nationalists take a special interest in meeting people's basic material needs. That is, to take self-determination seriously entails a genuine commitment to ensure that all nations enjoy the material conditions necessary for the exercise of national self-determination. As Nielsen has put it, failure to ensure that the preconditions of self-determination are secured universally is to make "a hollow mockery" of one's stated commitment to the universality of national self-determination (1999, p. 449). In short, on pain of contradiction, nationalists who accept the universality of national self-determination must also be committed to assisting nations secure the basic material conditions that are necessary for exercising their self-determination right. Political or legal recognition of the right to self-determination is not sufficient if some nations lack even very basic wealth and resources.

This point parallels Rawls's distinction between liberty and the worth of liberty. For Rawls, a lack of general means can affect the capability of a person to exercise a certain liberty, thus undermining the worth of that liberty for that person (Rawls 1971, pp. 204–5). I am arguing here, along similar lines, that the *worth* of the right to self-determination to a nation is distinct from its simply being granted that right in a formal sense. The right to self-determination will be less worthy to some than to others if not all are equally capable of making use of that right due to an inequality with respect to the necessary preconditions for the exercise of this right. The equal worth of the right to self-determination cannot be ensured when some societies are burdened by economic needs.

Equality versus basic needs

It could be objected that what I have shown above is not that liberal nationalists need to defend international equality as such, but that they have to ensure that all nations are able to achieve the level of economic development necessary for supporting the appropriate institutions for national self-determination. Accordingly, there would be no need to do more once all nations have achieved a basic or threshold level of development; inequality between nations as such is not a concern. Thus, there is no reason to be committed to international equality if we are mainly concerned with providing nations with the material resources for self-determination; we need only to take our duties of humanitarian assistance seriously, by making sure that no nations fail to meet certain basic economic conditions that are necessary for self-determination.

Theorists as diverse as John Rawls and David Miller have offered arguments along this line. Miller presents this view in terms of a contrast between "weak" and "strong cosmopolitanism," and argues that while weak cosmopolitanism which supports humanitarian duties is appropriate, strong cosmopolitanism which requires egalitarian distributive justice is not. Indeed, Miller says that this is all global justice can coherently demand. For Miller, therefore, one ought not to confuse global justice with global egalitarianism (D. Miller 1999a and 2000). And Rawls, as we have seen (chapter 3), emphasizes the need to assist peoples facing unfavorable conditions and who are hence unable to support well-ordered institutions. But this duty of assistance is not one of distributive equality; rather, it is a duty that ceases once a defined threshold of subsistence is secured.[9]

On first glance, the above seems right: if it is the lack of material resources rather than *inequality* as such that undermines self-determination, then a commitment to self-determination does not entail a support for international egalitarianism. But as I noted earlier (chapters 3 and 4), it is not always clear that basic deprivation can fully be understood in absolute terms without taking into account its comparative aspects.

---

[9] Rawls speaks in terms of providing peoples with the basic minimum for supporting well-ordered institutions rather than for supporting self-determining institutions. But the self-determination of peoples is presupposed in his argument, hence the importance of peoples being able to support their own well-ordered institutions.

There "is no clear or sharply defined threshold of 'serious deficiency' above which a concern to improve a person's material conditions simply ceases to operate" (Beitz 2001, p. 101).[10] That is, how one nation fares and what it can do with the resources and wealth it actually has is dependent in part on how much other nations have. Recalling the point made earlier (attributed to Sen), equality and poverty are closely interconnected because great inequalities between parties compromise the capacity of the worse-off to purchase necessary goods with the resources that they have, given their reduced purchasing power compared to the purchasing power of the better-off. That many developing countries are compelled by monetary incentives to replace subsistence agriculture with the production of commodities (like sugar, coffee, cacao) for markets in the developed world has put citizens in the developing countries in an especially precarious situation in which their ability to sustain themselves has become nearly wholly dependent on the prices of commodities in the global market, which is extremely fickle and contingent on various extraneous factors, including the betting patterns of speculators and brokers.

Thus, and directly on the point of self-determination, the claim that protecting basic needs is sufficient for securing nations' capacity for self-determination overlooks how differences in power relations between nations, which economic inequality engenders and sustains, obstruct the right to self-determination of the least advantaged. To the extent that nations interact in an increasingly interconnected global economic order, material inequalities will allow some nations to more easily exploit others, thereby compromising their right to self-determination. A nation that is able to meet its basic needs and is entitled to self-determination as a legal and political right, but that is poor compared to others, may still not be able to fully exercise this right in a situation of social and economic inequality. This is because wealth is, to a large extent, a relative factor rather than an absolute one in a shared economic space; the richer some are, the weaker the purchasing power of others, thus resulting in the different vulnerabilities of each with respect to the other. Indeed, inequalities make the alleviation of poverty more difficult. As Simon Caney aptly observes, it seems plausible "that some persons are impoverished at least in part because they have not had a fair start in life and that had they

---

[10] That a person's ability to meet her needs is determined in large part by how much others have is one of G. A. Cohen's objections to Nozick's claim that voluntary transactions between individuals in an initially just situation have to have a just outcome, even if this makes some immensely wealthier than others. Cohen objects (even if we accept such transactions to be fully voluntary) that this fails to notice that third parties who were *not* involved in such transactions are now faring worse relative to their initial situation because their relative purchasing power is compromised (Cohen 1978).

better opportunities, they could have been more likely to be able to earn a reasonable standard of living" (Caney 2001, p. 116). And to the extent that an impoverished society cannot properly or meaningfully exercise its right of self-determination, international inequality should be a concern for liberal nationalists.

Relative differences in power and vulnerabilities that arise when the gap between the rich and poor is too wide render self-determination difficult, if not impossible, for the worst-off. Indeed the relative vulnerability of some nations with respect to others makes them susceptible to coercion and deception, which is clearly anathema to self-determination. As Onora O'Neill writes, what makes coercion possible is:

> the *relative weakness* of their intended victims. It is not their absolute lack of capabilities and resources that constitutes vulnerability to coercion; rather it is that they possess fewer capabilities, powers or resources than others, and specifically than their coercers. Agents become victims not just because they are poor, ignorant, unskilled or physically weak or emotionally fragile, but because they are confronted by others who are richer, more knowledgeable, more skilful or physically or emotionally stronger, and prepared to exploit these advantages (2000, p. 95, my stress; also Satz 1999, p. 80).

Developing countries whose economies tend to be more dependent on exports of commodities or low-tech products are especially vulnerable to fluctuations in the global economy.

The power differential between nations, therefore, has an important impact on how nations are able to enjoy their independence and autonomy. As an example, consider the case of Indonesia. This was a country that, prior to the Asian economic crisis in 1998, had arguably met a basic economic threshold in development terms and was indeed touted by observers as a country on its way to becoming one of the region's economic "tigers." Yet because of the great inequality between it and the economies on which Indonesia depends (for its investments, for exports, for expertise, etc.), a fragile dependency that also bred corruption and mismanagement within, a regional economic downturn rapidly impoverished the country's economy, increasing levels of absolute poverty. Consequently, even its capacity to dictate its own domestic fiscal policies was further compromised on account of IMF impositions, whose intervention it found itself unable to refuse.

Inequality and the resulting differential power relations between countries can, therefore, have adverse implications for national self-determination. If one of the arguments for self-determination is that it allows for collective autonomy, and that it allows a people to express its way of life, then surely asymmetrical power relationships between

peoples affect their collective autonomy, just as differential power relations between individuals affect the ability of the disadvantaged to fully
exercise their autonomy (e.g., G. A. Cohen 1978). Thus, Beitz notes that
"some inequalities are objectionable because they express social relations
in which the advantaged exercise an unreasonably large degree of control
over others" (2001, p. 106). Accordingly, "[m]embers of economically
vulnerable societies – particularly the worst off among them, who lack private means to fall back on – are exposed, without any effective recourse,
to the consequences of decisions importantly affecting their life prospects
which originate elsewhere" (2001, p. 107).

The claim here is not that we need a global context in which countries
are able to fully exercise self-determination without intruding factors from
outside.[11] Rather, the point is that some countries are more vulnerable
to global market forces than others because of differences in power relations, and hence are unequally situated with respect to other countries
as a result. Their domestic policies are more prone to be influenced and
constrained by the process of globalization than those of countries in
stronger economic positions. To the extent that liberal nationalists take
self-determination to be a universal ideal, they should be exercised by the
inequality in relations between nations.

Indeed, a country's economic status directly determines the degree
of control and participation it can effectively have in global decision-
making, even in purportedly international organizations. To take just one
example, economic clout carries weight in IMF decision-making, where
a country's vote is weighted according to its financial contribution to the
organization. The European Union, the United States, and Japan com-
bined have a clear majority in determining the direction of the IMF (see
Sachs 1998). As another example, poor countries are less able to set terms
for their entry into WTO (membership in which certainly has privileges)
and other global trade arrangements and treaties. They are being pres-
sured, for instance, to accept the terms of the WTO agreement on intellectual property (Trade-Related Aspects of Intellectual Property Rights –
TRIPS) or face retaliation; they are asked to open up their markets to
imports or face similar moves in response that would have adverse effects
on their economies. In short, inequality between nations thus contributes
to what international theorists call the global "democratic deficit," that
is, the lack of democratic decision-making regarding decisions that have
global or at least regional effects. Global decisions are made that
have great implications for developing countries but over which they
have little democratic control.

---

[11] Miller presents this point as a rebuttal (Miller 2000, p. 163).

Thus economic inequality compromises self-determination in the brute sense in that it affects the material living standards of people, and so hinders their capability to dictate their national agenda. But economic inequality can also directly threaten the cultural life of a community by creating a pipeline in which cultural goods and influences flow only one way, from the rich to the poor. Rich countries are better able to produce, globally market and promote mass cultural products than poor countries. Simply put, global economic inequality makes for a highly unequal global cultural marketplace, making it difficult for some countries to protect their local cultural practices, thereby challenging their right to cultural self-determination. While import quotas on cultural products of different kinds (e.g., on Hollywood films) have been put in place by countries in the attempt to protect their cultural traditions and industries, the pressures of free trade make these quotas difficult for some countries to sustain. For example, while countries with developed economies like France and Canada are able to stave off demands on them by the US to lift import restrictions on American cultural products, countries like Thailand and even South Korea are less able to do so.[12] The economic costs of retaliation in response to their tariffs on cultural products may be too much for countries with more vulnerable economies to bear, even if lifting these tariffs means putting some of their local cultural practices at risk. So economic inequality not only makes the global cultural marketplace an uneven one, but it also limits the ability of individual countries to take steps domestically to counteract the marketplace inequality.

Indeed, it seems that, in the end, David Miller himself accepts this strong connection between inequality and the incapacity to exercise the right of self-determination. We recall that Miller is willing to defend what he calls "weak cosmopolitanism" which requires humanitarian duties between nations, but not "strong cosmopolitanism" which would require distributive principles between nations (D. Miller 1998, p. 176 and 1999a). Miller sees a crucial distinction between basic rights deprivation and material inequality, and holds that while the former imposes universal obligations on people, a concern for inequality is not universal in scope. Yet, he himself concedes at one point that inequality can lead

---

[12] There are ongoing negotiations in the WTO for what is called "cultural exceptions" to free trade – that is, the exemption of cultural goods from free trade agreements, thus allowing for their import restrictions. That negotiations are being undertaken (in spite of continuing US opposition), to the benefit of the cultural sectors of developing countries, is due to the powerful opposition of countries like France and Canada to American cultural imports. One could reasonably speculate that without the interests of countries such as Canada, France, and Japan in regulating cultural imports, there would be no serious consideration for cultural exceptions. Developing countries are getting a fighting chance to impose cultural restrictions on imports only because of the economic clout of other nations.

to exploitative relationships and consequently the failure to secure even basic rights. Miller writes "If we could equalize individuals' access to material resources, then on the one hand we would go a long way to ensure that everyone had the means to protect their basic rights, while on the other hand the power imbalances . . . that give rise to exploitation would disappear" (1999a, pp. 209–10). He thus rhetorically asks: "So haven't I arrived at the case for global equality by a different route?" (1999a, p. 210).

Miller's response to his own rhetorical question is that, unfortunately, there is no satisfactory account of global equality, even though inequality may lead to exploitation and so, in turn, would challenge even his weak cosmopolitanism (1999a, pp. 209–10). So it seems in the end that Miller's position is driven not so much by the distinction he sees between basic rights deprivation and inequality, as he claims, for he has conceded a strong causal connection between the two above, but by his general concern that there is simply no coherent basis for global equality.[13] But, as discussed in a previous chapter, this concern about the viability and coherence of global equality is too hastily put forth. To be sure, certain obstacles are in the way of a more egalitarian world order – including the lack of appropriate institutions and the lack of affinity between individuals across boundaries. But these are not insurmountable challenges; to take the world as it presently is to be a given, and assume that we have to constrain our aspiration on this basis, is to too easily surrender our hope for a better world. Indeed, as mentioned in earlier chapters, to hold justice to be limited by the reality of institutions already in place subverts our ordinary understanding of the relationship between justice and institutions (see chapters 2 and 4).

So, if liberal nationalists take the idea of self-determination seriously as a universal ideal, they must also be committed international egalitarians. The goal of self-determination can be achieved only in a context of, among other things, economic equality between nations. Meeting a predetermined basic needs level may not be enough to secure self-determination, given the fact of competitive interactions among nations. The arguments of some egalitarians that economic inequalities in the domestic context compromise the self-control of the less well-off has a natural global analogue (Scanlon 1997; Beitz 2001). Just as economic inequalities allow some individuals to subject others, thereby restricting their self-determination, economic inequalities between nations compromise the right to self-determination of worse-off nations.

---

[13] Miller says that global equality cannot be defined absent a world community, with rules governing holdings and the use of resources (2000, p. 210).

It might be pointed out that there is a potential tension between the argument presented in this chapter and my overall thesis in defense of cosmopolitan justice. Cosmopolitan justice would require a greater redistribution of resources to individuals currently less well-off, like individuals in China, and a transfer of resources away from individuals currently very well-off, e.g., the citizens in countries like New Zealand and Lichtenstein. Would this redistribution, given the relative difference in the size of their economies, not have the result of compromising the right to national self-determination of New Zealand and Lichtenstein relative to China's, while further enhancing China's? If so, cosmopolitan justice runs against the emphasis of the current chapter on protecting the equal right of self-determination for all nations.

But this tension between national self-determination and cosmopolitan equality can be mitigated if we keep in mind that the argument for self-determination supports the equal worth of self-determination and does not assume that all nations must be able to exercise self-determination to the degree that they currently are able. Specifically, the argument is for a global background context in which the right to self-determination can be meaningfully and equally claimed by all. The resource reallocation that this egalitarian international order requires will, of course, entail some reduction in the entitlements of some presently very well-off countries; but it is not clear that this immediately means that their right to self-determination is therefore *unjustly* restricted. So the tension between the cosmopolitan position and the national self-determination argument need not arise – both arguments can accept that there will be some restrictions on the scope to which some (rich) countries can carry out their right of self-determination.

The concern of this chapter is with what it would take, in terms of our international commitments, for self-determination to be equally claimable and exercisable by all nations. While it is clear that a country like, say, Sierra Leone will continue to find it difficult to exercise self-determination under the present global conditions, it is far from clear that a country like New Zealand would be unable to meaningfully exercise self-determination in a reformed world in which a country like India or China gains more economic clout due to greater global distributive justice while New Zealand experiences a reduction in its holdings. At present, a country like Singapore is able to trade extensively with China, which has a significantly larger economy, without having to submit to unfair trade terms thereby risking its right of self-determination.

There can be a tension between cosmopolitanism and national self-determination, but it is not as described above. It is not that cosmopolitan equality would undermine self-determination, but that cosmopolitan justice would set limits on how self-determination may actually be exercised. That is, a nation is entitled to the right to self-determination and the conditions under which this right has equal worth for all; but the exercise of this right must respect similar rights of other nations as well as the rights of individuals in the nation. But this limitation on self-determination, and on nationalism in general, is consistent with my defense of international equality. Just as equalizing individual wealth and income in the domestic context need not have the effect of allowing some households to dominate others when this equality requirement is understood to be part of a larger package of justice, so the cosmopolitan goal of equality between individuals need not unjustly undermine the self-determination of less populous countries.

Immigration and international equal opportunity

The first argument, the self-determination argument, is independent of whether one accepts a universalist version of liberalism or not.[14] As long as one is genuinely committed to the principle of national self-determination as a universal ideal, one must also, to be consistent, be committed to bringing about the preconditions that make self-determination possible. In the global context, one important precondition is that of economic equality between nations. If we like, what is doing the "globalizing equality" work is the universality of national self-determination and not liberalism per se.

But while the argument from self-determination should have appeal to all liberal nationalists irrespective of their understanding of liberalism, the next argument will have appeal only to those liberals who take the idea of equal opportunity to be a universally valid one. Nonetheless, this argument does not just try to show how equal opportunity as a liberal idea leads logically to global egalitarianism; instead it will try to show why the nationalist goals of liberalism provide liberal nationalists with collaborating and reinforcing reasons and motivations for supporting international equality. Given that some liberal nationalists are skeptical of international equality, revealing the peculiarly liberal *nationalists'* reasons for caring about international inequality will help assuage this particular skepticism.

I have not, of course, provided arguments here as to why liberals must be committed to global egalitarianism, nor is it my goal to repeat some

---

[14] For some "nonuniversalist" liberal positions, see Sandel (1996), Taylor (1992), and Walzer (1990a, 1990b, 1992). See, in particular, Walzer's description of the communitarian critique of liberalism as a *liberal* critique of one interpretation of liberalism. See also Taylor (1989).

of the well-known arguments to this effect.[15] My claim will be that for liberals who take global equality seriously, there is a potential tension between this global egalitarian commitment and the commitments of liberal nationalism, and my goal in this section is to show the implications of this tension for liberal nationalists.

The argument invokes the idea of nation-building discussed earlier. As mentioned, all states are nation-building states, including liberal ones. What differentiates liberal nationalism from illiberal forms of nationalism is how each defines and pursues their nation-building goals (Kymlicka 2001a, chap. 10). As we saw, Kymlicka notes nine features that can help us sort out more liberal ideas and ways of nation-building from less liberal ones. But among these acceptable nation-building strategies is that of regulating immigration into the liberal state (see chapter 5).

The claim here is not that nation states are permitted to firmly close their borders but that they may restrict movement of people into their country instead of maintaining fully open borders.[16] The belief is that it could be a legitimate nationalist goal to regulate immigration in order to protect and preserve a certain national identity that is necessary for sustaining and preserving important democratic political and public institutions. It is not that outsiders cannot in principle be integrated into the national culture so defined, but that the process of integrating outsiders into a common societal culture characterized by a common language and shared public institutions takes time and education, and, therefore, an absolutely open immigration policy might risk overwhelming a national culture at a given time. Regulating immigration thus allows a liberal state the needed interval of time to sustain and protect the national unity so crucial for grounding its democratic institutions.

Thus regulating immigration in itself is neither liberal nor illiberal, just nor unjust, on the liberal nationalist view. Whether an immigration policy is consistent or inconsistent with liberal justice depends on the criteria used for selecting (or restricting) immigrants and the reasons for this restriction. Immigration policies based on racial selection with the objective of preserving a racial identity of a nation would be plainly illiberal, whereas policies aiming at sustaining a nonracial national identity and which base their selection criteria on factors such as individuals' competency in the national language, occupational qualifications, family ties, or

[15] See, for example, the well-known arguments of Beitz (1999a); and Pogge (1989). I discuss these arguments in chapters 3 and 4 of this work (also Tan 2000, chap. 7).

[16] This need not apply to the special case of genuine refugees, who most liberals would say are entitled to unconditional admittance for humanitarian reasons. Needless to say, most liberal states do not live up to this requirement, contra the exhortations of the United Nations High Commissioner for Refugees.

familiarity with democratic culture are not necessarily inconsistent with liberal justice.[17] In short, some rationales for, and ways of, regulating immigration are more liberal than others; and a liberal conception of nationalism would strive to meet the requirements of the former.

But for liberals who hold that the liberal idea of equal opportunity applies transnationally, this nationalist justification for restricting immigration poses an awkward problem. One central reason for immigration in today's world is that of economic advancement. It is a common fact that immigrants tend to move from poorer countries to wealthier ones, the main purpose of which is to pursue economic opportunities. Thus, as Joseph Carens has argued, if we take the liberal idea of equal opportunity seriously, then we should seriously entertain the notion of open borders and free movement of people in the world. To allow states to restrict, or even regulate, immigration is to allow them to arbitrarily deny others the same access to resources its own citizens enjoy, and this would be a violation of equality of opportunity. Indeed, Carens points out, not allowing people to improve their conditions by allowing them to move countries is akin to the feudalist ideal that people's life chances are to be wholly determined at birth. Carens thus suggests that in a Rawlsian veil of ignorance globally construed, behind which individuals do not know their nationalities among other contingent facts about themselves, they will indeed opt for open rather than regulated national borders (Carens 1987).

The liberal *nationalist* idea that liberal states may regulate immigration, therefore, sits uncomfortably with the standard liberal commitment to equality. On the one hand, it is in the interest of liberal nationalists (for the most part) to regulate immigration in order to protect a certain shared national identity necessary for sustaining liberal democratic institutions; yet, on the other, doing so seems to quite clearly violate the liberal idea of equality. For this reason, Judith Lichtenberg wonders "whether, given the facts of global inequality . . . liberal nationalism can exist in practice as well as in theory" (1998, p. 183).

But what must be realized is that this "tragic conflict" between the commitments of liberalism and the strategy of nation-building is not inevitable. It is not an inevitable fact of our world that border closure necessarily means that equal opportunity cannot be had by all individuals of the world. This happens to be the case in our world because of an antecedently unequal global distribution of resources and economic opportunities. The obvious thing for liberal nationalists to do, then, is to ensure that such a dilemma need not arise by striving for a world in which

---

[17] Note the racially based immigration policies of Australia in the recent past and Germany.

wealth and resources are more equitably distributed to begin with. Once a more egalitarian international order is achieved, the liberal nationalist strategy of regulating immigration need no longer be in conflict with the liberal commitment to equal opportunity. Barring disadvantaged people from coming into one's borders need not violate equal opportunity if one is willing to move some resources from within one's borders out to them. Indeed, in such a world much of the motivation for immigration in the first place would be averted.

Moral conflicts or "tragic choices" of this sort prompt what Martha Nussbaum has labeled the Hegelian question: "is there a rearrangement of our practices that can remove the tragedy?" (Nussbaum 2000b, p. 1016). Tragic conflicts, in which some injustice or harm is inevitable no matter how we choose to act, should not make Buridan's Asses of us. They should, instead, move us to ask how such tragic choices may be avoided or their costs be minimized. We should ask if better institutional arrangements and planning can prevent such conflicts in the future.[18] In as far as certain moral conflicts arise primarily because of faulty institutional arrangements, we have an immediate moral obligation, in as far as these conflicts are genuinely *moral*, to correct these institutional failings. To be exact, hard choices have to be made once they have presented themselves; and we have the duty, in such cases, to ensure that the lesser evil we are forced to enact is minimized as far as possible. But the deeper challenge is to minimize the future occurrence of hard cases by "better social planning" (Nussbaum 2000b, p. 1017). Improving international equality is one institutional solution helping to avoid, or at least to minimize, the cost of immigration restrictions on individuals' access to equal opportunity.

Thus the liberal nationalist Yael Tamir notes that the right to regulate immigration in the name of nation-building is conditional on the duties of international distributive justice being satisfied. She writes:

Restricting immigration in order to retain the national character of a certain territory is only justified if all nations have an equal chance of establishing a national entity, in which its members will be given a fair chance of pursuing their personal

---

[18] Nussbaum calls this institutional resolution of moral conflicts a Hegelian move because Hegel recognizes "the political significance of tragedy." That is, there is the recognition of the institutional sources of moral conflicts, hence the political significance of these conflicts. According to Nussbaum, Hegel holds that tragedy "motivates us to imagine what a world would be like that did not confront people with such choices" (Nussbaum 2000b, p. 1013). Nussbaum refers to this passage from Hegel's *The Philosophy of Fine Art*: "The true course of dramatic development consists in the annulment of *contradictions* viewed as such, in the reconciliation of the forces of human action, which alternately strive to negate each other in their conflict" (Nussbaum 2000b). A just world would be one in which moral conflicts arising from institutional failures need not arise.

and collective goals. The right to preserve cultural homogeneity is therefore contingent on the welfare of other nations. Liberal nationalism thus implies that it is justified for a nation to seek homogeneity by restricting immigration only if it has fulfilled its global obligation to assure equality among all nations (Tamir 1992, p. 161).

Similarly, Robert Goodin notes that "if rich countries do not want to let foreigners in, then the very least they must do is send much more money to compensate them for their being kept out . . . [These capital transfers] are merely the fair recompense for their being blocked from doing something (that is, moving to a rich country) that could, and quite probably would, have resulted in their earning that much more for themselves" (1992, p. 9). If there is a recognized duty on the part of liberals to protect global equal opportunity, and it is also recognized that border restrictions contradict the ideal of equal opportunity, then liberals either give up their right to border restrictions or take steps to promote global equal opportunity in other ways. If liberals think that the costs of open borders are too great, or at least greater than moving resources to outsiders, then they should be prepared to call for a greater international redistribution of resources.

Adapting this general line of argument, Kymlicka adds an interesting twist to Carens' deployment of Rawls's original position reasoning with regard to the question of free movement and equality of opportunity. According to Kymlicka, among the general facts individuals will have access to behind the veil of ignorance, in addition to the general facts about the workings of economies and the fact that the world is radically unequal in terms of how resources and wealth are actually allocated between nations, is that individuals have a strong (and justifiable) interest in maintaining their national and political culture. Kymlicka points out that, under this scenario, it is more likely that individuals will not opt for open borders (contra Carens) but for regulated borders. However, because they also recognize the problem of global inequality, they will also insist that immigration restrictions must go hand in hand with a global resource redistributive scheme. That is, they would opt for a global institutional scheme in which protecting national culture (a legitimate goal) need not be at the expense of equal opportunity for all persons (Kymlicka 2001b, pp. 270–1).

Thomas Pogge arrives at a similar conclusion with different and more empirical arguments, and with different motivations (Pogge 1997). If our concern is with equal opportunity, Pogge says, it is in fact more effective and efficient to engage in resource transfer than to go for totally open borders. Instead of ensuring equal opportunity globally, open borders may actually undermine this ideal for the following reasons: only elites – the educated and upper class for instance – in developing countries have the means and resources (and contacts in countries where exit visas are necessary) to migrate, thus further worsening their countries' conditions and hence widening global inequality (UNDP 1999, p. 32). Also there are limits, in the end, on how many people are able to migrate into wealthier countries without undermining their carrying capacities and ability to generate wealth. Thus of the two options for promoting equality, the more effective option is to move resources to people, rather than people to resources.[19]

Veit Bader has argued, in response to Pogge, that we need to adopt both strategies – allow for some immigration (fairly open borders) as well as redistribute resources. That is, until resource distribution schemes are fully operational and fully complied with, liberal equality must demand some room for immigration (Bader 1997). I think most people will agree with Bader here. Under a nonideal context where equality between nations is far from being a reality, liberal states may have to admit more immigrants than they might otherwise have just cause to resist. And certainly, most liberal countries today (which is Bader's point) come nowhere near to admitting immigrants in the numbers that would undermine social cohesion and thus pose any threat to democratic institutions.

But Bader's apt observation need not repudiate Pogge's point, which is that completely open borders are not going to solve the inequality problem. The issue is not whether there has to be some entry permitted (a point which Pogge could support), but whether we ought to regulate immigration for the purpose of sustaining a national identity versus the complete opening of borders as advocated by Carens. So it is important to note that liberal nationalists are not necessarily justifying the actual immigration quotas of many liberal countries, but only that some regulation on immigration as opposed to open borders (as argued for by some) is a legitimate nationalist practice, and even so only under conditions of international equality. In sum, given the option of redistributing wealth or opening borders to equalize opportunity globally, redistribution is both a better strategy and one that is more consistent with the legitimate aspirations of peoples to sustain and protect their national ways of life.

---

[19] In short, while a country may regulate admissions into its borders only if it contributes to international justice, it does not follow that a country may refuse to contribute to international justice by opening its borders completely. Indeed given the problem of brain-drain in fully opening its borders, this country may be required to transfer even more resources outwards as a matter of compensatory justice, to make up to affected countries for the loss of their local talents.

What the above arguments show, then, is that the liberal nationalist interest in regulating immigration is a legitimate one given the legitimate ends of nation-building, but that it can be legitimately enforced only if it does not violate equality of opportunity. And this can be so only in the context of a more egalitarian world, a global order in which resources are more equitably distributed in the first place. Thus while liberal universalists have good liberal reasons for wanting to defend global equality, liberal *nationalists* have additional and independent reasons for wanting to promote global equality – they cannot otherwise legitimately realize their nation-building goals.

This need not mean that in practice no nationalist pursuits can be permitted given the fact of international inequality; such a rigoristic demand would rule out nation-building practices in the actual world where the quest for justice can only be an ongoing one. Thus Lichtenberg's exhortation to nationalists, "first you equalise resources [globally], then you can have your cultural belonging" (1998, p. 183), is most sensibly read as an affirmation of the primacy of international justice, rather than as a claim about how to prioritize public policies and goals. What the primacy of international justice implies is that the duties of international justice are to be taken seriously, and that national projects of well-off nations lose their legitimacy if these nations are not also doing their fair share as determined by their duties of justice.

Rawls in *The Law of Peoples* acknowledges the special problem of immigration. He writes that

an important role of government, however arbitrary a society's boundaries may appear from a historical point of view, is to be the effective agent of a people as they take responsibility for their territory and the size of their population, as well as for maintaining the land's environmental integrity . . . People must recognize that they cannot make up for failing to regulate their numbers or to care for their land by conquest in war, or by migrating into another people's territory without their consent (1999a, p. 8).

But he thinks that the main causes of immigration "would disappear in the Society of liberal and decent Peoples" (1999a, p. 9). Migration, he points out, is often motivated by religious, ethnic, or political persecution, famines, and population pressures. But in the ideal context of the Law of Peoples, Rawls argues, these problems are eliminated, thereby eliminating the main causes of migration.

But if it is true that inequalities can result in basic needs not being met, as I have suggested earlier, then allowing for inequalities will not stem the flow of migrants. Moreover, even if we have met basic needs, if we allow for gross differences in living standards between individuals of different countries, it is still likely to be the case that individuals from the less well-off countries would be motivated to move to countries where their living standards could be improved markedly. As mentioned earlier, deprivation has an important comparative aspect. So eliminating great calamities like famines and severe population crises, as required by the Law of Peoples, should stem the mass exodus of peoples. But as long as sufficient inequality remains, migration will continue to be a major global fact.[20] Preventing economic calamities may avert the tide of the difficult-to-define group often referred to as "economic refugees"; but immigrants on the move for better opportunities may still remain a fact of life to contend with as long as significant inequalities between nations remain.[21]

One appeal of the arguments made in the preceding paragraphs is that they can be seen as an outward extension of, and therefore consistent with, the influential arguments Kymlicka has made to defend minority rights. In his recent writings, Kymlicka notes that the nation-building efforts of states can have potentially illiberal effects on minority nations. The policies of public education, fostering a set of public institutions operating in a particular (i.e. majority) language, have potentially alienating effects on citizens who do not share the same societal culture. It is, in a sense, to compensate minority members that the liberal state should thus implement a policy of minority rights, to allow minority nations to establish parallel sets of institutions and immigrant members to more easily integrate into mainstream culture (through education, pluralizing the public sphere, etc.).

But just as a state's nation-building policies have potential illiberal effects on minority nations within its borders, so too can they have illiberal effects on other nations for the reason described above. These illiberal effects, as we saw, are in the first instance those of undermining equal opportunity for individuals in less well-off countries. Just as

[20] The right of exit is commonly treated as sufficient with respect to the case of oppressive societies or cultures. Yet most people want, it is reasonable to say, not so much just a right of exit as also the right to reform their culture or religious practices. Unless the situation is urgent and life threatening, what most people who find their societies or cultures oppressive want is the right to reform the practices of their societies or cultures, rather than just the right to exit their societies or cultures altogether. See, for example, Leslie Green's discussion on what he calls "internal minorities" (Green 1994, pp. 101–17).

[21] As mentioned, liberal states have strong reasons of justice as well as humanitarianism not to restrict the access of refugees as opposed to economic migrants. If a tension arises here for nation-building, this tension will be assuaged in a more just world in which the causes that lead to political persecutions that in turn lead to a refugee crisis would be eliminated, or contained at least. This important point can be inferred from Rawls, as discussed above.

the liberal state should take "compensatory" measures (by means of a policy of minority rights) to mitigate the negative effects of its nation-building efforts on minorities within, so the liberal state should take steps (by supporting a more egalitarian international order) to mitigate the potential illiberal effects of its nation-building policies on outsiders. In sum, nation-building carries potential injustices along two dimensions – on the domestic front (i.e., against minorities) and on the international front (i.e., against foreigners). A commitment to international justice, as well as minority rights, is the normative implication of *liberal* nationalism.

Conclusion

Liberal nationalists have reasons deriving from their nationalist commitments to take an interest in mitigating material inequalities between nations. Thus, not only is there no incompatibility between liberal nationalism and cosmopolitan justice, but liberal nationalists must also be committed international egalitarians if they take their own nationalist agenda seriously. To be sure, as I said in the opening of this chapter, international egalitarianism is only a step towards cosmopolitanism, for the latter requires not only equality between nations but also between individuals across national boundaries. But the attempted demonstration that liberal nationalists must be international egalitarians goes a long way towards correcting the common perception of liberal nationalism as antithetical to international concerns.

The aim of this part of the book has been to show why and how liberals can take cosmopolitan justice seriously even if liberals must also be liberal nationalists. This will reassure liberals that their cosmopolitan commitments are preservable even if liberalism has a hidden nationalist agenda. The primary goal here was to show that liberal nationalists need not give up on cosmopolitan justice. But to the extent that a common objection against liberal nationalism is that it fails to take global issues seriously, the discussions in the last two chapters, if successful, offer a defense of liberal nationalism against this common objection.

Yet some theorists will remain skeptical of this dependency and convergence of liberal nationalism and cosmopolitan justice. They will object that, its liberal inspiration notwithstanding, liberal nationalists cannot succeed in meeting the demands of international egalitarianism. This is because nationalism promotes, among other things, a sense of special commitment and solidarity among fellow members or conationals. A nationalism that does not encourage, let alone permit, loyalty to country and a special concern for one's conationals would be a rather empty form of nationalism. It is part of what it means to be a nationalist that you give priority to the claims of conationals over those of nonmembers. The problem, the objection continues, is that any special concern for conationals contradicts the impartiality of cosmopolitan justice. Thus, even liberal nationalism, by definition, cannot support egalitarian internationalism. For this reason, Bhiku Parekh writes that it is "naïve in the extreme" to think that liberal nationalism can be supportive of the demands of global justice. He writes: "It is difficult to see how a strong sense of nationhood sits easily with a concern for global justice. The nationalist privileges the moral claims of one's fellow nationals and assigns only a limited weight to those of outsiders" (Parekh 1998, p. 317; also Brock 2002, pp. 310–11; Lichtenberg 1998; Moellendorf 2002, pp. 51–4).

This problem about partial concern could in fact be turned around as an argument against cosmopolitan justice: because it is natural and expected for people to show special concern for their conationals or compatriots, the cosmopolitan ideal that all persons are to be treated with equal concern regardless of nationality or citizenship seems unrealistic, if not incoherent. It is to the problem of partial concern that we will turn in part III.

Part III

Patriotism

A common criticism of the cosmopolitan position in the contemporary debate is that it is unable to accommodate or account for the special and particular relationships and commitments that people have. One reason for this criticism is that some cosmopolitans themselves have generally tended to be dismissive or suspicious of special commitments, sometimes even treating them as instances of moral failure. Or, at any rate, they seem to give this impression.[1] As one leading proponent of the cosmopolitan position, Charles Beitz, acknowledges, "the philosophical weakness most characteristic of cosmopolitan theories . . . is a failure to take seriously enough the associative relationships that individuals do and almost certainly must develop to live successful and rewarding lives" (Beitz 1999b, p. 291). Adapting T. M. Scanlon's observation "that principles could reasonably be rejected on the grounds that they left no room for valuing other things that are important in our lives" (Scanlon 1999, p. 160), we might say that an account of global justice that does not allow sufficient space for the special ties and commitments that people reasonably find valuable is one which people may reasonably reject.

Patriotism is often presented as one of the important associative ties that individuals do and must develop which cosmopolitan theories do not take seriously enough. For this reason, many critics argue that the cosmopolitan position is an untenable or even an absurd one, given the prominence of patriotism and patriotic commitments in ordinary human life. This allegation that the cosmopolitan position is a *reductio ad absurdum* for failing to properly recognize and accommodate the ideal of patriotism is, to my mind, the central problem confronting the cosmopolitan position

[1] For instance, Nussbaum's cosmopolitan vision (1996) was interpreted by her critics as a cosmopolitan idea that does not take patriotism seriously enough (see the commentaries in J. Cohen 1986). Whether this is a fair criticism or not is a point that we will turn to below.

in the contemporary debate.[2] Unlike the early stage of the contemporary cosmopolitan project, which was concerned mainly with providing arguments for why justice has to be global in reach (e.g., Beitz 1999a; Pogge 1989), the principal challenge for cosmopolitans at this stage of the debate is to show how the aspiration for justice without borders can be reconciled with what seems to be a basic moral fact that people may, and are indeed obliged to, give special concern to their compatriots. Cosmopolitans are, thus, currently faced with what we may regard as a quintessentially philosophical task – that of showing how two seemingly conflicting commitments, in this case that of the ideal of cosmopolitan equality on the one hand and the patriotic ideal on the other, can be reconciled. My aim in part III of this work is to show how cosmopolitans can meet this challenge.

As we will see, while cosmopolitans are generally not guilty of denying the acceptability of patriotic practices altogether (*pace* some of their critics), some are in fact guilty of under-appreciating and undervaluing the moral significance of patriotism by treating the worth of patriotism as derivative of, or reducible to, cosmopolitan principles. That is, they can rightly be criticized for failing to take patriotism *seriously enough*. But, so I will argue, such a derivative or reductionist account of patriotism is not necessary to the cosmopolitan idea of justice. I hope to present an alternative understanding of the cosmopolitan position: one that can preserve the cosmopolitan global egalitarian commitments without at the same time stripping patriotism of its moral significance.

As said, I take the perceived inability of cosmopolitan theories to take seriously patriotic concern to be the foremost challenge facing the cosmopolitan position in the contemporary debate. In accepting that the burden is on the cosmopolitan to show how cosmopolitan justice can be reconciled with the ideal of patriotism in a way meaningful for both sides, I have thus granted the moral significance of patriotism (although I will also refer to some well-known accounts of patriotism in the literature so as to suggest its moral appeal and plausibility). My goal, to put it plainly, is not to praise patriotism but to defend cosmopolitanism by showing how it can take patriotic commitments seriously, *pace* its critics. But in the course of showing how patriotism can be meaningfully understood without being antithetical to the cosmopolitan ideal, my arguments, if sound, will also be of interest to theorists who want to advance a morally attractive account of patriotism.

---

[2] See Samuel Scheffler (2001). The problem of patriotism for cosmopolitanism is also the main theme in J. Cohen (1996) and Caney et al. (1996); and is one of the central topics addressed by the essays in Shapiro and Brilmayer (1999) and McKim and McMahan (1997). See also the relevant sections in C. Jones (1999a) and Moellendorf (2002).

The patriotic challenge

Patriotism is the love for and loyalty to one's country. One way this special regard for one's country is manifested is through the showing of special concern for one's compatriots. The belief that compatriots are entitled to special consideration is a deeply and widely held one, and can be said to be a feature of what some philosophers call "common-sense morality" (Scheffler 1988, p. 243). This idea of patriotic partiality or concern, as I will call such special concern for compatriots, is premised on the belief that compatriots take priority: that is, that the interests of compatriots can override those of strangers. Henry Shue has dubbed this the "priority thesis" (Shue 1996, pp. 131–2). Although the priority thesis does not exhaust the whole of the concept of patriotism, it reflects a crucial feature of it. It is this specific aspect of patriotism (i.e., patriotic partiality or concern) that I am especially interested in; but, for convenience, I will sometimes use the more general term "patriotism" to mean specifically the priority claim as the context determines.

It is often thought that patriotism presents a special challenge for cosmopolitan justice. Cosmopolitan justice, to recall, regards individuals as the ultimate units of moral concern and as being entitled to equal consideration regardless of their nationality or citizenship. As I am defending it, cosmopolitan justice holds that distributive principles ought to transcend membership considerations and should apply equally to all individuals of the world regardless of national membership or citizenship. Yet patriotic partiality, which entails that some individuals are entitled to special concern because they happen to be compatriots, appears to contradict this cosmopolitan impartialist ideal. There is thus a tension between the demands of cosmopolitan justice and the commonsense moral view that people may, or are even required to, give special consideration to the interests of their compatriots over those of foreigners.

In addition to being a feature of commonsense morality, some philosophers have also argued that patriotism is necessary for democratic politics and so is a political virtue of sorts. On this argument, democratic citizenship cannot function when individuals do not feel a special bond towards their compatriots. Democratic deliberation is prerequisite on a certain level of mutual respect and trust among citizens, especially if they also happen to have diverse and competing ends (as they normally would in pluralistic democratic societies). Mutual respect limits the kinds of claims citizens will make against each other, and the presence of trust allows them to accept democratic results not in their favor on the expectation that should results be different next time, their opponents would likewise honor these results (Kymlicka 2001a, pp. 226–7). In addition, democracy cannot successfully function when economic inequality within society is so great as to alienate some segments of society from the democratic order. The idea of reciprocity necessary for democratic politics will be strained in societies in which the gap between the rich and poor is very wide. To counter inequality, democratic societies must implement distributive policies; yet such distributive programs require a "high degree of mutual commitment" among individuals to be effective (Kymlicka 2001a; also Taylor 1996, pp. 119–20, quotation at p. 120). Patriotism fosters this sense of mutual indebtedness and mutual concern among individuals who are otherwise strangers to each other. Turning to more extreme cases, defending the democratic order can sometimes call on individuals to make the ultimate sacrifice – the risking or even the surrendering of one's life in defense of one's country – and patriots argue that only when citizens have a strong sense of fellow feeling for each other would they undertake such sacrifices (Tamir 1997; also MacIntyre 1984).[3]

Critics of cosmopolitanism, therefore, often accuse the cosmopolitan position of being a bloodless one for failing to acknowledge and accommodate this basic and morally significant feature of human life, which, moreover, serves as a precondition for democracy. Any conception of justice that does not provide conceptual space for the different special ties common to the lives of ordinary people, and the special commitments that these ties can generate, offends against our ordinary moral conception and experience. It would be radically out of touch with our commonsense morality that individuals do value and find meaning in certain special relationships and may legitimately pursue these special ends at the exclusion of other more impartial ends (e.g., Blum 1980).[4] An acceptable theory of cosmopolitan justice must, therefore, be congenial to the claims of commonsense morality. Cosmopolitans who reject the relevance of particular ties and special associations seem to prioritize a commitment to abstract principles over the concrete and personal values that make life worthwhile and meaningful. They call to mind Rousseau's

---

[3] Tamir argues that commitment to principles does not sufficiently motivate self-sacrificing acts for one's country because one need not necessarily be motivated to sacrifice one's life for a different country that shares the same values. See Tamir (1997, pp. 229–32).

[4] The problem of patriot partiality for cosmopolitan justice reflects a pervasive general problem in moral philosophy – how can the ideal of impartiality that is integral to ideal morality be reconciled with the commonsense morality that people have special attachments, ties, and relationships that they may be partially inclined toward? (See Herman 1993; Kelly 2000; Scheffler 1988.) Similarly, in discussions on justice, there is a debate in contemporary philosophy on how justice as impartiality is to be balanced against the personal pursuits and commitments of individuals that need not be impartially motivated (see Barry 1995; G. A. Cohen 2000; Nagel 1991). I hope that in confronting the special case of patriotism and cosmopolitan justice, we can help clarify some aspects of the general philosophical problem of partiality and justice.

well-known caricature of the "pretended cosmopolites, who in justifying their love for the human race, boast of loving all the world, in order to enjoy the privilege of loving no one."[5] More poignantly, if patriotism provides the "strong common identification" that is necessary for a democratic political community to function, the cosmopolitan dismissal of patriotism is morally irresponsible given "the [dangerous] alternatives to democracy in our world" (Taylor 1996, p. 120; also Gutmann 1996).

But, *pace* their critics, few cosmopolitans, if any, actually affirm an extreme impartialist position that denies any room for patriotic concern. Most cosmopolitan positions, when more carefully examined, do allow space for the exercise of patriotic commitments, even if on first impression these positions seem to rule out any space for such special concern. If there is any dispute between the patriots and the cosmopolitans, it is over the limits of patriotic concern and how this special concern is to be morally understood.[6]

Yet it remains unclear in the current literature how cosmopolitan theories can consistently accommodate and recognize the moral significance of patriotic and other forms of particularist commitments, while preserving the commitments of cosmopolitan justice. Because of the disunity and ambiguity among contemporary cosmopolitans themselves, critics of cosmopolitan theories have charged that even if cosmopolitans want to accommodate patriotic concern, it is far from clear that they can do so consistently with their professed cosmopolitan commitments.

My aim in this chapter is to show that, contrary to this criticism, cosmopolitan justice can accommodate and account for patriotic concern without sacrificing its own commitment to global egalitarianism. After some comments on the tension between impartiality and partiality, I proceed by assessing some common responses and reactions to the cosmopolitanism/patriotism tension. Evaluating some of the common responses in the literature has the virtue of allowing me to identify what I think are the common mistaken assumptions and beliefs about cosmopolitan justice and patriotism. The first position, which I will call "anti-cosmopolitanism," holds that because cosmopolitanism cannot successfully accommodate patriotic concern, it should be rejected as an implausible theory of justice. But the anti-cosmopolitan position, I will

---

[5] Quoted in Schlereth (1977, p. 91). The quotation is from the original manuscript of *Du contrat social*, in Rousseau (1915, I, 453).

[6] An example here is Martha Nussbaum's lead essay "Patriotism and Cosmopolitanism" in J. Cohen (1996). Some of Nussbaum's critics, whose essays are also included in the same volume, took her to task for not taking patriotism seriously. But in her "Reply" to her critics, Nussbaum makes it explicit that she was concerned with the limits of patriotism, not with the denial of patriotism as such.

argue, rests on certain mistaken assumptions about the limits and scope of patriotism that is entailed by commonsense morality, and so is confused about the demands of patriotism that cosmopolitan justice must accommodate. A second, more conciliatory, position tries to reconcile cosmopolitanism with patriotism by limiting the concern of cosmopolitanism to the provision of basic needs but not to promoting economic equality between persons as such. That is to say, cosmopolitan justice is reinterpreted to entail no global egalitarian commitment, and so there is no serious tension between patriotic partiality and cosmopolitanism. In short, this position makes space for patriotic concern by relaxing the demands of cosmopolitan justice; it abandons the traditional cosmopolitan idea that all persons are entitled to equal concern in matters of distributive justice. Yet this "restricted cosmopolitan" position, as I will call it, achieves the reconciliation of cosmopolitanism and patriotism by surrendering what for most cosmopolitans is the basic motivation for the cosmopolitan ideal. I will argue that this retraction of cosmopolitan equality is not only objectionable but also unnecessary for the purpose of rendering cosmopolitanism congenial to patriotism.

I will propose that cosmopolitan equality should set limits on the exercise of patriotism. This position is common to some cosmopolitans. But I will show, importantly, that this subordination of patriotism to cosmopolitan equality need not take patriotism to be reducible to or derivative of cosmopolitan principles. The "limited patriotism" position (as I shall call it) is able to preserve the cosmopolitan commitment to global egalitarianism without unreasonably restricting the exercise of patriotic concern; but, significantly, it can do so without denigrating the moral significance of this special concern. Indeed, as we will see, limited patriotism is consistent with our understanding of the relationship between justice and personal pursuits in more familiar contexts.

It is important to notice that while my argument assumes the commonsense moral view that patriotism is an important feature of our social world, it will challenge and reject the conventional perception and practice of patriotism that allows patriotic concern to limit the requirements of global justice. That is to say, while I take patriotism as such to be part of commonsense morality that any conception of global justice will have to take into account on pain of being a *reductio*, this is not the same as accepting patriotism as it happens to be currently accepted and practiced. To put the distinction perspicuously, commonsense morality is not the same as *conventional* morality. Cosmopolitan justice needs to be reconciled with commonsense moral views about patriotism but not necessarily with conventional views of patriotism. Indeed, I will be arguing that conventional patriotism runs against commonsense moral views about the correct limits of patriotic commitments and special ties in general.

Preliminaries

Before proceeding, let me make some preliminary remarks to clarify the terms and limits of the discussion ahead. First, I should acknowledge that a successful reconciliation of cosmopolitanism and patriotism does not alone establish the cosmopolitan position. As mentioned, the patriotic challenge takes the form of a *reductio ad absurdum*. It alleges that cosmopolitan justice is an absurdity because it does not mesh with a prominent feature of moral life. The task of the cosmopolitan with regard to the issue of patriotism is thus a defensive one – that of showing why the cosmopolitan position is not an absurdity as charged. So a successful reconciliation of cosmopolitan justice and patriotic concern does not alone demonstrate the truth of the cosmopolitan position, but only defeats one objection to it. By the same token, it is important to recognize the limited scope of the patriotic challenge. It challenges the cosmopolitan position as a whole by claiming that it is an absurd one for failing to accommodate and account for the ties that matter to people; but it does not directly challenge the positive arguments that have been given in defense of cosmopolitan justice (some of which we have already discussed in previous chapters).

Second, to be sure that I am not confronting a straw person, in rejecting conventional patriotism as mentioned above, I do not mean to reject only the extreme claim that any interests of one's compatriots take precedence even over the basic needs of strangers, or a form of "my country right or wrong" patriotism. This extreme position is difficult to defend morally speaking, and so is philosophically unchallenging and uninteresting; indeed few serious theorists of patriotism actually advance such a position.[7] It would have to be premised on some implausible claim, such as that no foreigners are entitled to any moral consideration, and that moral membership in the most basic sense derives from shared membership in a state. A rejection of extreme conventional patriotism alone will not get the cosmopolitan project very far. A more interesting and challenging version of conventional patriotism would accept that there are limits to what can be done to foreigners in the name of compatriots' interests, and that patriotism is not inconsistent with global humanitarianism. It would accept, for example, that foreigners are entitled to some assistance if they

---

[7] Now Alasdair MacIntyre does make some claims about patriotism that can be given an extreme interpretation. I will consider MacIntyre's arguments below.

are unable to meet their basic needs when the cost of this assistance is not too significant.[8] What the moderate version of conventional patriotism claims is that when it comes to distributive justice, and when it comes to ordering our institutions by which people's entitlements (beyond the basic minimum for subsistence) are to be determined, people's citizenship or nationality is a relevant factor to be taken into consideration (e.g., Miller 2000, pp. 172–4). It is conventional patriotism in this more plausible and philosophically interesting form that I intend to argue against. At any rate, everything I will say against moderate conventional patriotism will apply *a fortiori* to extreme conventional patriotism.

Third, the relationship between nationalism and patriotism and citizenship needs some initial clarification. For nationalist theorists, membership in a national community is that which provides the ultimate justification and motivation for patriotic partiality. Indeed, for nationalists, one of the goals of nationalism is to instil in individuals a sense of solidarity and mutual commitment towards their compatriots. But there are other contending accounts of patriotism that need not be nationalistic in their justification. One non-nationalist account of patriotism emphasizes the fact of shared *citizenship* in a constitutional state. Jürgen Habermas's "constitutional patriotism," in which patriotic partiality is justified in terms of a shared allegiance to a constitutional order rather than by reference to an underlying national culture, is an important example (Habermas 1992). Here, it is the shared commitment to certain abstract principles and democratic procedures that generates the affinity and special concern among compatriots in a liberal society.[9] I will discuss more fully the connection and distinction between citizenship and nationality and their relationship to patriotism below where it is relevant to my argument (chapters 8 and 9). For the present chapter, I will remain agnostic about the moral basis of patriotism, and will not assume that patriotism

---

[8] David Miller, for example, notes that it would be hard to justify England's "building a national football stadium, or a Millennium Dome" over helping "rebuild the economy of a foreign nation that has been shattered by foreign invasion or civil war" (D. Miller 2000, pp. 177–8).

[9] Some anti-nationalist theorists present patriotism as a morally defensible alternative to nationalism, which they take to be objectionable. But I think this way of contrasting the two positions obscures the fact that patriotism is one of the basic features of nationalism, and that nationalists are indeed interested in promoting patriotism. I think the contrast would be better understood not in terms of patriotism versus nationalism as such, but in terms of the forms of patriotism – *nationalist* patriotism or *constitutional* (or some other nonnationalist form of) patriotism. Treating patriotism as an alternative model of citizenship allegiance seems to commit a category mistake – for it compares the justification (of which nationalism is one possible source of justification) of patriotism with the practice of patriotism itself, as if there are competing and incompatible claims. For some discussion on the alleged contrast between patriotism and nationalism, see Vincent (2002) and Canovan (2000).

must be grounded on shared national culture or on some ideal of liberal citizenship. This is because my immediate goal is to determine how cosmopolitanism can accommodate patriotic partiality *independently* of how such partial concern may be justified. One of my claims will be that cosmopolitan justice sets the limits on patriotic concern no matter how this special concern is ultimately justified.[10] I will thus use the terms "citizens," "nationals," and the more general and neutral "compatriots," interchangeably in this chapter.

Impartiality versus partiality

Some people may object to my characterization of the tension between cosmopolitanism and patriotism in terms of justice as *impartiality* versus patriotic *partiality*. David Miller, for instance, thinks that couching this tension in terms of partiality versus impartiality misdescribes the issue. Showing special concern for conationals is not a case of partiality in his view because "impartiality has to do with even-handed application of rules – rules which may themselves require us to treat different categories of people differently. It is therefore possible to act impartially without giving equal weight to the claims of everyone affected by your actions in cases where the rule you are following requires you to discriminate" (Miller 1999b, p. 165). Thus, if there are "good moral reasons," as Miller puts it, for such discriminatory rules, then these rules may be impartial even if they command differentiated treatment of different persons (Miller 1999). To say that patriotic concern which involves the showing of special consideration to compatriots is a case of partiality is a misdescription of patriotism because there are good reasons for this special concern (also Blake 2002, p. 258).

But D. Miller's position, which seems to me to be no more than a "semantic shift," merely pushes the debate back a step. We still need to know what the justificatory bases of these discriminatory rules are. And good *moral* reasons for these rules have to start from some fundamental account of impartiality – that is, these must be reasons that are not arbitrary but that apply to all individuals in the same way under relevantly similar circumstances. In any case, describe the nature of this tension how we will, we still need to confront the fact that there are two potentially opposing demands – one which says that nationality is to be factored out (i.e., impartial about nationality), the other which says that nationality is a relevant point of consideration (partial about nationality). And

---

[10] Moreover, as we will see in later chapters, this agnosticism about the basis of patriotism is important because it avoids treating patriotic concern as being ultimately reducible to cosmopolitan principles.

this presents an apparent tension that needs to be explained. Thus, ultimately, the question is "impartiality or partiality with respect to what?"; and nationalists like D. Miller hold that there should be no impartiality with respect to nationality whereas cosmopolitans hold that there should be. So there is a real disagreement here about whether to be impartial or partial about nationality. Couching the debate in terms of partiality versus impartiality is not at cross-purposes if we are clear and agreed about *what it is that* we are claiming to be partial or impartial about.

Anti-cosmopolitanism

Some critics of the cosmopolitan position claim that because cosmopolitanism cannot accommodate patriotic partiality it is an incoherent position that should be rejected. The "anti-cosmopolitan" position takes the fact of patriotic partiality *alone* to be sufficient evidence against cosmopolitanism. The cosmopolitan principle that we regard *all* individuals equally, according to these anti-cosmopolitans, is incoherent because it cannot accommodate the widely and deeply held commonsense belief that we are permitted to show greater concern to compatriots than to strangers.[11]

But the anti-cosmopolitan argument rests on two assumptions: (a) that patriotism as conventionally understood must be accounted for by the cosmopolitan view, and (b) that commonsense morality would require that we forgo cosmopolitanism in the event that cosmopolitanism is incompatible with patriotism conventionally understood. Based on these assumptions, anti-cosmopolitans are able to argue that because cosmopolitanism cannot accommodate conventional patriotism, cosmopolitanism must be rejected.

Yet the first assumption, that cosmopolitan morality must accept patriotism in its conventional form, is mistaken. This mistake is illustrated, I believe, in David Miller's objection to Robert Goodin's attempt to reconcile a universalist moral perspective with conational partiality. Goodin has argued that dividing our duties along national affiliations is one *effective* way of coordinating and parceling up our general universal duties to individuals at large. But Miller rejects this "useful strategy" approach (as I will call it) because it is limited to just those instances in which countries are actually capable of providing for the needs of their own citizens, and so is far from "useful" or effective as a means of regulating our universal duties *in the real world* characterized by great economic and resource inequalities (D. Miller 1995, chap. 3). In short, Miller believes

[11] E.g., David Miller (1995, chap. 3); and Alasdair MacIntyre (1984).

that Goodin's attempt to reconcile moral universalism with compatriot partiality fails because it cannot accommodate *all* instances of such partiality. It cannot accommodate those cases of conational partiality that do not actually serve certain greater global good.

But this is a curious response to Goodin's position on Miller's part. Goodin's reason for wanting to situate compatriot partiality in the context of a universalist moral perspective is precisely to define the limits of this partiality. Goodin's intention is not to offer us a universalist justification of *conventional* patriotic partiality; rather he wants to show how our more universal duties ground, *and consequently* set conditions and constraints on the exercise of this partiality. For Goodin, then, as for most cosmopolitans, whenever compatriot partiality actually fails to live up to our universal duties to humanity, this partiality is illegitimate. As Goodin explicitly notes, "[i]n our present world system, it is often – perhaps ordinarily – wrong to give priority to the claims of our compatriots" (Goodin 1988, p. 686). Similarly, Martha Nussbaum's defense of partiality on the ground that it is a "sensible way to do good" is situated against a cosmopolitan theoretical background, and so when partial concern in fact violates the more fundamental cosmopolitan principles, the partial concern loses its moral ground (Nussbaum 1996, p. 136). As Goodin puts it elsewhere, against a background of distributive inequality, partial concern for people to whom we stand in some special relationship seems to be a "pernicious" form of prejudice (Goodin 1985, pp. 1, 6).

Miller's mistake, then, is that he seems to take it for granted that patriotic partiality need not be constrained, and that the conventional practice of patriotism is an acceptable one that must be accommodated within a cosmopolitan framework if cosmopolitanism is to be viable. So, because cosmopolitanism cannot provide a justification for unconstrained or conventional patriotism, cosmopolitanism is therefore an implausible doctrine. Yet, as mentioned, the very purpose of attempting a cosmopolitan justification of compatriot partiality is to define its moral basis so as to identify its limits. So arguing that cosmopolitan morality is a failed doctrine, because it does not succeed in accommodating conventional compatriot partiality in a world characterized by gross inequalities between countries, misses the motivation behind a cosmopolitan defense of moral partiality. While cosmopolitanism must allow space for patriotism, it need not be expected to allow space for the entire range of conventional patriotism. As Beitz writes, "the special responsibilities to compatriots that can plausibly be defended are not nearly as extensive as the priority for compatriots found in conventional morality" (Beitz 1999a, p. 213). The burden is on cosmopolitans to only accommodate and account for patriotism that does not violate independent moral requirements. Cosmopolitanism, like any other theory of justice, need not be accommodating of practices that are morally objectionable.

The belief that patriotism need not be constrained by cosmopolitan principles is related to the second questionable assumption of the anti-cosmopolitan argument. This is the assumption that in the event of a clash between cosmopolitan demands and our *conventional* moral view about patriotism, the latter automatically trumps. But why should this be the case? One could *as well* retort that in the event of such a conflict, so much the worse for conventional morality. Instead of rejecting cosmopolitanism, such a conflict could as well call on us to reconsider our special duties to compatriots. The burden of proof does not fall by default on the cosmopolitan, as the anti-cosmopolitan view has assumed. If convention holds that patriotism need not be constrained by the requirements of cosmopolitan justice, perhaps it is this convention that needs to be carefully reconsidered.

In other words, if some of our conventional moral convictions are incompatible with what morality requires, then it might be necessary to reexamine these convictions, and we should not assume that they are part of commonsense morality just because they happen to be conventional. That which may appear to be a feature of commonsense morality may be on closer examination discovered to be objectionable or at least dispensable without violating our notions of the kinds of values that are integral to any meaningful human life.[12] Thus one may ask if it is in fact the case that commonsense morality actually supports conventional compatriot partiality, as the anti-cosmopolitan argument seems to imply. To be sure, as we saw earlier, a moral theory that cannot accept any form of partiality defies commonsense morality, and so holds no appeal. But a moral theory that condones (let alone requires) unlimited partiality between individuals is just as defiant of common sense. Ordinarily, we do accept that one may give priority to one's own, but we also accept that there are limits on how far one may legitimately exercise such favoritism. We ordinarily value friendship and kinship, yet we also ordinarily regard cronyism and nepotism as vices rather than virtues. Commonsense morality accepts partial concern, but it *also* imposes limits on it. One can as well argue that given the current global inequality and poverty, it is the claim that compatriots may privilege each other's interests to the point of resisting any demands for global redistribution that flies in the face of commonsense notions of rightness and wrongness.

In short, when adjusting our ethical theories or theories of justice to conform to commonsense moral viewpoints, it is important to recognize that commonsense morality is not coextensive with morality as

---

[12] This recalls Rawls's idea of reflective equilibrium.

conventionally perceived or as accepted by the majority. Commonsense moral views are not just views that are widely held, but are also views that can be endorsed on due reflection and whose denial runs against our deep moral convictions about the sorts of values and commitments a meaningful and worthwhile life may have. Conventional morality, on the other hand, is just simply the morality that is currently being practiced by people, and this need not be what commonsense morality would require or even permit. On due reflection, a conventional moral practice may be discarded or rejected as mistaken without offending against our understanding of what counts as a good human life. So while conventionally many people in developed countries may hold a more permissive view of patriotic concern, this need not be in line with commonsense moral views concerning patriotism. While it is easy to see that patriotic partiality as such is an aspect of commonsense morality (and that a conception of justice that does not allow patriotism of any form would be at odds with our considered views about what is valuable and important for human beings), it is hard to see how a conception of patriotism that allows compatriotic relationship to determine what is owed to each other is an aspect of commonsense morality, in the sense that its denial would entail a morally impoverished picture of human life. That cosmopolitans need to recognize the value of patriotism in order to conform to commonsense morality does not mean that they must endorse patriotism as it is conventionally practiced. In short, the anti-cosmopolitan position misunderstands what commonsense morality permits of patriotism, thinking that it would reflect more or less conventional patriotism, thus falsely seeing the challenge for cosmopolitans to be that of reconciling their ideal of justice with patriotism currently understood.

A similar set of arguments can be made against Alasdair MacIntyre's appeal to patriotism in his criticism of the ideal of moral impartiality that he associates with liberalism. In his essay "Is Patriotism a Virtue?" MacIntyre points to "conflicts that arise from scarcity of essential resources," and argues that the "standpoint of impersonal morality [which] requires an allocation of goods such that each individual person counts for one and no more than one" cannot accommodate the patriotic view that one strives "to further the interests of" one's respective community, even to the point of going "to war on one's community's behalf" if necessary (MacIntyre 1984, p. 6). That is, moral impartiality is a flawed ideal because it cannot allow for patriotic concerns of these sorts that are very much part of the fabric of our ordinary moral thinking.

Again, the mistaken assumption here is that the moral impartialists must be capable of accommodating patriotism in the conventional sense, including an extreme form of patriotism that motivates waging war in order to defend scarce resources in extreme cases. The impartialist's response here, as we have seen, could be that if this is what patriotism entails (going to war to settle disputes over resources), then so much the worse for patriotic partiality. Cosmopolitans need not accept that the burden of proof is on them to show how the waging of war on patriotic grounds can be accounted for in the cosmopolitan framework. There are other arguments, besides cosmopolitan ones, as to why the extreme patriotism of the sort MacIntyre refers to is morally objectionable. The burden of proof is less on the cosmopolitans to account for such extreme patriotism within their theory of justice, but more on these extreme patriots to defend their patriotic commitments. As I have argued above, it is far from clear that conventional patriotism (let alone the extreme form MacIntyre is alluding to) is part of commonsense morality to which cosmopolitan justice must be reconciled, let alone be a virtue. MacIntyre's mistake, then, like D. Miller's, is that he believes that cosmopolitans must accommodate and account for patriotism as conventionally understood. Accordingly, he thinks that because cosmopolitanism cannot be compatible with extreme forms of patriotic commitments, cosmopolitanism must be rejected. In sum, in his rejection of cosmopolitanism MacIntyre is guilty of the same two mistakes identified above – (1) he too quickly dismisses the capacity of an impartialist moral theory to account for patriotism, because (2) he wrongly thinks that impartialists want and must be able to account for patriotic practices as conventionally understood.

There could be other arguments against cosmopolitanism (and I have certainly not offered any positive defense for the cosmopolitan view here); but my point here is that the fact of compatriot partiality in *itself* does not compel one to abandon cosmopolitanism; on the contrary, the cosmopolitan ideal should tell us how we should understand and conceptualize that fact.

A more interesting anti-cosmopolitan challenge does not simply say that cosmopolitans cannot accommodate patriotism, but claims that cosmopolitans accommodate patriotism by morally impoverishing it. Cosmopolitans, because of their commitment to impartialist principles, can justify patriotic partiality only by treating this partial concern as merely instrumental for meeting the requirements of the impartialist principles. The worth of patriotism is ultimately reduced to certain impartialist principles on the cosmopolitan view. But this reductionist view of patriotism, the argument continues, misdescribes and undervalues the nature of patriotic ties, for such ties do have "intrinsic ethical relevance" for the majority of people (D. Miller 1999b, p. 165). Just as it would be crass to reduce the worth of the relationship of friendship to the merely instrumental one of promoting the greater good, likewise it would be a serious misdescription of the moral worth of common citizenship if we think it is merely an administrative device for discharging our general duties to humanity. Certain associative ties and their corresponding duties have a moral independence in the sense that they cannot be explained by or grounded on certain principles of justice external to the associations. Their moral worth, and the force of their commitments, derive from the relationship itself and not from some external principles of right and wrong.

Thus Ronald Dworkin notes that an instrumental argument for partial concern "fails to capture the intimacy" of most special relationships and commitments (Dworkin 1986, p. 193). Likewise, Samuel Scheffler rejects (what he calls) "extreme" cosmopolitanism which cannot recognize the independent worth of certain special attachments and commitments (Scheffler 2001, pp. 114–15). He writes that "it is pathological to attach nothing but instrumental value to any of one's personal relationships . . . [And] if one values one's relationship to a particular person non-instrumentally, one will inevitably see it as a source of reasons for action . . . for treating that person differently from others" (Scheffler 2001, p. 121).

Hence, the objection here is not that cosmopolitans cannot *accommodate* patriotic partiality within its framework in the sense of not allowing adequate space for the practice of patriotic concern, but that it cannot *account* for this partiality in a way that does not strip patriotism of its moral significance. For D. Miller, the fact that a person is my compatriot provides "a basic reason for action" that ethical universalism cannot properly explain (1995, p. 50). To say that caring specially for one's compatriots is justified because it is an effective way of doing good for humanity at large risks missing the true point of patriotic relations.

This is an important argument on the part of the anti-cosmopolitans, and they are indeed right to remind us of the irreducibility of certain special relational ties and commitments of people. So if cosmopolitans are indeed forced to hold that special ties like shared nationality have *merely* instrumental worth on account of how these ties successfully serve other moral ends, the anti-cosmopolitans have a point against them. But my argument above intends only to illustrate one false assumption of the anti-cosmopolitan position – that conventional patriotism must trump cosmopolitan considerations. The "useful strategy" argument of cosmopolitans like Goodin and Nussbaum provides one way of bringing together cosmopolitanism and patriotism without undermining the force of cosmopolitan commitments; but this argument is consistent with the claim that there are other *irreducible* reasons for patriotic partiality. The cosmopolitan could accept that there are aspects of certain personal relationships, including possibly that of shared nationality, whose worth is not reducible to the greater good principle or some other general idea of justice, and that to explain these ties in terms of certain external moral features is to underestimate and undervalue the moral independence of special relationships. What is to be concluded from the above discussion is not that patriotism has to be morally reduced to certain general principles of justice, and that it can have only derivative moral worth; rather, the conclusion to be drawn is that patriotism can be limited or constrained by certain principles of justice.

These are distinct claims. It is one thing to say that the worth of a relationship is *reducible* to some impartial principle of justice (which cosmopolitans are not forced into saying), and quite another to say that the moral legitimacy of that relationship is *conditional* on its not violating this principle (which cosmopolitans, I am suggesting, must claim). We do not seek to explain a person's conception of the good in terms of some general and abstract universal principle, but we nonetheless hold that the pursuit of that conception of the good is to be limited against certain standards of justice that are external to and independent of that conception of the good. As Erin Kelly notes in her instructive discussion on morality and personal concern, the impartialist need not deny that people can have non-universalist but specific historical or cultural reasons for their "sense of unity"; the impartialist "merely holds that promoting a collective good must meet a certain test of moral compatibility with the interests of outsiders" (Kelly 2000, pp. 134–5). Justice sets the limiting conditions on people's conceptions of the good even as it recognizes that these conceptions are morally independent in that they need not be justified ultimately by reference to (i.e., reduced to) the principles of justice. In short, justice plays a limiting rather than a justificatory role with respect to people's conceptions of the good.

To illustrate this point, consider again the instructive case of friendship. Impartialists need not reduce the entire worth of friendship to a set of general principles (so we are in agreement with the anti-cosmopolitans here about the independent worth of certain associative ties); nonetheless they can demand of any display of friendship that it does not transgress the boundaries of justice if the friendship is to be a morally legitimate one. It is thus important not to infer from the (possibly correct) belief that patriotism has certain irreducible moral worth the false conclusion that patriotism cannot be constrained against certain more general and external moral considerations. In short, cosmopolitans are only claiming that the practice of patriotism must be constrained by the considerations of global justice, not that the entire worth of patriotism is reducible to and explainable by these considerations.

To say that partial concern has to be limited or constrained by certain external principles is not the same as saying that the partial concern must be explainable ultimately by reference to these principles.[13] One could still claim, with D. Miller and Scheffler, that the fact that a person "is my sister" or "my conational" is a basic relational fact that provides one with a basic reason for action; but this does not mean that this reason for action need not be balanced against other claims, including the claims of people outside that relationship. Cosmopolitans need not deny the irreducible nature of the ties of nationality (that some nationalists want to claim); they need only insist that the expression and exercise of these national ties be constrained by cosmopolitan principles. How cosmopolitanism can and ought to constrain patriotism is a question that I will turn to later. Before doing that, however, let me consider a different response to the cosmopolitanism/patriotism tension.

Restricted cosmopolitanism

A position that has been forwarded in the recent literature tries to reconcile cosmopolitanism with patriotism, not by limiting the scope of legitimate patriotism but by relaxing the demands of cosmopolitan justice. That is, the position tries to show that cosmopolitan justice properly understood does not require global impartial egalitarianism, and so cosmopolitanism can easily accommodate the favoring of compatriots even in matters of distributive justice. Cosmopolitanism, on this restricted view, as I will call it, does not call for distributive principles that transcend borders; instead, it permits (and even requires) people to privilege their own citizens' well-being, even if this comes at the cost of a more egalitarian world.[14] For these cosmopolitans, it is the view that cosmopolitan justice requires global egalitarianism that needs to be revised in light of the patriotic challenge.

One interesting defense of this general strategy has been proposed by Richard Miller.[15] R. Miller's basic point is that the cosmopolitan ideal

---

[13] See, e.g., Simmons (1996, p. 268).

[14] The restricted cosmopolitan and the anti-cosmopolitan views thus arrive at the same general conclusions concerning global distributive justice from different moral starting points. In some ways, this divide seems to differentiate liberal theorists who reject cosmopolitan global justice, like Rawls, on one side, and those whom we may call "communitarian" theorists like Miller, Sandel and Walzer, on the other (Rawls 1999a; Walzer 1995; D. Miller 1998, 1999a; and Sandel 1996).

[15] For other arguments along *somewhat* similar lines, see Blake (2002). For Blake, a concern for "relative deprivation" as opposed to "absolute deprivation" arises only among those who "share liability to a coercive system of political and legal institutions" (Blake 2002, p. 260; also pp. 281–2). I will focus on R. Miller because he explicitly rejects the ideal

of equal respect does not entail equal concern for *all*. He argues that universal respect will require, on the contrary, that we accord *greater* concern to those with whom we share common institutional schemes, i.e., compatriots. This is because (a) we need to foster greater mutual respect and trust among fellow participants in these schemes, and because (b) we need also to be able to give them incentives for complying with these (sometimes coercive) schemes that we are helping to impose on them (R. Miller 1998, pp. 203–4).

What is important, according to R. Miller, is that this showing of special concern to compatriots *does not* mean that we are denying the moral worth of strangers; i.e., we are not granting them less than equal respect. Given that noncompatriots will also recognize the importance of fostering mutual respect and trust among individuals sharing a common cooperative scheme, they too can accept our "patriotic bias" as reasonable (1998, p. 204). This point holds too, Miller argues, even if these noncompatriots belong to economically worse-off social schemes (1998, pp. 204–5). A citizen of a poor country can *reasonably* accept a distributive scheme that allows for the privileging of membership, even if this means that her own social scheme remains relatively deprived as a consequence. As he claims, such a person "could accept this rationale even though he suffers from the worldwide consequences of . . . this sort of patriotic bias, because his own moral responsibility leads him to accord a special importance to the kind of social and political relations [others seek], an importance that entails allowing others to treat the pursuit of such relations in their own lives as a basis for choice among rules for giving" (R. Miller 1998).

In short, the ideal that we treat individuals with equal respect *and* concern is interpreted by R. Miller to mean only that we treat *fellow citizens* with equal respect and concern. Among strangers, we need only treat them with equal respect *but not* necessarily with equal concern. It is important to remember that patriots are not saying that outsiders count for nothing; in fact they readily accept that people have certain (positive) duties to strangers with respect to basic subsistence rights. But restricted cosmopolitanism insists nonetheless that the cosmopolitan ideal does not require equal concern for all individuals globally, and that when it comes to allocating entitlements and benefits beyond those which are needed

---

of global distributive equality while explicitly defending the cosmopolitan framework. I should note also that David Miller's more recent position too is more accurately categorized under this heading, I believe. D. Miller now makes a distinction between "weak cosmopolitanism" which he supports, and "strong cosmopolitanism" which he rejects (D. Miller 1998 and 1999a). The weak cosmopolitanism he holds can be classified under what I here call restricted cosmopolitanism. What I will say about R. Miller's arguments will also apply generally to the positions of Blake and D. Miller.

for basic human survival, shared citizenship can rightly be invoked here as a decisive factor.

It is important to stress that R. Miller does not assume that the existing global distributive scheme is beyond criticism. The current scheme is one in which the basic needs of many people are not adequately met and so is one in which the ideal of equal respect for all is not realized. R. Miller would demand substantive global reforms in the name of cosmopolitan equal respect. But what Miller nonetheless accepts, and what many cosmopolitan egalitarians would regard as a reneging on the cosmopolitan commitment, is that there is no compulsion for global egalitarianism. That is, Miller accepts the conventional idea that when it comes to *distributive justice*, compatriots have special claims that foreigners do not. So while the basic needs of persons are to be universally respected, there is no requirement of justice to ensure that the inequality between the haves and the have-nots not be too wide, once the required level of subsistence as would be needed by the ideal of equal respect is provided for all persons. It is in this sense that R. Miller's cosmopolitanism has more restricted demands than those of cosmopolitans like Beitz or Pogge, and in this qualified sense we can say that Miller modifies the cosmopolitan position so as to accommodate the conventional view about patriotism.

Thus R. Miller wants to *restrict* the cosmopolitan ideal to cover only the principle of equal respect, and not the more demanding principle of equal concern, and this distinction therefore allows him to defend cosmopolitanism while allowing patriotic concern to influence our conception of global justice. But R. Miller's attempt to drive a conceptual wedge between the ideals of equal respect and equal concern seems question begging. It assumes that one can always show greater *concern* to some (i.e., compatriots) *without* showing less than equal *respect* to others (i.e., strangers) as a consequence. But this assumption overlooks the fact that the practice of partial concern has to be considered within a larger social context before it can be determined whether or not it does *in fact* violate the principle of equal respect (Friedman 1985, pp. 58–9; Pogge 1998). In a context of equality in which resources and wealth are equitably and adequately allocated between individuals across different countries, it is probably right that greater concern for compatriots need not offend against the ideal of equal respect. If a person is justly entitled to her holdings, it is hard to dispute that she may utilize her holdings in ways, if she so wishes, that privilege her fellow members, or her other personal projects and attachments (provided, of course, that the terms of justice are not upset by this privileging of personal and associative ends).

But in a world marked by stark international inequality, it is implausible that citizens of richer countries may show greater concern to compatriots without *simultaneously* undermining the ideal of universal equal respect. Because of an unfair global distribution of wealth and resources to begin with, the practice of compatriot partiality in our world undermines equal respect straightaway because it permits the withholding of basic resources and goods from those who have a just claim to them. Part of what it means to give a person due respect is that we treat her justly, and that her rightful claims be recognized. So if the practice of patriotic partiality means that we are in fact withholding resources from certain noncompatriots who have a legitimate claim to them, then this patriotic partiality clearly undermines the principle of equal universal respect because we are treating these noncompatriots unjustly.

Thus partiality towards compatriots in an unegalitarian global order fails to meet the cosmopolitan ideal of equal respect precisely because such partiality takes place in a global context that is antecedently unjust, and it, moreover, perpetuates and rationalizes this existing injustice. The failure of R. Miller's argument, as it appears to me, is that he assumes that the cosmopolitan ideal of equal respect is separable from the ideal of equal concern *independently* of the background conditions against which people interact. If there is a prior commitment to global equality, then special concern for compatriots will not translate into disrespect for others only if this special concern is exercised in a global framework that has met the requirements of global egalitarianism.

R. Miller would reply that my objection puts the cart before the horse: his whole point in justifying the practice of patriotic bias is to show why a nonegalitarian global distributive order – a distributive scheme that allocates resources and wealth principally on the criterion of citizenship – is legitimate. That is, he wants to show that the answer to the question "what counts as a just global allocation" cannot be decided independently of the special claims of compatriots, and that a conception of global justice has to build into it the ideal of compatriot partiality.

But this response assumes a default position that cosmopolitans should question. Why should the claims of compatriots be "factored in" at the basic level of deliberation about global distributive justice? R. Miller argues for this by conceptualizing cosmopolitanism in such a way that it entails this special consideration for compatriots. But this seems to be tinkering too much with our theory to accommodate facts that we should want to call into examination.

Indeed, if R. Miller's reason for caring about domestic equality is because of the coercive schemes compatriots are helping to impose on each other, then there seem to be good reasons for caring about global equality as well. As I noted earlier, individuals participate in "complex international economic, political and cultural relationships that suggest the existence of a global scheme of cooperation" (Beitz 1999a, pp. 143–4). If this claim about global interdependency is acceptable, then R. Miller's starting premise, that we should foster mutual respect among individuals participating in common institutions, and that we must give them incentives to comply with these institutions, has to be applied globally as well as domestically. Ironically, then, given this fact of global interdependency, R. Miller's recommendation fails to give due respect to needy individuals of poorer countries on his own terms: they have not been given good reasons for accepting and complying with the global social and economic schemes which we are helping to impose on them. So, contra R. Miller, instead of finding the patriotic bias of the rich reasonable and acceptable, needy citizens of poor countries would find such partiality an affront to their participation in common global schemes.

The driving argument behind R. Miller's thesis is that mutual trust and solidarity within a society can be fostered only when domestic institutions are designed in such a way as to privilege the needs of members over those of nonmembers. But if it is correct that treating one's own with greater concern in an unequal global context comes at the price of treating strangers unjustly, then the practice of compatriot partiality might in fact undermine mutual respect and trust rather than encourage these virtues. One might conjecture that the sorts of attitudes that would condone treating outsiders unjustly are those that would encourage treating insiders unjustly as well. As Daniel Weinstock has pointed out, the limitation of equal concern to one's compatriots risks "corroding" that community's view of justice (Weinstock 1999, p. 533). Plato's observation that there will be dissension and differences among thieves, and that injustice "whether among free men or slaves, will make them hate each other and quarrel," speaks to this point.[16] Or consider Engels's observation that "a nation cannot become free and at the same time continue to oppress other nations."[17] If this is right, then in order for patriot bias to actually nurture mutual respect and trust among compatriots, it must first be shown that this bias does not result in treating outsiders unjustly. R. Miller's whole point, of course, is to show that injustice towards outsiders does not follow from partiality towards insiders. But my argument is that the justness of the global context must be first independently identified *before* we can with confidence conclude that special concern for compatriots does not entail injustice for foreigners.

The mistake of the restricted cosmopolitan view, in sum, is that it takes a global distributive scheme that is informed by patriotic partiality to reflect an *acceptable* distributive allocation (even as it rejects the current

---

[16] See Plato, *The Republic*, 351c–351e.   [17] Quoted in Cunningham (1994, p. 104).

distributive scheme in which basic needs for all are not met), and so falsely sees the principal philosophical task to be that of reconciling *this* distributive scheme with the cosmopolitan ideal. And this side-steps the problem, for the fundamental issue is whether a global distributive scheme that is informed and limited by patriotic partiality is a just one in the first place. To mold and temper the concept of cosmopolitanism so that it meshes with and rationalizes this conventional understanding of patriotic partiality is to be getting hold of the wrong end of the stick. Justice aims to assess our existing practices, not the other way around.[18]

The fact of people's particular citizenship, and its effects on the global distribution of wealth and resources, is a fact that should be evaluated against our theory of justice, rather than a fact that may *determine* that theory. *Justice ought to constrain and (re)shape our institutions; not the other way around.* To say that we have to begin our theorizing about justice from currently accepted institutional arrangements and practices as they are *as if* these are given or inevitable, and that our conception of justice has to accommodate this existing reality, is to misconstrue the role and point of justice.

Limited patriotism

The above discussion, I hope, has clarified for us what cosmopolitan justice needs to accommodate and what it demands. Cosmopolitan justice does not need or seek to accommodate patriotism as conventionally practiced; commonsense morality does not require this. Nor should cosmopolitans attempt to reconcile cosmopolitanism with patriotic concern by abandoning the cosmopolitan concern for global egalitarianism. An idea of cosmopolitan justice that does not require global equal concern for all individuals would be cosmopolitan in name only; it would defeat the reason for wanting to take cosmopolitanism seriously as an

---

[18] What I am calling the wrong starting point is also present in Blake (2002). Blake begins his paper by saying that there is a tension between the liberal theoretical commitment to universal equal concern and respect, and the liberal practice of protecting borders and favoring compatriots. Blake then sees the philosophical challenge to be that of reinterpreting liberal theory so as to make sense of and justify this liberal practice of exclusion (Blake 2002, p. 257). What I am arguing above is that this assumption as to what the challenge is is too quick; that there is the alternative, which should be considered, of examining and criticizing the practice of exclusion in light of what liberal theory demands. To put it differently, the method of reflective equilibrium sometimes requires us to tinker with our theory to make it fit our considered judgments; other times, however, it can compel us to reconsider and examine some of our practices, which we may have wrongly believed to constitute a moral fixed point, in light of our theoretical commitments. The burden is not always on theory to accommodate practice; the burden can, on due reflection, be on practice to change in order to conform to theory.

account of global justice that is motivated by the problem of global inequality.

Let me turn now to the "limited patriotism" position that I think provides the most appropriate way of understanding and balancing the demands of cosmopolitan justice and patriotism. To start, it will help to clarify the scope of justice as impartiality. Justice as impartiality does not demand strict impartiality across the whole of people's lives. That is, justice as impartiality does not aim to regulate individuals' day-to-day interaction with each other as such; rather it aims to define and regulate the background social context within which such interactions occur. As I noted above, a theory of justice that does not provide any (or even sufficient) space for personal and partial pursuits would be a rather unappealing, and indeed alien, conception of justice – one that appears to neglect the rich complexities and interconnection of ordinary individual lives. Indeed, theories of justice begin from the assumption that personal and partial pursuits are what give meaning and worth to individual lives, and that the aim of principles of justice is not to rule out these partial commitments and pursuits as such, but to define the social context within which individuals may freely and fairly pursue their own projects. As Rawls has pointed out, "while justice draws the limit, and the good shows the point, justice cannot draw the limit too narrowly" (Rawls 1996 [1993], p. 174).

Following Brian Barry, we can say that justice as impartiality demands "second-order" impartiality – that is, it requires that the rules and principles of institutions be impartial with respect to individual preferences and choices. But justice as impartiality does not entail "first-order" impartiality – that is, it does not require "impartiality as a maxim of behaviour in everyday life" (Barry 1995, p. 194). Or, to put it differently, justice requires impartiality at the "foundational level" where we determine people's baseline legitimate entitlements and claims; but it does not require impartiality at the substantive or "intermediate level" within the constraints set by foundational impartiality (Beitz 1999a, p. 208).

Cosmopolitans accept the ideal of impartiality in the same way, as a second-order claim or a claim about institutional arrangements, rather than as a substantive claim or a claim about specific interaction within the rules of institutions. Accordingly, the aim of cosmopolitan impartiality is not to eliminate all forms of national and other associative concerns, interests, and pursuits, but to determine the global context and rules within which such concerns and interests may be legitimately pursued. And as people may opt to pursue and realize special ends and associative ties within the rules of a just institutional setting, so may individuals pursue particular ends and ties, including the commitment of patriotism, within the limits of a just global institutional arrangement. Citizens may use resources that rightly belong to their country to favor the claims of their compatriots. So cosmopolitan impartiality does not, to repeat, deny the importance of patriotism but only serves to establish the parameters within which patriotic concern may legitimately take place. Rather than ruling out the ideal of patriotism, impartial cosmopolitan justice serves to define and secure the global background conditions under which individuals may legitimately favor the demands of their compatriots as well as pursue other nationalist and partial projects.

Thus cosmopolitan impartiality constrains the practice of patriotic partiality by holding that partial concern is permissible (not to say obligatory) only when the appropriate conditions of justice are met, and that only when the global "playing field" is level may one privilege one's special ties (Pogge 1998, pp. 466–72). To express the limited patriotism position in a principle, we might say that people may take their patriotic commitments seriously only in a background global context in which the needs of all persons are impartially considered. Legitimate patriotic partiality is necessarily a patriotic partiality exercised in a world limited or regulated by impartial principles.

The crucial question, then, is what does impartiality require at the global level? Adopting a global perspective, among the sorts of claims that justice needs to adjudicate are claims that are tied to nationality, namely the claims members of nations make against members of other nations. In other words, a theory of global justice aims, in part, to adjudicate the demands and interests of different nations against each other. Hence, following from the above observation about the purpose of justice, we would want to factor out nationality at the basic level of deliberation. To allow a conception of global justice to be shaped by nationally based factors is to corrupt its role as the arbiter of national disputes. This means that when we decide on people's basic and legitimate entitlements from the global standpoint, we are to treat individuals as equals regardless of nationality (in addition to factoring out other historical and contingent facts about them, as we do in the domestic case).

At the foundational level of deliberation about global justice, impartiality requires that we do not allow people's nationality to influence our views on what people's baseline entitlements are. This is what the cosmopolitan ideal of impartial justice calls for. A person's nationality, a mere accident of birth, cannot by itself be a reason for giving her greater consideration at the foundational level. To allow this is to permit a claim that is the very subject of adjudication (i.e., the claim of nationality) to influence the terms of the adjudication, which would be self-defeating.

To illustrate the above point, let us suppose that global justice requires a global resource tax (GRT), as proposed by Thomas Pogge, which would require countries to pay a resource extraction tax to a global development fund (Pogge, 1994). In saying that justice sets the limiting conditions on patriotic obligation, I mean that a country would be able to favor its own citizens only after doing its share as required by the terms of the GRT, just as, in domestic justice, families may favor their children only with their post-tax income.[19] But once the requirements of justice are met, partial concern for compatriots (just as in the case of partial concern for one's family members) is not only to be expected but is unreasonable to deny. Thus the real challenge for defenders of global justice is not whether patriotic obligations per se are permissible, but whether patriotic obligations may determine and limit the demands of justice.

This understanding of the relationship between the impartiality of justice and the special commitments of people is thus consistent with how we conceive of justice in the domestic context. We want the institutions of a society, and the rules and principles that underpin them, to be informed by the ideal of equal consideration for all citizens, and that the institutions we establish "should be based on an impartial consideration of the claims of each person who would be affected" (Beitz 1999b, p. 287). We try to achieve this ideal of impartial treatment by putting aside those facts about individuals that are "arbitrary from a moral point of view," such as their gender, race, social or caste status, and so on (Rawls 1971, p. 15). These contingencies are seen as mere accidents of birth and ought not to affect individuals' entitlement at the institutional level. Yet within the rules and limits of impartially defined institutions, individuals may utilize their rightful resources as they wish, including favoring personal projects and special social commitments. Justice does not necessarily ground but only sets the limits within which people may engage in personal and other special pursuits. As Marilyn Friedman writes, "impartiality does not a priori require each of us to devote substantial moral attention to those we do not love or for whom we feel no special attachment." It is our background institutions "that must be impartially morally justified" (Friedman 1985, p. 82).

The cosmopolitan view of justice extends this understanding of the relationship between justice and personal pursuits to the global context. It is just that, in moving to the global plane, nationality becomes a contingency to be factored out when deliberating the baseline entitlements of people, even though it is a presupposed (and necessary) context in the case of domestic justice. Nationality is one of the accidents of birth that has grave implications for people's life chances; indeed it may be an even more pernicious accident than others, given the starker real inequalities

---

[19] For more on the latter point, see Murphy and Nagel (2002).

of wealth and resources between individuals across national boundaries than within, when we adopt the global point of view. While it is a necessary background assumption in deliberations about *domestic* justice, nationality becomes a serious contingency whose effects we must strive to nullify when thinking about justice *globally*.

Notice that none of the above commits the cosmopolitan to the view that the moral worth of patriotism must be traced back to some cosmopolitan principles: that is, that the value of patriotism must be explainable ultimately in cosmopolitan terms. This reductive account of patriotism, as we saw earlier, is the source of much discontent among defenders of patriotism, and rightly so because it misdescribes and underappreciates the ethical significance of nationality. What cosmopolitan principles do, however, is constrain the practice of patriotism by establishing the limiting conditions for its practice. Cosmopolitanism plays a limiting role with respect to patriotism, not a justificatory role as such. To repeat a point made earlier, we can deny that patriotism (or any special obligations) must be reduced to certain external principles of justice without denying that the practice of patriotism (or any special commitments) must be constrained by principles of justice.

As mentioned previously, the idea of the moral independence of special obligations refers to its justificatory basis, not to its moral unconstrainability. This, too, is consistent with how Rawls understands the relationship between the moral powers of individuals – the capacity for a sense of justice and for a conception of the good. People's conceptions of the good can have a certain moral independence; they need not derive ultimately from the principles of justice. Yet justice sets limits on the conceptions of the good that people may have and how they may pursue these conceptions. To recall a point made earlier, while there has to be what Kelly calls a "moral compatibility" between people's personal concern and the requirements of impartiality, this does not require that personal concern has to be rationally justifiable by reference to these requirements (Kelly 2000, pp. 116f).

The basic claim of the cosmopolitan is that we must first determine what "rightly" belongs to whom, and to do this we must adopt a point of view that is impartial with respect to nationality. In this sense, the practice of patriotism is to be subordinated or limited by the principles of cosmopolitan justice impartially arrived at. Now this does not mean that the practice of patriotism in our existing highly unequal world is ruled out from the cosmopolitan viewpoint until ideal global justice is achieved. Complete justice in our world is a goal to strive for rather than a state that we can actually achieve. So, to require that patriotic concern be forestalled until we have reached a truly just world order is in effect to rule out patriotic concern in the real world. What the limited patriotic thesis requires, when applied to the nonideal world in which justice is never fully realized, is that patriots ought also to take their duties of global justice seriously, and that they should be striving actively towards a more just world arrangement, if they want their practice of patriotic favoritism to be legitimate. They may show compatriots special concern, but they must also be sincerely attempting to minimize the background injustices by working towards a more egalitarian world.

To be sure, the priority of cosmopolitan justice needs to be further defended. For instance, some nationalists will argue that nationality provides one of the basic factors to be taken into account when determining the terms of justice. My point here is that justice can set the limits on the good, including the good associated with patriotism, without having to pretend to be providing an explanation for the good. Why justice – in particular, cosmopolitan justice – deserves priority over patriotic pursuits and nationalist claims will be further discussed in chapter 9.

Conclusion

To some defenders of patriotism, the requirement that patriotism be exercised *within* the bounds of justice may sound like an over-demanding one, because now patriots would have to both work towards global equality and exercise special concern for their compatriots. But if this seems over-demanding, it is only because it is taken for granted that patriotic partiality may indeed limit the demands of global equality. Cosmopolitan justice of course imposes demands on the patriot, but the principal question is whether these are reasonable demands. As Rawls has pointed out, to take responsibility for one's ends is to exercise one's moral capacity to revise and reform one's conception of the good in light of one's legitimate claims.[20] So if it is indeed the case that taking one's duties of global justice seriously would mean that one has fewer resources left to favor one's compatriots, then the onus is on the patriot to reformulate the extent to which she may favor her compatriots. Of course, just as we do not want a domestic theory of justice that is so rigoristic as to leave insufficient space for personal pursuits, so we do not want a cosmopolitan theory that leaves virtually no room for national partiality. But this does not mean that we must capitulate to people's existing and unexamined sense of entitlements when conceptualizing our theories of justice. To pursue national ends, including those of patriotic partiality, within the constraints of justice, with resources that are rightly allocated, is part of what it means to

[20] See, e.g., Rawls (1999b, p. 371).

pursue these ends successfully. If we accept that the critical success of one's personal projects is compromised if one pursues them without concern for the injustices in one's domestic society (cf. Dworkin 1992, p. 222), likewise the practice of patriotism becomes morally questionable, and its critical success compromised, if people continue to favor their compatriots without concern for the larger global background injustices against which this partiality is expressed. To put it differently, the cost of patriotism in an unequal world is continued injustices to noncompatriots. To offset this cost, the morally sincere patriot has the duty to try to bring about a new global arrangement in which the injustices of patriotism can be mitigated or avoided.

Another way cosmopolitan justice may be seen as too demanding is that it offends against our deeply held perception of the moral significance of certain associative ties, of which patriotic ones are an example. So, just as a theory of justice that can accommodate the particularity of friend-ship by attaching only instrumental value to it will violate our ordinary perception of friendship, so a cosmopolitan theory that can account for patriotism by attaching only instrumental value to it risks violating our ordinary perception of patriotic commitments. But I have tried to show that cosmopolitan justice imposes limits on patriotic concern without taking a stance on the bases of such concern. The moral independence of patriotism is compatible with the cosmopolitan requirement that the exercise of patriotism be bounded by the requirements of justice.

Patriotic concern thus has a place within a cosmopolitan theory of justice; but cosmopolitan justice defines its limits. The conventional view that what counts as a just global distribution of wealth and resources may be determined in part by people's national affiliation or citizenship need not be accepted by cosmopolitans.[21] Special concern, to be morally acceptable, must, among other things, be exercised against a background of justice in which the entitlements of all persons are impartially consid-ered. Commonsense morality does not require otherwise.

---

[21] Pogge points out the different ways this assumption is instantiated in the real world. Pogge (1998, 1992a, 1992b).

8   Citizenship and special obligations

The previous chapter tried to show that cosmopolitanism can accommodate the exercise of partial concern among compatriots, and that the *partiality* of patriotism can be reconciled with the *impartiality* of cosmopolitan justice. This reconciliation is best achieved, I argued, by confining the scope of patriotism within the framework of cosmopolitan justice, rather than by limiting our cosmopolitan commitments against the patriotic ideal as conventionally understood and practiced. This subordinating of compatriot partiality to the principles of cosmopolitan justice sits well with our considered views about the relationship between justice and partial concern in more familiar social contexts (e.g., in the context of domestic society).

This subordination of patriotism to cosmopolitanism does not mean that patriotism is reducible to cosmopolitan principles (in the sense that the worth of patriotism is understood to derive ultimately from these principles). If it did, defenders of patriotism could rightly accuse the cosmopolitan position of failing to take seriously into account the moral significance of patriotic ties and concern. But it does mean that the practice of patriotism ought to be limited by the parameters defined by cosmopolitan justice. And, as mentioned, taking patriotic commitments to be constrainable by cosmopolitan principles does not mean that patriotic commitments are to be reducible to cosmopolitan principles.

We, therefore, have a general structure for reconciling cosmopolitanism and patriotism that does not compromise the global egalitarian commitments of cosmopolitanism. On this reconciliation structure, we say that the showing of special concern for compatriots is permissible (not to say obligatory) to the extent that this partiality is expressed in a context of global justice (defined on cosmopolitan terms).

But it might be thought that patriotic concern is not merely a prerogative but an obligation grounded on reasons of justice. That is, compatriots not only may care specially for each other, but they also have obligations of justice towards each other that are distinct from the global duties they owe to strangers. And it might be thought that because the demands of justice between compatriots are stronger than the duties of justice between strangers, whenever there is a conflict between justice for compatriots and justice for strangers, the former takes priority. To illustrate this claim, assuming a fixed amount of resources, it might be thought that the duty to improve public healthcare in one's own society is an obligation of justice owed to compatriots that overrides the duty to provide basic healthcare services for people in foreign countries who lack even minimum facilities. Thus patriotic obligations, as I will call the special obligations of justice between compatriots, may limit what global justice can require of people. That is, there are supposedly reasons of domestic justice for limiting the demands of global justice. Taking patriotism to be a claim grounded on justice, therefore, seems to present a stronger limiting case against the demands of cosmopolitan justice. We are not simply pitting an option or prerogative against the claims of justice, but two claims of justice against each other; and one of these claims, that of patriotism purportedly, is more strongly grounded than the other.

Given this challenge, some defenders of cosmopolitan justice see their main task to be that of showing why the common arguments offered in defense of patriotic obligations fail. For instance, Charles Jones writes that compatriot favoritism (as he calls special concern for compatriots) is "clearly lacking any general, defensible rationale" (Jones 1999b, p. 134; see also Brock 2002, pp. 310–11; Lichtenberg 1998): that is, on this approach, cosmopolitanism is protected against the patriotic challenge by showing that there is no rational basis for any distinctly and specially grounded obligations towards compatriots. Cosmopolitan justice is defended by defeating arguments in defense of patriotic obligations.[1] Yet such an outright rejection of patriotic obligations, as I noted, would count as a weakness rather than a strength of the cosmopolitan view. As we saw in the last chapter, the perceived failure of cosmopolitan theories to take seriously the claims of patriotism is seen to be one of their chief weaknesses.

I want, therefore, to adopt a slightly different strategy in defense of cosmopolitan justice against the challenge of patriotic obligations. I will shift the question somewhat and ask *not* whether there are good arguments for special obligations as such, but whether the arguments for special obligations give us good reasons for limiting the demands of cosmopolitan justice. My approach will thus differ from that frequently adopted in defense of cosmopolitan justice. Often, when faced by the patriotic challenge, cosmopolitans will try to show, even if they are receptive of limited

[1] In the debate between global justice and special obligations, the situation is often in deadlock, with one side attempting to show why there are special obligations, and the other claiming that the arguments in defense of special obligations ultimately fail.

scope for patriotism, that only certain kinds of arguments for patriotism are defensible (e.g., those grounding patriotism on the basis of shared commitment to universal principles), whereas other arguments are not (e.g., those grounding patriotism on national membership).[2] My view is that, for the purpose of cosmopolitan justice, the rational foundations of patriotic obligations may be put to one side – the issue is whether and how patriotic obligations can be justly exercised and discharged.

The crucial question, in other words, is not whether patriotic obligation can be rationally defended, but whether it is reasonable. What I mean by this is that, from the point of view of justice, what is relevant is that patriotic obligations respect the bounds of some appropriate understanding of justice (i.e., that they are reasonable), not what kinds of arguments people can give in their favor. The concern is with the *moral limits* of patriotism rather than with the *rational basis* for patriotism. Accordingly, people may see themselves to be specially obliged to their fellows *for whatever reasons* so long as the expression of this obligation respects the boundaries of what is morally acceptable. The basis of special obligations need not be at issue, so long as such obligations are reasonable with respect to justice.

By refocusing the debate in this way, by seeing that the question concerns the *limiting conditions* of patriotic obligations rather than the *justificatory basis* of such obligations, we can avoid two difficulties that have tended to complicate the debate on global justice. First, we can avoid the *reductio* (as described above) of rejecting patriotic obligation or patriotism altogether in order to defend cosmopolitanism. As we saw, critics of cosmopolitanism often (and rightly) take such an outright rejection of patriotic ties (or other partial commitments) as a point against global justice. Or, even if cosmopolitans do not reject patriotism completely, but reject only certain purported justifications for patriotism, such as those that appeal to certain intrinsic features of nationality or membership in a state, they can be accused of undervaluing the various forms of associative ties and relationships that matter to the lives of many people. Second, by focusing our attention instead on the *limits* or *terms* within which people may legitimately realize their ends, we can avoid moral and philosophical controversies about the worth or good of the attachments and social ties that characterize individual lives. Such controversies have tended to stall rather than advance the debate. On my approach, the burden imposed on the patriots is not the unreasonable one of requiring

---

[2] For example, Simon Caney, Judith Lichtenberg, and Jeff McMahan reject arguments for patriotic partiality that are based on shared nationality. Caney refers to these kinds of arguments as "value-independent" arguments (Caney 1996; Lichtenberg 1998; and McMahan 1997).

them to explain and justify their special ties and commitments to the cos-mopolitan's satisfaction, but the more reasonable one that they exercise such ties and commitments within the bounds of cosmopolitan justice.[3] To put it colloquially, it is not the business of cosmopolitans to tell peo-ple how to rationalize and understand their patriotic commitments; their business is only to clarify and establish the bounds of justice that any reasonable patriotism must respect.

With the crucial question in sight, I will examine some common argu-ments in defense of patriotic obligations to see if any of these provide reasons for rejecting cosmopolitan justice. In the present chapter, I will consider two arguments that appeal to the special features of common citizenship as the justificatory basis of patriotism. One is what I will, for reasons to be explained below, call the "instrumental" argument; the other is the "institutional" argument. Against these arguments, I will make two claims. The primary claim is that these arguments, even if they do succeed in providing an account of special obligation, do not provide one that may limit the demands of cosmopolitan justice. On the con-trary, as I hope to explain, these arguments succeed only by affirming the *priority* of global justice. The secondary claim is that, ultimately, these arguments suffer from an *explanatory gap*, and that this gap can be filled only by appealing to a prior shared membership among individuals that makes common citizenship possible.

In the recent literature on citizenship, some theorists have argued that shared nationality provides the common membership that is necessary for forging a citizenry. The nationality argument for patriotism is, thus, of quite a different class of argument from the citizenship-based arguments. Instead of appealing to the administrative and institutional aspects of cit-izenship for the purpose of justifying patriotism, the nationality argument appeals to the underlying shared nationality of persons that allegedly pre-cedes and underpins common citizenship. I will consider the nationality argument separately in the next chapter, and I will argue that even if the nationalist argument is right – that shared nationality is the ultimate explanation for the special obligation among citizens – shared nationality does not provide an account of patriotism that may limit the demands of cosmopolitan justice.

My aim with respect to the instrumental and institutional arguments is to see whether they provide arguments that may limit the demands of global justice, however global justice might be understood. So I will

---

[3] Defenders of global justice who see their goal to be that of rejecting patriotic obligations *in toto* have assumed for themselves a heavier than necessary philosophical burden because the task of showing that *there are no* rationally defensible grounds for patriotic obligation can never be conclusive.

use the more general term "global justice" below so as not to prejudge that global justice has to be cosmopolitan in content. The central aim of this chapter is mainly to preserve the priority of (global) justice over patriotic obligations. If global justice is indeed cosmopolitan justice (as argued in earlier chapters), the instrumental and institutional arguments for patriotic obligations on their own do not tell against it.

The instrumental argument

According to the instrumental argument, special obligations provide an efficient and effective strategy for coordinating and apportioning our general duties to humanity at large. As Robert Goodin writes, "[s]pecial responsibilities are . . . assigned merely as an administrative device for discharging our general duties more efficiently" (Goodin 1988, p. 685). Special obligations thus serve as a useful means of dividing up our moral labor by assigning and locating our otherwise complex and indeterminate general duties within specific groups of individuals and institutions: e.g., among fellow citizens and their shared state institutions (Goodin 1988, p. 679; also Shue 1988, pp. 695–9; and Nussbaum 1996, p. 13).

On this argument, the special obligations that citizens have towards members – obligations that could be both stronger and more specific than their general duties to others – are ultimately instrumental to the purpose of discharging the general duties people have to all others at large. Special obligations thus derive their moral force from the *preexisting* general duties people have; we are expected to care especially for our fellows not because they are entitled as such to special treatment, but because this is how we can best collectively discharge our duties to all individuals.

But, as should be evident from the above, the instrumental argument succeeds in defending special obligations only in as far as giving compatriots special consideration does in fact satisfy, or at the very least does not contradict, certain predefined and preexisting general duties people owe to each other. Because special obligation, on this view, is ultimately a *strategy* for meeting the goals of greater justice, a "sensible way of doing good" as Nussbaum puts it, any practice of patriotic concern that subverts or contradicts this general end straightaway loses its moral ground.

It is useful to recall Mill's remarks in *Utilitarianism*, that it is natural for a person to first tend to the interests of those close and dear. This is not necessarily inconsistent with the principle of maximizing utility, as Mill points out. What is crucial, however, is that "in benefitting them, he is not violating the rights – that is, the legitimate and authorised expectations – *of anyone else*" (Mill 1997b, chap. 2, my emphasis). That is, there is the prior issue of the existing legitimate claims of others that any exercise of special concern for particular persons must respect. Special obligations are limited by general obligations, not the other way around.

So, far from proposing an account of patriotic obligation that could resist the demands of global justice, the instrumental argument presupposes the force of certain universal duties, and takes special obligations between citizens to be a means towards fulfilling these duties. Indeed defenders of the instrumental argument readily acknowledge that in light of existing global inequalities, "some of our general duties to those beyond our borders are at least sometimes more compelling, morally speaking, than at least some of our special duties to our fellow citizens" (Goodin 1988, p. 663; also Nussbaum 1996). The instrumental argument, therefore, does not provide an account of patriotism that may trump the demands of global justice.

Of course nothing in my discussion above proves the existence of cosmopolitan duties. The point is that the instrumental argument *presupposes* that people in general have equal claims on each other regardless of membership, and that it is in the spirit of servicing this general equality that we divide our special obligations along patriotic lines.

One may here propose that, if we adopt an indirect consequentialist strategy, we could say that patriotic obligation, even in instances where it conflicts with duties of global justice, is warranted because the ends of global justice are best realized in the long run if people accept the principle of partial concern. That is, it is a useful general policy for people to favor their own citizens even in particular cases when doing so does not result in greater good.[4] But it is not clear if this argument can apply to forms of patriotism that are clearly violating "the legitimate and authorized expectations" of others. It is highly doubtful that patriotic obligations that involve the using of resources to favor compatriots' interests among those in well-off countries at the expense of the basic needs of strangers, without examining if these resources are justly distributed globally in the first place, can serve as an indirect strategy for maximizing the global good; and it is not clear if this position can in good faith be defended by reference to an indirect strategy for meeting greater good.

Note that the point being argued for is not that a division of labor among compatriots is never permissible in a context of global inequality. It is possible that dividing up our moral labor even in a context of injustice is sometimes a useful strategy for allocating and distributing the burdens of justice, and that even in the context of injustice, a division of labor along citizenship lines might be the best way of righting existing injustices. This is especially so if those unfairly disadvantaged specially look out for each

---

[4] See Railton (1993) and Sumner (1987) for accounts of indirect strategy consequentialism.

other. Special obligation here indeed would have the aim of rectifying injustices. My claim is that an argument that is derived from the idea of a division of labor does not limit what global justice can demand. The division has to be at least consistent with, if it does not directly service, the demands of justice if the rationale for this division is that it furthers the ends of justice. My aim here, to stress, is not to show that the instrumental argument does not succeed in grounding patriotism in our unequal world; my claim is that the instrumental argument does not ground a form of patriotism that may limit the demands of global justice.

The institutional argument

An alternative to the instrumental argument for special obligations is the argument that appeals to the fact that compatriots, as fellow citizens of a state, participate in a range of common *institutions* (social, economic, and, particularly, political).

One interpretation of the institutional argument that I will not examine in great detail here says that absent an existing institutional arrangement, there can be no discussion of justice. According to this interpretation of the argument, the fact that there are institutional arrangements *within* domestic society (i.e., within a single state), but not in the international arena, shows that the only claims of justice there are are those between compatriots. Special obligations that derive from participation in shared institutions, in short, are all the obligations of justice individuals have.

With regard to this skeptical argument, I will only briefly recall two points already made elsewhere in this work. First, the premise that there are no global institutions is quite exaggerated. Even if we were to begin from the idea that justice presupposes an existing institutional scheme, there do exist various *global institutions* that impact on individual lives profoundly, and so considerations of justice are relevant and indeed most pressing in the global context (see Beitz 1999a).

One might reply here that even if it is true that there are global institutions, they are not of the same degree of intensity as domestic ones, and therefore the duties of justice these global institutions entail are necessarily very weak duties, compared to duties within domestic society. The response to this reply takes us to the second point, and this is that the skeptical argument assumes that the boundaries of justice are to be restricted by the boundaries of institutions. But this misconstrues the relationship between justice and institutions. While considerations of justice are *necessary* where there are institutional arrangements, institutional arrangements are not necessary in order for considerations of justice to have great relevance. On the contrary, we have a duty of justice – what

John Rawls calls a "natural duty of justice" – to establish appropriate institutions where none exist (to recall a point made in chapter 2). So rather than being limited by the scope of existing institutions, justice can call on us to extend the reach of these institutions, and to create new ones, where necessary. This point has also been argued for by Beitz and Shue; and it is a view that goes back at least to Immanuel Kant, who noted that considerations of right and wrong become immediately relevant wherever there is interaction between individuals. For Kant, it is this fact of interaction that gives us the duty to leave the state of nature (i.e., an institution*less* situation) and to enter into statehood.[5]

So I will leave behind this extreme interpretation of the institutional argument. The kind of institutional argument I want to examine in greater detail does not take the idea of justice to be tied to existing institutions, but claims nonetheless that there are special *institutionally given* reasons why compatriots have additional obligations to each other. So, on this argument, while the existence of institutions is not a necessary condition for justice, the existence of institutions does create special obligations of justice. There are broadly speaking two different ways of understanding the nature of state institutions, and hence two distinct ways of presenting the institutional argument. On one understanding, state institutions are seen as a *cooperative* scheme that generates mutual benefit (we will call this the *mutual benefit argument*). On another understanding, state institutions are seen as a coercive scheme that in turn generates a *strong* commitment to the ideal of reciprocity, for reasons to be given below (we can call this the *argument from reciprocity*). I will explain and examine these arguments in turn.

The mutual benefit argument

It is sometimes said of the state that it is a mutually beneficial association, and so, in exchange for the mutual advantages of common citizenship, citizens bear certain special obligations to their fellows.[6]

One feature commonly associated with the idea of mutual benefit is that of "voluntariness." The idea is that the benefits and the corresponding

---

[5] Kant writes that we ought to unite ourselves institutionally with all others with whom "we cannot avoid interacting" and subject ourselves "to a public lawful external coercion" (Kant 1993 [1797], p. 124). My point here is not that we have to enter into a global statehood (i.e., create a world state) due to the fact of interaction, but that we need, at the very least, to create global institutions to regulate and facilitate this interaction. Neither, of course, does Kant support a world state.

[6] See Hobbes, Rousseau, and Locke on one interpretation. For a contemporary view, see Dagger (1985).

burdens of citizenship are freely consented to, and so the special obligations of citizenship are especially binding because these obligations have been freely assumed. Just as my freely making a promise imposes on me a special obligation towards my promisee, so individuals, in accepting the mutual benefits of citizenship, have consented in a sense to certain obligations to their compatriots that they would not otherwise have done.

Now the claim that citizenship is mutually beneficial in any strict sense is highly contentious, hence the difficulties with the traditional social contract theories. Indeed, mutual benefit associations need not even be voluntary; though one could say that by freely accepting the benefits of participation, one is in practice consenting, albeit tacitly, to one's membership.[7] But I will leave these points aside for the moment, and ask: does voluntary consent on the part of citizens generate special obligations that can limit their duties of global justice?

It does not appear so. While the criterion of "voluntariness" provides a necessary condition for certain kinds of obligations (it is certainly true that there are certain obligations one need not have without freely agreeing to them), it does not serve as a sufficient condition. Consider the example of promise-making: does a freely made promise always impose an obligation on the promisor? Not necessarily. A promise to perform an act that would violate any prior duty the promisor has cannot generate an obligation on the promisor to perform that act. For instance, a promise to commit a violent crime cannot impose on the promisor an obligation to carry out the crime, for this would be in violation of the promisor's general duty to third parties.[8] An obligatory act has to be a permissible act in the first place, and so promises to execute impermissible actions cannot by definition generate an obligation, free consent on the part of the agent notwithstanding. What this shows is that a necessary condition for free consent to generate a special obligation is that the discharge of that obligation does not violate any outstanding duties an agent has.

It is not enough, then, to simply say that citizens have voluntarily consented (assuming, again, the plausibility of voluntary consent as the basis of citizenship) to privilege and favor each other's interests over the interests of foreigners, and therefore have assumed certain special obligations towards one another that may limit what outsiders can claim of them. People may freely acquire special obligations towards their fellow citizens

---

[7] Arguments for special obligations that appeal to mutual benefit need not rely on voluntary *consent*, but on the voluntary *acceptance* of benefits (i.e., a principle of fair play). But both versions of this argument take citizenship to be a mutually beneficial one in some straightforward way, and participation to be voluntary in some sense (see Simmons 2001, chap. 1, pp. 46–7).

[8] See Scanlon on promising (1999, pp. 199–200).

only if they do not consequently neglect their preexisting duties of justice to others. In sum, for voluntary consent to ground an account of patriotic obligation that may restrict the demands of global justice, it has to provide the further argument that individuals have no prior duties of justice to strangers absent free consent. As presented, however, it is an argument for patriotic obligation that presupposes that the background conditions of justice are appropriately preserved.

The above discussion applies to the notion of mutual benefit in general, whether or not we adopt the voluntary consent model of mutual benefit. The fact that an association mutually benefits its members says nothing about the extent or limits of its members' outstanding duties towards nonmembers. On the contrary, we would say that the sorts of mutual benefit associations people may form – and hence the sorts of corresponding special duties they may incur – are to be limited against their prior general duties to all individuals.

The mutual benefit argument thus, at best, gives us an account of special obligations that is limited by the general duties of justice people have towards each other. Instead of limiting global justice, special obligations, on this argument, are to be constrained against the demands of global justice. If citizens of well-off countries can be said to be members of a mutually beneficial association, the legitimacy of their association is contingent on whether they relate to others *on just terms*. Hence, the mutual benefit argument endorses rather than rejects the priority of global justice.

The argument from reciprocity

The mutual benefit model of citizenship is not the most common way of understanding the normative status of citizenship; and in fact few contemporary theorists actually endorse this model. First, citizenship is rarely voluntary (e.g., Rawls 1996 [1993], p. 136), and second, and more to the point, citizenship is *not*, strictly speaking, mutually beneficial in that, in practice, the burdens and benefits of living together qua citizens are not always evenly shared (R. Miller 1998, pp. 203–4; Goodin 1988, pp. 675–8). Rather than stressing the benefits of common citizenship, some theorists point to the potentially coercive and involuntary nature of living together under shared political institutions.[9]

Accordingly, some have argued that it is precisely because of the involuntariness and coerciveness of shared citizenship that citizens are required to show each other special concern. As Richard Miller writes, it is the need

---

[9] This is how Rawls's difference principle is best understood. See Rawls (2001, p. 43); also Anderson (1993) and J. Cohen (1989).

"to provide adequate incentives for compatriots to conform to the shared institutions that one helps to impose on them" (1998, p. 204) that warrants and justifies the practice of what he calls "patriotic bias," that is, the favoring of compatriots over noncompatriots when it comes to distributive issues.

This argument can be described as an argument from reciprocity for the following reason. The ideal of reciprocity says that, because social institutions are potentially coercive and involuntary, we should only impose such institutions on people that they can reasonably be expected reasonably to endorse (Rawls 1996, p. xliv; cf. Scanlon 1999).[10] And one way of acquiring this reasonable endorsement is through the adoption of special obligations and patriotic bias among fellow citizens (R. Miller 1998; also Blake 2002, pp. 281–2). To put it plainly, membership in a state has its cost, but it comes with certain privileges to sufficiently offset this cost.

But two counter-points can be made against the reciprocity argument. First, it could be claimed that there is in fact an involuntary and coercive *global* scheme – a fact that is accentuated by the advent of globalization in recent years – that affects profoundly and pervasively the life prospects of most individuals in the world (e.g., Pogge 1999, 2000). Thus the ideal of reciprocity applies also internationally – foreigners are to be given good reasons, which they can reasonably accept – for the coercive global scheme that others (in particular members of powerful countries) are helping to impose on them. Accordingly, there is no reason why compatriots should be specially favored if special obligations derive from the ideal of reciprocity on account of people's involuntary participation in coercive institutions. On this view, all should be favored, meaning, effectively, none.

Indeed, the reciprocity argument's allusion to shared *institutions* is only a red herring. In the end, what is really at issue, morally speaking, is the fact of *coercion* between persons, whether or not there is a preexisting institutional scheme. Fundamentally, the duty of reciprocity requires that we act only in ways that those who would be affected by our actions could themselves reasonably accept. If this is right, the duty of reciprocity comes into play the moment we occupy a single physical or geographical space in which our actions have implications for each other, independently of the fact of any social arrangement. So, even if we were to reject the claim that there are global institutions that we are imposing on one another, it is hard

---

[10] As Rawls writes: "The reasonable is an element of the idea of society as a system of fair cooperation and that its fair terms be reasonable for all to accept is part of its idea of reciprocity" (Rawls 1996 [1993], pp. 49–50).

to deny that global relations are in many respects coercive for many people in poorer countries (see O'Neill, 2000, chap. 5; also Satz 1999, pp. 76–7). Thus, if reasonable endorsement of a potentially coercive relationship or state of affairs is that which really generates special obligations among compatriots, it would also generate similar duties between individuals across state boundaries, i.e., between citizens and noncitizens.

The degree of global interdependency is such that even if we were to accept that there are no significant global institutions that we are helping to impose on each other, domestic decisions regarding tax laws for businesses, consumption, and the deployment of technology that have environmental implications, and so on, have potentially grave implications for others beyond the borders of the countries in which these decisions are made. The requirement of reciprocity would demand that such decisions be made only under conditions in which it would be reasonable for outsiders (who would be affected) to accept these decisions, even if there were no global institutions mediating the interaction of countries.

To illustrate this point about the requirements of reciprocity even in a pre-institutional condition, imagine that you and I are in a natural setting without any background institutions or agreed on rules governing our interaction. But imagine also that I happen to live upstream on a river and so how I exploit this resource would have grave implications for you who are living downstream. The principle of reciprocity would require, even in the absence of any prior institutional scheme regulating our relationship, that I use this resource only in ways that you can reasonably accept. Indeed, the fact that how I act can have serious repercussions for you would generate a duty on me to enter into an institutional relationship with you in order to regulate my use of the river. As Kant has noted, considerations of justice come into play the moment our actions can affect another: "The concept of Right, insofar as it is related to an obligation corresponding to it (i.e., the moral concept of Right), has to do, first, only with the external and indeed practical relation of one person to another, insofar as their actions, as facts, can have (direct or indirect) influence on each other" (Kant 1993 [1797], p. 56). That my decisions and actions will have an impact on you gives you a rightful claim grounded on justice against me.

Second, and more fundamentally, even if we grant that the ideal of reciprocity is restricted to our fellow citizens on account of our shared coercive scheme, we still need to ask why we are imposing that scheme on *this* particular group of individuals and not on another. This question is especially poignant when our scheme, its coerciveness on participants notwithstanding, is comparatively more advantageous than other similar schemes; and, most significantly, it is a scheme that actively keeps

nonmembers out (e.g., through immigration policies and border polic-
ing that restrict membership for many who would be happy to pay the
price of membership). To say that sharing a social scheme justifies favoring fellow members is therefore question-begging in a context of global
inequality, for the very act of sharing a social scheme with some and not
with others (as in the case of rich but exclusive countries) is already an
act of favoritism that needs to be accounted for. To paraphrase Onora
O'Neill, in justifying the boundaries of special obligation, the arguments
for the special obligation cannot be defended in ways that presuppose
these boundaries (O'Neill 2000, p. 178). The justness of maintaining
that scheme and its boundaries turns, among other things, on the moral
implications of that scheme *for others*. The reciprocity argument assumes
that institutions define the boundaries of justice, when it is the justice of
these boundaries that needs to be first examined.

In short, the expression of partial concern cannot be considered in
isolation from the background conditions of justice. If the *criterion of reciprocity* demands that I show you special consideration because of our
joint participation under a coercive scheme, the *criterion of justice* would
demand that I use *only* resources that are rightly mine when doing so.
That is, before we can know what I may rightly give to my fellow members, we must first agree on what is rightly mine. And to establish what
is rightly mine, we need to take into account the claims not just of fellow members but the claims of nonmembers as well. As Henry Shue has
written: "[i]n order to talk about specific duties of domestic justice one
must assume that one knows how much wealth and resources the members of the domestic unit (such as the nation state . . .) are entitled to"
(Shue 1983, pp. 604–5). So, instead of presenting us with an account
of special obligation that may resist the demands of global justice, the
reciprocity argument can support patriotic obligation only if this show of
favoritism is consistent with the demands of justice in the larger global
context.

One might point out that forms of coercion in the domestic and international contexts are distinct and therefore generate different kinds of
distributive considerations in each context. For instance, in his stimulat-
ing discussion on legal coercion and distributive justice, Michael Blake
writes that there is "no ongoing coercion of the sort observed in the
domestic arena in the international legal arena" (Blake 2002, p. 280).
For Blake, there is "a web of legal coercion" in the domestic arena that is
sanctioned by the state, whereas international coercion, the fact of which
Blake does not deny, is of a different kind. If the international domain is
coercive, it is not, however, coercive through the imposition of legal rules
sanctioned and enforced by a political entity with a monopoly on the use

of force. What Blake means is that coercion in the international sphere is not institutionally sanctioned, whereas state coercion in the domestic sphere is, of course, institutionally sanctioned. So while coercive domestic institutional arrangements generate a concern for distributive equality among participants of the institutional scheme in order to legitimize their coercion, coercion in the international domain does not generate such a concern.

Here one might ask if international law in practice is not only coercive but also ongoing and institutional in a way that requires similar legitimization to legal coercion in the domestic context. After all, international coercive actions are not confined to just those actions outside the bounds of international law (as in illegitimate interventions and illegal trading practices that violate, say, WTO rules), but more often than not also include actions that are sanctioned and, indeed, often required by international law. International laws regulating sovereignty and intervention that allow corrupt regimes to be tolerated by powerful countries with economic and political interests in sustaining these regimes, WTO rules on free trade and patent rights that impose unfair terms on those with weaker bargaining power, and so on, are international legal norms that impose themselves on an ongoing basis on individuals and that create conditions of domination and coercion in international relations. I think, therefore, that it is a false description to say that international coercion is not "institutional coercion" in the relevant ways that domestic state coercion is.

But, more significantly, the fact that countries impose border restrictions is already an explicit legal restriction that affects primarily nonmembers, and so needs to be accounted for to nonmembers who are adversely affected by such restrictions. As Debra Satz writes, "saying that citizens of a state have these obligations to one another does not mean that they have the right to determine the conditions of entry and exit from their state" (Satz 1999, p. 79). That states do in practice impose border restrictions is a form of legal coercion that must be justified to those who are being kept out (Satz 1999, pp. 79–80). That is, border restrictions on the part of well-off countries can be justly maintained only in a context of a global arrangement that those being kept out can reasonably accept as reasonable. This would require, among other things, a more egalitarian global distribution of wealth and resources. Border restrictions in a world marked by great inequality are a form of institutionalized coercion on members of less well-off countries. To legitimize this legal imposition on them, global conditions must be corrected so as to make their exclusion from well-off countries not unreasonable. This would support a concern for global distributive equality.

Now Blake anticipates and counters this point by saying that while exclusion could be potentially coercive, there is still "the distinction between prospective and current membership," and only the latter, Blake says, "gives rise to legitimate concern for relative deprivation" (2002, n30). Yet, once it is acknowledged that outsiders can also be coerced in an ongoing legal way by means of their exclusion from membership in well-off countries, it becomes unclear what sustains the distinction between prospective and current membership. If the fact of legal coercion is that which warrants the concern for relative deprivation among members, then to say that nonmembers are not entitled to this concern, even though they are also coerced legally because they are nonmembers, seems to be question-begging. It presupposes the very claim – i.e., the moral significance of boundaries and membership – that the argument is meant to defend.

The missing nationalist premise

Let me summarize the discussion so far. The instrumental and the institutional arguments succeed (to the extent that they do) in defending special obligations but only by presupposing the validity/force of certain global demands. The instrumental argument defends special obligations on the ground that special obligations best meet global needs; the institutional argument, in its different forms, successfully supports special obligations only when the appropriate background conditions of justice are preserved. Therefore, rather than presenting accounts of patriotic obligations that may resist the demands of global justice, these arguments presuppose the *priority* of global justice for their very success.

But there is another problem with these arguments (this is the secondary claim that I said I was going to make in the beginning of the chapter; and this is why I said a moment ago that the arguments succeed only partly). Besides presupposing the priority of global justice, the above arguments must also presuppose a prior sense of shared *identity* among citizens. As mentioned in the previous chapter, the reduction of special obligations to a mere strategy for achieving global goals, as suggested by the instrumental argument, does not provide a fully satisfactory account of patriotic ties and obligations. It is not to be denied that allocating certain important duties to one designated group of individuals can indeed help meet certain general goals. But reducing the ties of citizenship to the merely instrumental one of servicing the greater good misdescribes and undervalues the nature of such ties, as one would undervalue and misdescribe the ties of friendship if one were to reduce the commitments between friends to mere strategies for realizing larger societal ends or to certain general duties such as the duty of gratitude and so on.

To be sure, friendship and citizenship are very distinct kinds of associations; still, to insist that special obligations between citizens are wholly instrumental misses something morally significant and important about shared citizenship (D. Miller 1988, 1995; Dworkin 1986). Indeed, most people do not think that their duties to compatriots are simply "administrative devices" for discharging their general duties to humanity at large. On the contrary, they believe that there is something special about such commitments that *cannot* be fully explained without some appeal to certain particular features of their relationship, e.g., their sense of common history, sense of common belonging, shared destiny, and so on.

Thus patriotic obligations, as I noted earlier, may be treated as "associative obligations" (Scheffler 2001, p. 49). Associative obligations, as understood by some philosophers, refer to a subclass of special obligations that, unlike the instrumentally or institutionally derived special obligations discussed so far, derive their moral force from the particularities of the special relationship itself, and not from features external to it. The history of that relationship and the norms governing that type of relationship are what account for the special commitments among individuals so related. Thus instead of explaining patriotic obligations by referring to the greatest good of humanity or the obligations stemming from institution-sharing, understanding patriotic obligations as associative obligations locates the source of the obligations in the nature of the ties between compatriots. The special relationship itself, it is said, provides the basic reasons for action (Scheffler 2001; D. Miller 1995, p. 50).

Besides failing to do justice to our ordinary understanding of patriotism, the instrumental argument owes us a story as to why we are to assign special obligations to a designated group of persons but not to another. After all, there are presumably other effective ways of allocating and parceling out our general duties, other than on the criterion of citizenship; and indeed different ways of demarcating our *administrative* institutional boundaries consequently. So why assign these obligations to those whom we now consider to be compatriots, and not to others?

Similarly, as already alluded to, the institutional argument is unable to tell us why a given institutional scheme that confers mutual gain or that is potentially coercive but exclusive should be established among a particular group of individuals, and, indeed, why others are often to be (forcefully) kept out. To complete the argument, there must be a criterion of membership, of who is to count as a participant in the institutional scheme, hence to be accorded special concern (either on the ground of

mutual benefit or reciprocity). In other words, there is a more fundamental question of membership that must be first addressed in order to
explain the boundaries of institutions and the significance of membership.

Thus both the instrumental and the institutional arguments as presented are incomplete in that they do not fully account for the subjects of
special obligations. What is presupposed in these arguments is a notion
of a *shared membership* that can help explain why we should divide up
our moral labor along certain lines, or why we should establish common
institutions with some people but not with others. In the contemporary
literature on citizenship, a growing number of theorists believe that the
shared membership necessary for binding a citizenry together is that of a
common *national culture* (Kymlicka 1995, chap. 9; D. Miller 1995; Tamir
1992). On this nationalist view, compatriots owe each other special duties
ultimately because they share a common nationality. On this argument, it
is not the fact in itself that individuals are fellow citizens (participating in
common institutions as members of a state) that generates special obligations, but the fact that they belong to a shared cultural community that
precedes their common citizenship. I turn to the nationality argument in
the next chapter.

9   Nationality and justice

As I noted in the previous chapter, one common view in contemporary theories of citizenship, which is gaining an increasing number of adherents, is that a shared *nationality* provides the crucial common denominator for a functioning liberal democratic citizenship.[1] While this acknowledgment of the connection between nationality and democratic citizenship has come to the fore only comparatively recently in contemporary debate, the importance of common nationality for democratic citizenship was recognized by earlier liberals. J. S. Mill, for instance, famously wrote: "Free institutions are next to impossible in a country made up of different nationalities. Among a people without fellow-feeling, especially if they read and speak different languages, the united public opinion, necessary to the working of representative government, cannot exist" (Mill 1977a, p. 547).

Along the lines suggested in this quotation from Mill, contemporary nationalist theorists argue that a national *culture* provides the sense of membership that undergirds a common citizenship or membership in a state. This shared identity provides the historical "ties that bind" an otherwise diverse and pluralistic population (Kymlicka 1995, chap. 9). Common nationality provides the collective pride and humiliation, the common history, and the common sympathies that provide the motivation for individuals to establish, and participate in, common political institutions together (cf. Mill 1977a, pp. 546–8). To share a nationality is to share an understanding or vision of where one fits in historically and culturally in the story of humanity, and to share a *cultural* framework within which one formulates, pursues, evaluates and revises one's purposes and goals in life (Kymlicka 1989, 1995; Miller 1995; Tamir 1992). As David Miller writes, "identifying with a nation, feeling yourself inextricably part of it, is a legitimate way of understanding your place in the world" (Miller 1995, p. 11). Nations are, thus, what one

---

[1] For one excellent survey on citizenship and nationalism in contemporary political philosophy, see Kymlicka and Norman (1994).

might call a "historic community" (Walzer 1980), within which individuals acquire and cultivate their moral agencies and capacities (Walzer
1980; also MacIntyre 1984).

It is for this reason that the nation is said to constitute an ethical community, or a "community of obligation" whose members see themselves to
be mutually indebted and obligated to begin with (Miller 1995, pp. 83–4;
also Kymlicka 2001a, chap. 12; and Tamir 1992). Shared membership
in a nation alone is sufficient for grounding mutual concern among individuals. And, for this reason, conationals see themselves to have certain obligations to each other that they do not have to nonmembers. To
quote from Miller again, "in acknowledging a national identity, I am also
acknowledging that I owe special obligations to fellow members of my
nation which I do not owe to other human beings" (Miller 1995, p. 49).

Indeed, as we saw in chapter 5, nationalists argue that a sense of
national solidarity – what Mill calls the "common sympathies" that exist
between conationals but not "between them and any others" (Mill 1977a,
p. 546) – is crucial for the purposes of social justice within a country. Common sympathies provide the motivation for ordinary individuals to extend
the scope of their moral concern beyond the narrow and intimate circle
of the family, kin, and tribe, but to include also fellow citizens with whom
they have no direct personal ties. The perceived failure of contemporary
liberal theories of justice to take into account the importance of communal solidarity for distributive justice is often invoked as a point against
liberalism by its "communitarian" critics (e.g., Sandel 1992, p. 22).

The national culture that is invoked here need not be defined thickly
in terms of ethnicity, religion or shared moral values, although some
nationalist theorists endorse such a view. Minimally, a nation reflects
what Kymlicka calls a "societal culture" – a set of public institutions
and practices operating under a common language and a shared sense
of history and destiny among members (Kymlicka 1995, 2001a). Liberal
nationalism, according to its main proponents, permits a plurality of cultural practices, traditions, affinities, and rituals within the terms of its
national societal culture (Kymlicka 2001a, p. 211; also D. Miller 2000,
chap. 8). Nonetheless, national membership is centered around the fact
of a shared societal *culture* that gives a nation its distinct identity.

One might object that the cultural basis for patriotism invoked by the
nationality argument is a false description of the real world. Most states
are multicultural states and so do not have the common cultural basis
on which to ground patriotic commitments as required by the nationalist position. But this point can be deflected by the nationalist side. As
mentioned earlier (chapter 5), nationalist theorists are not ignorant of the
fact that citizenship and nationality rarely coincide. On the contrary, this

common incongruity between nationality and citizenship is, in a sense, the motivation for their nationalist thesis – that states ought to actively inculcate a sense of common nationality among citizens for the purpose of strengthening the sense of obligation between them, among other things. The asymmetry between nation and state is not a case against the nationalists, but is in fact the problem that nationalism is meant to solve. For some nationalists, the ideal state is one in which citizens share a common national identity. They warn against the threat to patriotism that arises because of the failure of states to inculcate a strong sense of nationality (e.g., MacIntyre 1984); and they will point to existing patriotism in spite of diversity as evidence of the success of state nation-building, and not a case against it.

Treating the nation as the pre-institutional or the "historic community" that underlies the democratic state and which makes it possible does not imply that national identities are primordial and natural. The imposition of a common language (e.g., as in the formation of the French nation), and the creation and promulgation of a national history for the purpose of inculcating in individuals a sense of belonging to a historical community (as in most liberal democracies, including the United States), are very much political activities.[2] For nationalists, this does not make nationality any less real – what is crucial is that there are present certain objective traits (shared language, common history, and so on), however these traits are cultivated or acquired, that can allow individuals to see themselves as constituting a distinctive historical community or people (Miller 1995; 2000, pp. 28–9). The creation of national traits, or the process of "people-making" as Rogers Smith aptly describes it, is thus a "basic dimension of all political activity" (Smith 2002, p. 19).

In opposition to the nationalist argument, it might be argued that what provides the sense of membership for grounding patriotic commitments is not shared national culture but a shared commitment to abstract principles. Jürgen Habermas's concept of "constitutional patriotism," for example, explains patriotic commitments in terms of the special attachment liberal citizens have to a constitutional order, and how this common attachment generates a special allegiance towards compatriots. Constitutional patriotism, sometimes refered to as the "new patriotism," is presented as a morally more inclusive and universalistic alternative to an idea of patriotism based narrowly and exclusively on nationality (see Vincent 2002, chap. 5; Canovan 2000). If what makes common citizenship possible is a shared commitment to abstract principles and democratic

---

[2] On the importance of national myth-making for democratic citizenship, see Yack (1999). See also Rogers Smith's (2002) account of "people-making."

procedures, then no person may be disqualified from citizenship on the basis of her ethnicity or race.

But there are two difficulties with constitutional patriotism according to defenders of nationalist patriotism. First, shared principles are not sufficient for generating special concern. After all, individuals across state borders can affirm the same abstract principles without seeing themselves as mutually committed.[3] In any case, even if shared principles were sufficient for generating special obligations, it would not explain patriotic obligations, for any boundaries of special obligations based on shared values would extend beyond the boundaries of patriotic obligation. The second and related difficulty is that shared principles alone cannot identify the political community to which, and to whose members, one owes special allegiance. Given that the bounds of patriotism are narrower than those of the set of people committed to the same ideals, a prior understanding of the relevant community is necessary for solving what some commentators call the "identity problem" – that of defining the community and the membership to which the constitutional order applies. Referring to what is often considered to be the quintessential example of a constitutional patriotic state, Margaret Canovan notes that in spite of the appearance that Americans are brought together by a commitment to the principles of the American constitution, it must be recognized that these principles, for Americans, are recognized as "our" principles, "handed down to us by our forefathers, biological or adopted" (2000, p. 425). Canovan goes on to say that to treat Americans as a people "bound together by constitutional patriotism rather than by nationhood is to overlook inheritance – inheritance not only of citizenship, but of the Constitution, the principles, the national mission, the American Way of Life." That is, there is a pre-defined American "people" to whom the American constitution applies (Canavan 2000; also Kymlicka 2001a, pp. 242–5). American patriotism is not ultimately understood in terms of constitutional patriotism but in terms of common nationality. This is consistent with Rawls's view of a people, which he takes to be analogous to a nation and "distinct from the idea of a government or state" and "characterized by a pattern of cultural values described by Mill," that is, the possession of a common history, common sympathies, collective pride and so on (Rawls 1999a, p. 25n).

The reference to a shared nationality and not simply shared values does not discount the point that for liberal nationalists, patriotic ties are

---

[3] Thus Kymlicka notes that joint commitment to abstract principles did not keep countries such as Sweden and Norway from splitting up, nor Quebec sovereigntists from demanding secession from the rest of Canada (Kymlicka 1995, chap. 9). See also Yack (1999).

worthwhile only if they are also based on nationalist commitments that are just by liberal standards. The point, rather, is that the fact of shared principles alone does not sufficiently account for patriotic obligations. Nor, importantly, should liberal nationalists be misunderstood to treat ethnicity coextensively with nationality. As mentioned above, nationality is defined in terms of a public political culture, organized around a common language, that need not have a narrow ethnic or religious character.

The argument from nationality supposedly completes the earlier arguments for patriotic obligations in the following ways. Unlike the instrumental argument, the nationality argument does not reduce the ties and commitments of citizenship to mere instruments for attaining greater moral good. And, unlike the institutional argument, the nationality argument provides us with an account of why people would want to establish and support an institutional scheme with one definitive group of individuals rather than with another. The shared nationality argument, therefore, provides the strongest argument for patriotic obligations, and our question here is whether patriotic claims deriving from shared nationality – what I will call "national obligations" – may resist the demands of cosmopolitan justice.

As mentioned in chapter 8, what is distinctive about national obligations, compared to the instrumental or institutional special obligations discussed in the previous chapter, is that national obligations are what some philosophers call "associative obligations." Associative obligations are special obligations that do not merely derive from features external to a relationship, such as the principle of utility or the principle of reciprocity, but are special obligations that arise from features particular to the relationship itself. For instance, the fact that one is my sibling or a friend provides a basic reason (indeed *the* reason in some cases) for action (see D. Miller 1995; Scheffler 2001, pp. 6–7). Part of what it means to be kin or friend is that those so related have certain special claims on each other that are not reducible to general principles.

The nationalist's point is that, like those of friendship or kinship, the ties of nationality cannot be "reduced to obligations deriving from promises or agreements, or from any discrete interactions among the participants" (Scheffler 2001, p. 6; D. Miller 1995). Reduce the moral ties of nationality to external principles (such as the principle of greater good or the principle of reciprocity or gratitude) and we empty the ideal of nationalism of much of its meaning, as we would, say, the ideal of friendship if the special obligations between friends are treated as merely instrumental for promoting the common good.

One might object that nationality is distinct from friendship or kinship in crucial ways, one of the most obvious being that friendship or kinship ties are intimate and directly personal in ways that ties of nationality plainly are not. So, it might be thought that common nationality is not the sort of relationship that can generate associative obligations. But it is the members' perception of any given relationship, rather than some externally observable features about it, that determines its salience for participants. After all, if members of a nation feel themselves to be mutually indebted and obligated, then they feel that way regardless of the actual direct intimacy or lack thereof between them. The nation is, in Benedict Anderson's well-known phrase, "an imagined community" in that even though conationals are generally not intimate with each other, "in the minds of each lives the image of their communion" (Anderson 1993, p. 6). Indeed, the closeness of a given relationship, and hence its ability to generate associative obligations, is ultimately a matter of its members' understanding of that relationship rather than a matter of any tangible facts about the relationship. Associative obligations arise from "relationships that one has reason to value" (Scheffler 2001, p. 7), and actual personal intimacy is not a necessary condition for having such a reason. In as far as the nation is an "imagined *community*," then conationals can identify themselves as members of a community that they have reason to value. Indeed, one of the main goals of nationalism is to instill this strong sense of community among conationals through various public policies, national myth-making, the promotion of a national language and common history, and so on. So it is not that objective features are unnecessary and that members' perception is all that matters for the kinds of claims members feel they owe to each other. Rather, the objective features can be "constructed" to reinforce in the minds of each the "image" of their union (see Miller 1995, pp. 33–5).

   The thesis that shared nationality underpins common citizenship and that it is the sort of relationship that can generate associative obligations (in spite of its impersonal nature) are points of contention in the literature on citizenship and nationalism. I have noted some of these, and the possible replies on the part of the nationalists to indicate its plausibility.[4] Admittedly, more needs to be said to defend the nationalist thesis. But for my current purpose I need not pursue the matter further. I want to go on to argue that even if the nationalist defense of patriotism holds, it does not provide a limiting case against cosmopolitan justice. So I shall grant the nationalist defense of patriotism and evaluate the implications of this position for cosmopolitan justice. To the extent that nationalist patriotism is often thought to be the greatest obstacle to cosmopolitanism,

---

[4] For further debate on nationalism and patriotism, see the collection of essays in Beiner (1999); McKim and McMahan (1997); Couture et al. (1998). See also Kymlicka (2001a).

in granting the nationalist position, I am granting the most challenging case against my thesis. Thus, assuming that patriotic obligations derive from the shared nationality of citizens, I want next to ask if this argument presents an account of special obligations that may override the demands of global justice.

The limits of nationality

Some nationalists do not think so. These nationalists, whom we may call *liberal nationalists*, argue that conationals may favor one another only if they are *also* doing their part with respect to cosmopolitan justice. Kymlicka, for example, explicitly points out that the nation-building policies of liberal states, such as the regulation of immigration, must be balanced against considerations of global justice, and that states may control entry into their borders only if they are also doing their part to mitigate the great global inequality that motivates much immigration in the first place (Kymlicka 2001b; also Tamir 1992, p. 161). For liberal nationalists, national partiality is permissible, not to say obligatory, only if the exercise of this partial concern does not violate the fundamental duties of justice that people owe to each other at large. Cosmopolitan justice sets the limiting terms for national obligations. Liberal nationalists take the relationship between national claims and global justice to be analogous to the relationship between personal pursuits and justice in the domestic context. As personal pursuits are to be limited by principles of justice impartially arrived at in the domestic sphere, so too should national pursuits and commitments be limited by global justice principles impartially arrived at.

So while nationalists will hold that the fact that "a person is my fellow member" is *a basic reason for action* that is not reducible to more general principles or commitments (cf. D. Miller 1995, chap. 3), liberal nationalists would maintain that this basic reason must be balanced against other considerations, including the consideration of justice towards nonmembers. Liberal nationalists, therefore, allow for special obligations between conationals, but, for them, these obligations are to be constrained by the requirements of global justice *impartially defined*.[5] In short, on this view, what we owe to conationals must be limited against what we owe to individuals at large.

---

[5] This subordination of pursuit of interest to the requirements of justice impartially defined is consistent with how we understand the relationship between personal pursuits and justice in the domestic context. We say, for example, that people may favor their family members but only with resources that are rightly theirs, and what counts as rightly theirs is defined independently of the claims of familial ties.

That national obligations are to be limited by considerations of justice for other nationals does not contradict the claim that national obligations are associative obligations. As mentioned in chapter 7, that an expression of a special commitment must be limited against certain principles of justice does not mean that the worth of this commitment is ultimately reducible to these principles. Constrainability and reducibility are distinct requirements, and liberal nationalists can accept the associative nature of national obligations while maintaining that these obligations are to be constrained by obligations of cosmopolitan justice.

The problem for cosmopolitans, however, is that other nationalists – call them "communitarian nationalists" – reject this privileging of cosmopolitan justice.[6] Indeed, against the liberal nationalist position described above, communitarian nationalists would argue that the purported analogy between global justice and domestic justice is deeply mistaken. While justice may constrain personal pursuits in the domestic setting, global justice cannot constrain national pursuits for the reason that global justice claims cannot be determined independently of national commitments. What we owe to others, on this nationalist view, is to be determined in light of what we owe to members. On the communitarian nationalist view, the liberal nationalists are too quick in claiming a compatibility between national pursuits and cosmopolitan justice. On their view, nationalist commitments properly understood are not subordinated to global demands in the way liberal nationalists hope.

For the communitarian nationalists, the nation constitutes a *distinctive* "ethical community," a distinctive "sphere of justice," against which other considerations of justice need to be balanced (Miller 1995, chap. 3; cf. Walzer 1983). So unlike the liberal nationalists who allow for special obligations only within the terms of global justice impartially defined (as would be required by the cosmopolitan view), communitarian nationalists argue that the terms of global justice should not be impartially defined, as cosmopolitans insist. On this view, within the limits of humanitarianism, the more urgent claims of nonnationals may be limited by the less urgent interests of conationals.

---

[6] Some of these so-called "communitarian nationalists" think of themselves as liberal nationalists. As the liberalism versus communitarianism debate has unfolded, we have seen that the communitarian position is really not an alternative to liberalism but an alternative account of liberalism. But still each position stresses different features of liberal theory. Thus the label "communitarian" is not altogether without significance. "Communitarians" tend to endorse the view that there are different and possibly conflicting "spheres of justice" applicable to different human activities, associations, and communities. The "communitarian nationalists" I am discussing, such as David Miller and Michael Walzer, hold this point. Thus, in spite of taking his nationalism to be a form of liberal nationalism, Miller also refers to his own position on nationality as "communitarian" in "a broad sense" (D. Miller 2000, p. 5).

Nationality and moral agency

One common argument invokes the "communitarian" claim that it is within a particular cultural context, the nation in this case, that a person is "characteristically brought into being and maintained as a moral agent" (MacIntyre 1984, pp. 10–11). As it is qua member of a particular national community that I acquire my moral agency and understand my moral obligations, I therefore owe my primary allegiance to that community and its members. Nationality, in other words, endows people with their moral identities and hence is normatively basic for this reason. Undermine this community and we undermine the basis of my moral agency.

But as liberals like Beitz and Kymlicka have pointed out, this communitarian argument conflates the distinction between moral agency and moral education, on the one hand, *and* the nature and demands of morality, on the other (Beitz 1991, pp. 252–4; also Kymlicka 1989, pp. 57–60). The fact that one acquires one's moral learning and agency within a particular communal context does not mean that one's moral obligations and reasoning must remain confined within that community's boundaries.[7] And the fact that people's moral motivation is sometimes (or even often) limited to those with whom they share a common culture, does not mean that it is inevitable that it remains thus limited, and that the scope of their moral concern is fixed and nonextendable. As an analogy, it is a common fact that the moral learning and education of children begins at home. Yet we do not say that moral reasoning and the scope of moral concern are thus restricted to the home, or that each person's family presents a privileged moral viewpoint that should constrain deliberations about justice for society. The moral community that the nation constitutes, and with which people may identify, is thus not exhaustive of the scope of moral reasoning (see also Moody-Adams 1997, p. 192).[8]

The irreducibility of national allegiance

Another argument one might offer for the ethical status of the nation points to the irreducible worth of national membership and ties. As we saw, one of the inadequacies of the instrumental argument is that it takes

---

[7] Thus, while Will Kymlicka holds that one's national culture provides one with the "context of choice" within which to form, pursue, and revise one's conception of the good, one can also step back and critically evaluate aspects of one's culture (Kymlicka 1989, p. 53).

[8] Proponents of the moral identity argument, therefore, owe us some arguments as to why one's cultural community, even if this is where one learns to be moral, has a limiting effect on what nonmembers can demand of us. They may appeal to some form of ethical relativism here, but at this point they should be ready to defend their position against the standard rebuttals against relativism.

special obligations to derive from certain features *external* to the ideal of citizenship: for example, that of the general good that special obligations can help realize. Nationalists are perhaps right in rejecting this reductionist view of special obligations. To recall a point made earlier, to treat all of our important ties and obligations as merely "administrative devices" for serving impersonal ends and principles misses the intimacy of some of these ties (Dworkin 1986; Nagel 1979, 1986; Scheffler 2001; Hardimon 1994). As I have noted, certain valued individual relationships (e.g., friendship, kinship, and so on) are said to be normatively independent in that they resist attempts to be explained or justified by reference solely to external and general principles. Associative obligations are irreducible to external principles, and hence are said to enjoy a certain normative independence. Thus nationality enjoys a certain moral independence, and this presents a moral point of view that may oppose the impartial standpoint of cosmopolitan justice (Nagel 1991, chap. 15; also Scheffler 2001).

But this argument from irreducibility and the independence of nationality does not fully succeed in showing that national commitments need not observe the limits of global justice. The argument seems to wrongly assume that, just because some attachments are irreducible in the sense described above, they cannot thus be limited by external considerations. But, as we saw in chapter 7, it is one thing to hold that some of our special relationships are morally independent in that they provide us with independent sources of reasons for action, it is quite another thing to conclude that the exercise of these relationships need not be balanced against considerations of justice. While principles of cosmopolitan justice may not provide the *justificatory basis* for national commitments, they can provide the *limiting conditions* for such commitments.[9] The ties of nationality, even if irreducible, may be constrained by the requirements of justice.

Here, one might ask: why should the exercise of national ties be constrained by the requirements of justice? Even if national commitments are to be limited against other considerations, why should cosmopolitan justice be that dominant value? Or, to put the point in a different way, why can the national point of view not be taken directly into account when

---

[9] Recall the example from friendship: while we do not take the moral worth of friendship, and the special commitments between friends, to be justified entirely in terms of general impersonal principles, we nonetheless hold that cronyism is wrong because it is an expression of friendship that has exceeded the bounds of justice. The ties of friendship are nonreducible to the principles of justice, yet the exercise of these ties ought to be constrained by principles (Friedman 1985). See also Scanlon's point that friends have moral standing independent of friendship, and that this moral standing ought to be accorded to others (i.e., non-friends) as well (Scanlon 1999, chap. 4).

determining the terms of global justice, as some nationalists suggest (e.g., Miller 2000, pp. 167ff)?

The response to this challenge, I believe, turns on our general understanding of the role and concept of justice. If we understand the role of justice to be that of a fair adjudicator between competing partial standpoints or claims, then the terms of justice against which these claims are to be assessed and adjudicated must be as neutral or as impartial as possible between these competing claims. Our terms of adjudication can hardly be described as fair, or even useful, if they are informed or shaped by one or the other of the views under contention.[10] The ideal of impartiality is thus central to the concept of justice, and any plausible conception of justice must express this ideal in some appropriate way. As Kymlicka neatly puts it, to reject the ideal of justice as impartiality is to propose "an alternative to justice, not an alternative account of justice" (Kymlicka 1990b, p. 103). Thus, what Jeremy Waldron calls the "primacy of justice" with respect to particular claims follows from the very concept of justice (Waldron 2003). The terms of justice are to be determined impartially with respect to particular and special demands if the purpose of justice is to evaluate these demands.

Extending this common understanding of justice to the global context, the terms of global justice ought to be as impartial as possible with respect to national standpoints; they could not be appropriately called terms of global justice otherwise. This is because, in the global arena, the partial and competing standpoints that principles of justice are meant to impartially adjudicate are national standpoints. Again, this is not to say that partial national commitments cannot be pursued; it only says that national goals/projects are to be pursued within the terms of global justice impartially arrived at. This means that particular national commitments and conceptions of the good cannot be appealed to at the fundamental level of determining the legitimate claims and entitlements of individuals. Only at the intermediate level, only within the rules of a global order regulated by impartial principles, may nationalistic pursuits, including the giving of special concern to conationals, be legitimate (Beitz 1999a, pp. 208–9). The insistence of the communitarian nationalist that the claims of conationals may limit and influence the terms of global justice, therefore, subverts our common understanding of justice. The priority of impartial global justice over national claims derives necessarily from

---

[10] Or if we prefer a more cooperative model of justice, we can say that its purpose is to establish *fair terms* of *social cooperation* so as to allow persons (individually or in associations) to best pursue their conceptions of the good. And this would require that the *terms* of cooperation must be as impartial or neutral as possible with respect to people's conceptions of the good. The ideal of *fair cooperation* cannot be attained otherwise.

the purpose and role of justice. It seems, then, that to deny that global justice needs to be impartial with regard to nationality (as advocated by cosmopolitans) is not to offer an alternative conception of global justice but to reject the very concept of global justice.[11]

Conflicting claims of justice

David Miller thinks that the analogy between domestic justice and global justice is misleading. According to Miller, unlike individuals who are to limit their particularistic personal pursuits against the terms of justice in society (so that "justice features only on one side of the balance"), nation states are engaged in the pursuit of social justice for their members, and so a conflict between different conceptions of justice arises because justice "features on both sides" of the equation – on the domestic side and the global side (D. Miller 2000, p. 167). In short, Miller says that the priority of justice in the global context does not follow from the priority of justice in the domestic context because there are competing accounts of justice in the former but not in the latter.[12] Global justice is simply one "sphere of justice" among others and so need not have dominance.[13]

But Miller's claim seems to miss the mark. To be sure, within different spheres of human associations (both national and subnational), different distributive principles are at play, and what these principles are is in part determined by the nature of the activity in question. Nonetheless, the pursuit of justice in any one sphere must, among other things, not violate other principles of justice that also apply to that sphere. For instance, an association within a society could have a distributive principle that says "to the greater contributor goes the greater benefit." Following Rawls (following Elster), we can call this "local justice," which applies only within an association, as distinct from "domestic justice," which applies to society at large (Rawls 2001, p. 11). But this does not mean that this association need not respect the principles of domestic justice that also apply to it, in particular, those principles that regulate its dealings with other associations and nonmembers. For one, this association may not

---

[11] This usage of the "concept of justice" to refer to the idea of justice, and "conceptions of justice" to refer to different accounts of the idea of justice is, as is well known, from Rawls (1971, p. 5).

[12] The main arguments for Miller's thesis, that there are conflicting claims of justice in the global context, is that the domestic and global spheres offer different ideas as to the subject matter of justice (the goods to be distributed) and the criteria of just distribution (the principles we should use). What the appropriate criteria of justice are is dependent on the social context at hand (2000, pp. 168–70).

[13] The idea of "spheres of justice" is of course Walzer's (1983).

misappropriate the property of other associations and then distribute that property according to the local principle of "greater contribution" among its members. And, to take a specific example, if the difference principle were in effect in the society in which this association operates, then the association would have to comply with this requirement with respect to the rest of society, its claims of local justice notwithstanding. Thus the association-specific principle (local justice), that the greater contributor receives the greater benefit, is constrained by other principles binding the association (domestic justice). A distinct sphere of human activity is not sheltered from principles governing its relationship with other societies.[14] So there may be two different (and conflicting) spheres of justice – local and domestic – and yet it makes perfect sense to say that the former needs to be constrained by the latter.

The rejection of the priority of global justice, therefore, does not succeed if the claim is simply that there are distinct spheres of justice to which distinct ideas of justice apply. As we saw earlier, what members of an association owe to each other entails, first of all, that the association is able to determine what rightly belongs to it. This requires subordinating internal claims of justice to claims of justice at large. Now, the rejection of the priority of global justice may succeed if it is the case that nationally based justice is all there is – that there is no basis for justice in the global context. One might claim that the lack of global consensus on the goods to distribute, on the principle of distribution, etc., rule out the possibility of global justice. But this is an argument about the *lack* of global justice and so is a different argument from the one Miller has specifically offered here about the conflicting claims of justice; and, as I have tried to show earlier (chapters 2 and 5), this argument is too hasty.

In the end, then, Miller's claim, that in the global context there is a conflict of justice claims, whereas in the domestic context justice features only on one side of the equation, is misleading. In both the domestic and the global contexts, there are different claims of justice (justice features on both sides in both contexts) – local versus domestic justice in the case of the nation, and national (as well as local) versus global justice in the case of the global context. And just as we do not reject the priority of domestic justice in the context of the nation, in spite of competing claims of local justice, because we accept that there are ways of ordering claims of justice, so we have no reason to reject, contra Miller, the priority of global justice just because there are competing (national) claims of justice. If domestic justice has precedence over local justice because one of the functions of domestic justice is to adjudicate the competing claims of

---

[14] Indeed, to claim otherwise entails, implausibly, that criminal organizations may claim that their internal distributive practices have an equal standing alongside principles of justice that regulate society as a whole.

different associations within society, then so should global justice have precedence over national claims of justice, if we accept that the function of global justice is to adjudicate competing national claims. The fact of the presence of competing claims of justice alone does not deny the priority of some claims of justice over others.

The national perspective

One might resist this prioritization of cosmopolitan justice by pointing out that individuals have the prerogative – what Scheffler calls "agent-centred prerogatives" – to privilege personal and particularist projects, including tending specially to the needs of their conationals (and other special and personal commitments and attachments), even if this does not best advance the goal of global equality (Scheffler 1982; Nagel 1991, p. 14). This may suggest that there are "some constraints that any adequate formulation of cosmopolitanism may need to respect" (Scheffler 2001, p. 110).

This tension between pursuing particularist ends and the end of justice reflects the general problem, identified by Thomas Nagel, of reconciling the competing perspectives of the personal point of view and the impersonal point of view required by justice as impartiality.[15] While there is the possibility of a political solution to this ethical problem in the domestic context, by creating "a set of institutions within which persons can live a collective life that meets the impartial requirements of the impersonal standpoint while at the same time having to conduct themselves only in ways that it is reasonable to require of individuals with strong personal motives" (Nagel 1991, p. 18), the problem is less soluble in the global context. This is because, thinks Nagel, of the "extreme" diversity of values and the "enormous gap between rich and poor" in the world (1991, p. 170). Thus advocates of global egalitarianism have to, at some point, accept that citizens of rich countries could legitimately resist further global redistribution, in favor of their prerogatives (and indeed obligations) to support their national commitments and interests. "In cases of extreme inequality the poor can refuse to accept a policy of gradual change and the rich can refuse to accept a policy of revolutionary change, and neither of them is being unreasonable in this" (1991, p. 171). In short, nationality constitutes a legitimate moral point of view that may rightly limit the demands of the impersonal point of view of cosmopolitan justice.

[15] Nagel writes that "[a]t some point the natural demand for egalitarian impartiality has to come to terms with a recognition that legitimate claims of personal life exist even for those who are not in need" (1991, p. 18).

An immediate response to this objection, however, is that the alleged tension between the national and cosmopolitan standpoints does not even arise in our world because the cosmopolitan view is, as yet, far from being adequately expressed. As Beitz points out, we are far from the point where national prerogatives may limit the requirements of impartial global concern. "Any defensible version of the priority thesis would have to be trimmed back from the form in which it presents itself in ordinary morality and be qualified in ways that leave room for the operation of international principles" (Beitz 1999a, p. 214). Nagel himself notes that "[w]e would have to move a considerable distance toward improvement in the condition of most human lives before the claims of the better-off presented a serious challenge to the pursuit of further equality at their expense" (1991, p. 19). He goes on to say that the "collective pursuit of prosperity and justice for themselves by the citizens of a nation remains under a shadow while it goes on in a world like ours, where a minority of nations are islands of relative decency in a sea of tyranny and crushing poverty, and the preservation of a high standard of life depends absolutely on strict control on immigration" (1991, p. 179; see also Scheffler 2001, p. 108). The nationality argument need not, therefore, support patriotism as it is currently practiced and accepted in our world. A great deal of progress towards global equality is in order before the nationality argument – before the tension between the national point of view and the demands of impartial global justice – comes into play. To resist moves towards greater equality in light of the current situation is to unduly privilege the national viewpoint by paying insufficient heed to the demands of the cosmopolitan ideal.

Still, the objection would claim that once the cosmopolitan point of view is adequately realized – once, say, individuals of the world are able to meet their basic subsistence – national interests may rightly resist further demands for global egalitarianism. Yet it remains unclear why national prerogatives should enjoy this special status vis-à-vis the demands of justice, when familial and friendship relationships do not. As we may not invoke the ideal of friendship to justify the using of resources that are not rightly ours to favor friends, so we may not claim conationality to resist what global justice would require of us. While we should accept that "in acknowledging a national identity, I am also acknowledging that I owe special obligations to fellow members of my nation which I do not owe to other human beings" (Miller 1995, p. 49), we should reject the claim that such special obligations need not be limited by considerations of justice absent further arguments. If the claim is that the nation constitutes a distinctive and independent sphere of justice, there is still the question, left unanswered, why this sphere of justice need not be limited by other considerations of justice. And, as we saw earlier, considerations of cosmopolitan justice have dominance because the legitimacy of the claims of justice of conationals cannot be assessed in isolation from the claims of justice of outsiders. To put it in a different way, the reasonableness of the practices of a nation depends in part on how that nation relates to others.

Thus Nagel's own point about the possibility of an "institutional solution" for the problem of conflicting moral viewpoints should be taken more seriously than it seems Nagel himself does, as an option for solving the cosmopolitanism and nationalism tension in the global context. Before hastily concluding that the tension between global equality and national commitments is intractable, we should explore the possibility of creating a global order in which this tension can be assuaged. A global order regulated by principles conceived independently of national standpoints would provide a fair context for national pursuits without itself being in violation of the national point of view if we agree that what counts as legitimate national points of view and pursuits cannot be identified without first settling on the question of what claims nonnationals have against each other.

Samuel Scheffler, in *Boundaries and Allegiances*, while sympathetic to the cosmopolitan view, worries that it is not necessarily straightforward for the cosmopolitan ideal to be reconciled with the more local and particular allegiances people have. He writes: "I believe that there is a deep and persistent tension between these two features of our moral thought, and nothing in the non-reductionist position [on special obligations] guarantees that we will be able simultaneously to accommodate both features to our own satisfaction" (Scheffler 2001, p. 109). Yet it seems to me that if we treat cosmopolitanism foremost as a claim about justice (a position that Scheffler himself identifies) rather than a claim about individual identity, we can perhaps better appreciate the special and confined scope of cosmopolitan demands. As a claim about justice, cosmopolitanism only makes demands against institutions rather than the choices people make within the rules of institutions. And *within* the rules of institutions, people can see themselves as having special obligations to whomever on whatever ground and however this special obligation is to be properly understood. As a claim about justice, cosmopolitanism does not demand that people explain their special commitments by reference to cosmopolitan principles. The only requirement is that these commitments be exercised within the bounds of justice. Cosmopolitanism, so understood, does not pretend to be offering a "unified" moral outlook, and can accommodate a diversity of commitments, including nonreductionist accounts of patriotic commitments. It only requires that national obligations and pursuits be discharged and exercised within a global basic structure that is regulated by the same kinds of egalitarian principles that we would require of our domestic basic structure. Scheffler is right to reject an extreme form of cosmopolitanism that does not acknowledge the independent moral significance of patriotic and national ties and obligations; and he is right to urge in its place a moderate cosmopolitanism that appreciates the irreducible plurality of special commitments. What I am suggesting is that a strong cosmopolitan position about justice, that is, one that takes global egalitarianism to be a concern of justice, can still be a moderate cosmopolitanism in this respect.

The point above is not that a concern for justice at home need not come into conflict with a concern for justice abroad. Rather, the point is that how we may combat injustices at home cannot be determined independently of the justness of the global context. This point holds even if the injustices at home are injustices for which we are directly responsible. As it would be wrong to steal from one person in order to compensate another for the harm that we have inflicted on her, so it would be wrong to satisfy the demands of justice of compatriots by violating our outstanding duties of justice to outsiders. What this means in a world that is far from just, as I mentioned earlier, is not that we may not care about injustices at home. What it means is that to make such partial concern for national justice morally acceptable, it must not be at the expense of our duties of justice to others.

So the response to the argument from the prerogative of national justice is not to withdraw our demands for justice, but to stress the basic point that people may do as they wish, and that they may exercise their prerogatives, as long as the overall rules of justice permit it. This point extends to our special commitments of justice: how we are to live up to our duties to those to whom we are specially related is limited by whatever general duties of justice we have to all others. To deny this point is to suggest a highly counterintuitive view that one may unilaterally renege on one's outstanding duties of justice to some by taking on special commitments and obligations to others.

Let me summarize the central points advanced. On a liberal nationalist view, nationality-based special obligations do not limit the requirements of global justice; indeed it is the other way around. The "communitarian nationalists," on the other hand, claim that people's particular nationality ought to be among the factors to be taken into account when deciding on what is owed to others. But I have tried to suggest that arguments in defense of this view do not work. The argument from moral agency confuses morality with moral learning; and the argument from the normative independence of nationality and the argument from national prerogative distort our ordinary understanding of the relationship between justice and partial commitments and pursuits. That there are distinct spheres of justice does not mean that there are no dominant criteria of justice that should adjudicate between these distinct spheres. And that people can have special obligations of justice does not alone mean that their general obligations of justice may be overridden.

Conclusion

In this and the previous chapter, I have not tried to show that arguments for patriotic obligations fail altogether. What I hope to have shown is that such obligations are to be limited against the demands of cosmopolitan justice. Cosmopolitan justice, beyond establishing the limits of patriotism, need not take a stance on the moral basis of patriotism. This understanding, that principles of cosmopolitan justice impose only limiting conditions and not justificatory conditions on patriotic pursuits, is consistent with how we normally understand the relationship between justice and personal pursuits in more familiar contexts. As Rawls tells us in *Justice as Fairness*, "within the framework of background justice set up by the basic structure, individuals and associations may do as they wish insofar as the rules of institutions permit" (Rawls 2001, p. 50; Kelly 2000). The ideal of justice as impartiality is directed at the institutions of society and not at individual conduct within the rules of institutions per se. So long as people act within the rules of a just basic structure, they are not required to further explain themselves.[16]

Extending the same reasoning to the global context, we can say that, within the rules of a just global structure, individuals may favor their compatriots for whatever reasons so long as the rules of cosmopolitan justice permit. Indeed, as mentioned at the beginning, a theory of cosmopolitan justice that does not allow space for patriotic expressions of any form lacks plausibility, or may itself be reasonably rejected by reasonable persons. Cosmopolitans, I am suggesting, need not be concerned with the rational bases of patriotic obligations as such but with the reasonableness of such commitments. The task for cosmopolitans is not to show that patriotic commitments per se are rationally indefensible, but to show that defensible forms of patriotism do not violate the demands of cosmopolitan justice. Partial concern in itself is not a problem for global justice. The crucial question for global justice is how the rules of the global structure are to be determined. It is impartiality at this level of global institutional design that defenders of cosmopolitan justice must preserve; and I have tried to show that the standard arguments for patriotic ties on their own do not contradict this commitment.

[16] I discuss this in Tan (2004).

10   Conclusion

Contemporary accounts of cosmopolitan justice have been criticized for
failing to take seriously the ties and commitments of nationalism and
patriotism. The criticism can be put in the form of a dilemma: either we
reject the cosmopolitan idea of global equality or we deny that nationalist
and patriotic commitments are admissible. In this book, I have tried to
show that cosmopolitan justice, properly understood, can accommodate,
in a nontrivial way, liberal forms of nationalism and patriotic commitments. Cosmopolitan justice does not require a world in which national
boundaries and patriotic commitments have to recede and wither away.
The basic features of nationalism most often thought to be antithetical
to cosmopolitan justice – the principle of self-determination, and the
ideas of national partiality and national solidarity – are compatible with
cosmopolitan principles if these nationalist demands are kept within the
parameters of *liberal* nationalism. And the patriotic idea, that compatriots show special concern to each other, does not pose a real threat to
the cosmopolitan idea of justice. On the contrary, I have argued that our
ordinary understanding of the relationship between justice and personal
pursuits would require that patriotic commitments be limited against
the demands of cosmopolitan justice. Limiting patriotism against cosmopolitan justice does not imply a reductionist account of patriotism. It
can still be accepted that patriotism has more than merely instrumental value, and that it can acquire its moral significance independently of
cosmopolitan principles or commitments. Cosmopolitan justice need not
take a stance on the moral foundations of patriotism even as it establishes
the framework of justice within which such partial commitments must be
situated.

The crucial issue for cosmopolitan justice, then, is not whether nationalism and patriotism are morally grounded per se, but whether the
demands of patriotism and nationalism may influence the terms of global
justice. I have argued that if we accept the coherence of global justice – and
I have tried to show that liberals should – it distorts the meaning of justice

to say that the national or patriotic perspective may influence the terms of global justice. The very concept and idea of justice precludes the distortion of its principles by the particular points of view whose adjudication is the very function of justice. Adapting Kymlicka's general point about the impartiality of justice, to insist that the national point of view may be taken into account when determining the terms of global justice is not to propose an alternative to the *cosmopolitan* account of global justice but to propose an alternative to global *justice* (cf. Kymlicka 1990b, p. 103). What this means, simply put, is that global justice has to be cosmopolitan justice.

Liberal nationalism presents a compelling view of the world in which the identity and well-being of individuals is connected to the flourishing and self-determination of their national cultures. Not only is this view of the world not incompatible with the cosmopolitan ideal, but, as I have tried to show, anyone who endorses the liberal nationalist view of the world should also endorse some of the central commitments of cosmopolitan justice, for it is only under conditions of international equality that it will be possible for all nations to sustain their cultures and to exercise their right to self-determination (and for individuals to benefit from the exercise of their nationhood). The choice for nationalists is not between an inequitable world organized around national communities or an equitable cosmopolitan one without national borders. The real choice is between the inequitable global status quo in which only individuals in rich developed nations have the means to exercise self-determination, often at the expense of other nations, and a cosmopolitan order in which members of all nations are able to participate as equals in a global society of nations. Those who find liberal nationalism compelling should be prepared to defend cosmopolitan justice, and not argue against it as some tend to do.

Similarly, patriotic concern is an attractive feature of our common-sense moral world. Indeed, a world devoid of patriotic ties might be a world in which the common bonds necessary for democratic politics are absent. Yet in a world marked by injustices, patriotic concern among citizens in well-off countries is at odds with the idea that people use only resources that are rightly theirs to realize their special commitments and ties. Just entitlements must be established and secured before personal commitments and projects may be pursued, if the integrity of such pursuits is to be preserved. Special concern shown to particular others that favors those who are already relatively well-off is morally problematic in a context of injustice. Anyone from a rich country who takes patriotism seriously must, therefore, be motivated to strive for a just world if she wants to discharge her patriotic duties in good conscience.

If the arguments in this book are acceptable, then the common concern that cosmopolitan justice is too rigoristic or bloodless because it rules out nationalistic and patriotic pursuits is assuaged. If it is really the case that cosmopolitan justice cannot by definition accommodate and account for such particularist demands, the problem is not with cosmopolitan justice per se but with the very idea of justice as impartiality. But so long as we think that justice in the domestic context is a coherent notion in spite of the variety of personal pursuits and partial commitments that citizens in liberal democracies have (in fact, it is this diversity of personal ends that makes the concept of justice pertinent), we can also accept the coherence of cosmopolitan justice. To think that the diversity of national points of view should rule out cosmopolitan justice, when the diversity of personal pursuits is not normally seen to rule out domestic justice, is to be guilty of double standards in our understanding and practice of justice.

Accordingly, citizens in affluent liberal countries have a significant obligation to promote greater global equality. Difficult questions remain, however, as to the precise terms of this obligation and how they can be effectively implemented. Some may think that cosmopolitan justice is inapplicable without a world state to enforce the terms of justice. And given the practical and theoretical shortcomings associated with the notion of a world state, the idea of cosmopolitan justice is consequently a non-starter. There is also the worry that a cosmopolitan world order must presuppose a world of democratic (perhaps even liberal) states; yet the task of achieving a world of democratic (let alone liberal) states is itself fraught with political challenges. Related to this point, there is the problem of what obligations liberal citizens owe to individuals in poor but corrupt and tyrannical societies. Can foreign aid to poor countries be a matter of justice if this is not only going to be wasteful but also potentially hurtful of the individuals most in need of help?

These are pressing questions that any serious attempt to implement cosmopolitan justice in the real world will have to confront. I have hinted in different parts of this book how some of these concerns may have to be addressed. By way of conclusion, I will recall some of these remarks as well as making some additional tentative observations. Regarding the issue of enforcement, various theorists have proposed alternative forms of global institutions short of a world state that can conceivably motivate compliance with the terms of cosmopolitan justice. The UN, the WTO and other extant global institutions are able to implement terms of cooperation and exact compliance with these terms, albeit not always perfectly.

Existing global institutions, properly reformed and democratized, could provide the basis for a democratic global governance that cosmopolitan justice would need. Still the concept and practicality of the idea of global governance without global government, an idea receiving growing attention in the literature on international relations, will have to be further developed and explored.

Concerning corruption and inefficiency in certain developing countries, it is important to note that cosmopolitan justice is not primarily a call for resource transfers to disadvantaged persons (though it will have that effect) but the creation of a global context in which all persons are treated with equal concern and respect. There are some obvious steps that can be taken in this regard: the dismantling of tariffs by affluent countries on imports from developing countries, reforming patent laws especially for therapeutic drugs, sharing more evenly the economic costs of dealing with global warming, and so on are just some examples. Cosmopolitan justice, thus, is not about extracting "handouts" from affluent countries to give to less-developed countries, but about reforming the global structure (with its unfair terms of trade, internal laws and practices that favor powerful interests, the problem of democratic deficit, and so on) that unfairly restricts the life options of many individuals. Moreover, it is important not to overlook the global factors that contribute to corruption and domestic inefficiency, and the remedial steps that the global societies of nations must and can take to counter this problem (see, e.g., Pogge 2002, chaps. 6 and 8). Cosmopolitan justice, therefore, does not deny that countries have to take some responsibility for their own development; what it rejects is the common belief that countries are solely at fault for their own poor showing. Still, the creation of a just world may have the result of increasing the resource holdings of poor countries, and causing the problem of local corruption and inefficiency as described above to reappear. In these cases, tact and sound political judgment must be exercised so as to best assist individuals without at the same time entrenching the authority of corrupt governments. As pointed out in chapter 4, sometimes assistance may have to be stalled if continuing assistance does not help the people for whom it is meant but can in fact hurt them. The point to note, however, is that there might be prudential reasons to withhold what rightly belongs to another, which is different from saying that there are reasons of justice not to give. What justice requires does not become unfixed just because it is not prudent or politically wise to act on the demands of justice at a given time.

I point out some of these difficulties to show that the realization of cosmopolitan justice is not going to be easy. A philosophical aspiration is of course pointless if there is no possible way of seeing how one can realize the aspiration. But I have also tried to show that there are ways of trying to surmount these practical challenges, even if the details would have to be worked out and tested. If the vision of cosmopolitan justice I have presented is a morally plausible and attractive one, then we should be motivated to see how that vision can be brought about.

References

Aikens, William and H. LaFollette (eds.) (1996). *World Hunger and Morality* (Prentice Hall, Englewood Cliffs, NJ).

Alston, Peter (1990). "The Fortieth Anniversary of the Universal Declaration of Human Rights: A Time More for Reflection than for Celebration," in Jan Berting et al. (eds.), *Human Rights in a Pluralist World* (Netherlands Commission for UNESCO, The Hague) (Middelburg: Roosevelt Study Center, London: Meckler), 1–13.

Anderson, Benedict (1993). *Imagined Communities* (Verso, New York).

Anderson, Elizabeth (1999). "What Is the Point of Equality?" *Ethics*, 109: 287–337.

Archibugi, Daniele, D. Held and M. Kohler (1998). *Re-imagining Political Community: Studies in Cosmopolitan Democracy* (Stanford University Press, Stanford, CA).

Avineri, Shlomo and A. de-Shalit (eds.) (1992). *Communitarianism and Individualism* (Oxford University Press, Oxford).

Bader, Veit (ed.) (1997). *Citizenship and Exclusion* (St. Martin's Press, New York).

Barry, Brian (1974). *A Liberal Theory of Justice* (Oxford University Press, Oxford).

(1982). "Humanity and Justice in Global Perspective," in J. Roland Pennock and J. W. Chapman (eds.), *Ethics, Economics and the Law*, NOMOS, vol. XXIV (New York University Press, New York).

(1989). *Theories of Justice* (University of California Press, Berkeley, CA).

(1995). *Justice as Impartiality* (Oxford University Press, Oxford).

(1998). "International Society from a Cosmopolitan Perspective," in Mapel and Nardin (1998).

(1999). "Statism and Nationalism: A Cosmopolitan Critique," in Shapiro and Brilmayer (1999).

Barry, Brian and Goodin, R. (eds.) (1992). *Free Movement: Ethical Issues in the Transnational Migration of People and of Money* (Pennsylvania State University Press, University Park, PA).

Beiner, Ronald (ed.) (1999). *Theorizing Nationalism* (State University of New York Press, Albany, NY).

Beitz, Charles (1983). "Cosmopolitan Ideal and National Sentiment," *Journal of Philosophy*, 80/10: 591–600.

(1991). "Sovereignty and Morality in International Affairs," in David Held (ed.), *Political Theory Today* (Stanford University Press, Stanford, CA).

(1999a [1979]). *Political Theory and International Relations*, 2nd edn (Princeton University Press, Princeton, NJ).

(1999b). "International Liberalism and Distributive Justice: A Survey of Recent Thought," *World Politics*, 51: 269–96.

(1999c). "Social and Cosmopolitan Liberalism", *International Affairs*, 75/3: 515–29.

(2000). "Rawls's Law of Peoples," *Ethics* 110: 669–96.

(2001). "Does Global Inequality Matter?" *Metaphilosophy*, 32/1 and 2: 95–112.

Bell, Daniel (1996). "The East Asian Challenge to Human Rights: Reflections on an East West Dialogue," *Human Rights Quarterly* 18/3: 641–67.

(2000). *East Meets West* (Princeton University Press, Princeton, NJ).

Belsey, Andrew (1992). "World Poverty, Justice and Equality," in Robin Attfield and Barry Walkins (eds.), *International Justice and the Third World* (Routledge, London), 35–49.

Blake, Michael (2002). "Distributive Justice, State Coercion, and Autonomy," *Philosophy and Public Affairs*, 30/3: 257–96.

Blum, L. A. (1980). *Friendship, Altruism and Morality* (Routledge and Kegan Paul, London).

Brilmayer, Leah (1994). *American Hegemony: Political Morality in a One-Superpower World* (Yale University Press, New Haven, CT).

Brock, Gillian (2002). "Liberal Nationalism Versus Cosmopolitanism: Locating the Disputes," *Public Affairs Quarterly*, 16/4: 307–27.

Buchanan, Allen (2000). "Rawls's Law of Peoples," *Ethics*, 110: 697–721.

Caney, Simon (1996). "Individuals, Nations, and Obligations," in Caney et al. (1996).

(2001). "Cosmopolitan Justice and Equalizing Opportunities," *Metaphilosophy*, 32/1 and 2: 113–34.

(2002). "Cosmopolitanism and the Law of Peoples," *Journal of Political Philosophy*, 10/1: 95–123.

Caney, Simon, D. George and P. Jones (eds.) (1996). *National Rights, International Obligations* (Westview Press, Boulder, CO).

Canovan, Margaret (1996a). *Nationhood and Political Theory* (Edward Elgar, Cheltenham, UK).

(1996b). "The Skeleton in the Cupboard: Nationhood, Patriotism and Limited Loyalties," in Caney et al. (1996).

(2000). "Patriotism is Not Enough," *British Journal of Political Science*, 30: 413–32.

Carens, Joseph (1987). "Aliens and Citizens: The Case for Open Borders," *Review of Politics*, 49/3: 251–73.

Cassese, Antonio (1986). *International Law in a Divided World* (Oxford University Press, Oxford).

Clark, Ian (1999). *Globalization and International Relations Theory* (Oxford University Press, Oxford).

Cohen, G. A. (1978). "Robert Nozick and Wilt Chamberlain: How Patterns Preserve Liberty," in J. Arthur and W. Shaw (eds.), *Justice and Economic Distribution* (Prentice Hall, Englewood Cliffs, NJ).

(2000). *If You're an Egalitarian, How Come You're So Rich?* (Harvard University Press, Cambridge, MA).

Cohen, Joshua (1989). "Democratic Equality," *Ethics*, 99: 727–51.

(ed.) (1996). *For Love of Country* (Beacon Press, Boston).

Cornia, G. A. et al. (1987). *Adjustment With a Human Face: Protecting the Vulnerable and Promoting Growth (A Study by UNICEF)* (Oxford University Press, New York).

Couture, Jocelyn, K. Nielsen, and M. Seymour (eds.) (1998). *Rethinking Nationalism* (University of Calgary Press, Calgary).

Crocker, David A. and Toby Linden (eds.) (1998). *Ethics of Consumption: The Good Life, Justice, and Global Stewardship* (Rowman and Littlefield, Lanham, MD).

Cunningham, Frank (1994). *The Real World of Democracy Revisited* (Humanities Press, Atlantic Highlands, NJ).

Dagger, Richard (1985). "Rights, Boundaries, and the Bonds of Community," *American Political Science Review*, 79: 437–47.

DeMartino, George (2000). *Global Economy, Global Justice: Theoretical Objections and Policy Alternatives to Neoliberalism* (Routledge, London).

Donnelly, Jack (1989). *Universal Human Rights in Theory and Practice* (Cornell University Press, Ithaca, NY).

Dreze, Jean and Sen, A. (1989). *Hunger and Public Action* (Clarendon Press, Oxford).

Dworkin, Ronald (1977). *Taking Rights Seriously* (Harvard University Press, Cambridge, MA).

(1984). "To Each His Own: Review of Michael Walzer's *Spheres of Justice*," *New York Review of Books*, 14 April: 4–6.

(1985). *A Matter of Principle* (Harvard University Press, Cambridge, MA).

(1986). *Law's Empire* (Harvard University Press, Cambridge, MA).

(1992). "Liberal Community," in Avineri and de-Shalit (1992). Originally in *California Law Review* (1989), 77/3: 479–504.

(2000). *Sovereign Virtue* (Harvard University Press, Cambridge, MA).

Dyzenhaus, David (1996). "Liberalism After the Fall," *Philosophy and Social Criticism*, 22/3: 9–37.

(1998). "Critical Notice of Charles Larmore, *The Morals of Modernity*," *Canadian Journal of Philosophy*, 28/2: 269–86.

Feinberg, Joel (1980). "The Nature and Value of Rights," in J. Feinberg, *Rights, Justice, and the Bounds of Liberty* (Princeton University Press, Princeton, NJ).

Fishkin, James (1982). *The Limits of Obligation* (Yale University Press, New Haven, CT).

Freeman, Samuel (2003). "Introduction: John Rawls – An Overview," in S. Freeman (ed.), *The Cambridge Companion to Rawls* (Cambridge University Press, Cambridge).

(2004). "Public Reason and Political Justifications," *Fordham Law Review* 62/5: 2021–72.

Friedman, Marilyn (1985). *What Are Friends For? Feminist Perspectives on Personal Relationships and Moral Theory* (Cornell University Press, Ithaca, NY).

Galbraith, James K. (1999). "The Crisis of Globalization," *Dissent*, Summer: 13–16.

Gewirth, Alan (1988). "Ethical Universalism and Particularism," *Journal of Philosophy*, 85/6: 283–302.

Goodin, Robert (1985). *Protecting the Vulnerable* (University of Chicago Press, Chicago).
  (1988). "What Is So Special about Our Fellow Countryman?" *Ethics*, 98/4: 663–86.
  (1992). "If People Were Money . . . ," in Barry and Goodin (1992).
Green, Leslie (1994). "Internal Minorities and Their Rights," in Judith Baker (ed.), *Group Rights* (University of Toronto Press, Toronto).
Gutmann, Amy (ed.) (1994). *Multiculturalism* (Princeton University Press, Princeton, NJ).
  (1996). "Democratic Citizenship," in J. Cohen (1996).
Habermas, Jürgen (1992). "Citizenship and National Identity," *Praxis International*, 12/1: 1–19.
Hardimon, Michael (1994). "Role Obligations," *Journal of Philosophy*, 41: 333–63.
Hardin, Garrett (1996). "Lifeboat Ethics: The Case Against Helping the Poor," in Aikens and LaFollette (1996), 5–25.
Held, David (ed.) (1991). *Political Theory Today* (Stanford University Press, Stanford, CA).
  (ed.) (1993). "Democracy: From City-States to a Cosmopolitan Order?" in D. Held (ed.), *Prospects for Democracy* (Stanford University Press, Stanford, CA).
  (ed.) (1995). *Democracy and the Global Order: From the Modern State to Cosmopolitan Governance* (Stanford University Press, Stanford, CA).
  (2000). "The Changing Contours of Political Community: Rethinking Democracy in the Context of Globalisation," in Holden (2000).
Herman, Barbara (1993). *The Practice of Moral Judgment* (Harvard University Press, Cambridge, MA).
Hirst, Paul and Grahame Thompson (2000). "The Myth of Globalisation," in Frans Buelen (ed.), *Globalisation and the Nation State* (Edward Elgar, London).
Hoffmann, Stanley (1995). "Dreams of a Just World," *New York Review of Books*, 2 November: 52–7. Reprinted in Stanley Hoffman (1999). "Ideal Worlds," in *World Disorders* (Rowman and Littlefield, Boston).
Holden, Barry (ed.) (2000). *Global Democracy: Key Debates* (Routledge, New York/Canada).
Hume, David (1977 [1751]). *An Enquiry Concerning Human Understanding* (Hackett Publishing Co., Indianapolis).
Huntington, Samuel (1996). *The Clash of Civilisations and the Remaking of World Order* (Simon and Schuster, New York).
Hurka, Thomas (1997). "The Justification of National Partiality," in McKim and McMahan (1997).
Hurrell, Andrew and Ngaire Woods (eds.) (1999). *Inequality, Globalization, and World Politics* (Oxford University Press, New York).
Hutchings, Kimberly (1999). "Political Theory and Cosmopolitan Citizenship," in Hutchings and Dannreuther (1999).
Hutchings, Kimberly and R. Dannreuther (eds.) (1999) *Cosmopolitan Citizenship* (St. Martin's Press, New York).

Ignatieff, Michael (1993). *Blood and Belonging: Journeys into the New Nationalism* (Penguin Books, Toronto).

(2001). *Human Rights as Politics and Idolatry*, ed. Amy Gutmann (Princeton University Press, Princeton, NJ).

Ikegami, Eiko (1999). "Democracy in an Age of Cyber-Financial Globalization: Time, Space, and Embeddedness from an Asian Perspective," *Social Research*, 66/3: 887–92.

Jones, Charles (1999a). *Global Justice: A Cosmopolitan Defense* (Oxford University Press, Oxford).

(1999b). "Patriotism, Morality, and Global Justice," in Shapiro and Brilmayer (1999).

Kant, Immanuel (1991 [1795]). "Perpetual Peace," in *Kant's Political Writings*, ed. and trans. Hans Reiss, 2nd edn (Cambridge University Press, Cambridge).

(1993 [1797]). *The Metaphysics of Morals*, trans. Mary Gregor (Cambridge University Press, Cambridge).

Kateb, George (2000). "Is Patriotism a Mistake?" *Social Research*, 67/4: 901–24.

Kelly, Erin (2000). "Personal Concern," *Canadian Journal of Philosophy*, 30/1: 115–36.

Kiely, Ray (1998). "The Crisis of Global Development," in Kiely and Marfleet (1998).

Kiely, Ray and Phil Marfleet (ed.) (1998). *Globalisation and the Third World* (Routledge, London).

Kitching, Gavin (2001). *Seeking Social Justice through Globalization: Escaping a Nationalist Perspective* (Pennsylvania State University Press, University Park, PA).

Kleingeld, Pauline (1999). "Six Varieties of Cosmopolitanism," *Journal of the History of Ideas*, 60/3: 505–24.

Kuper, Andrew (2000). "Rawlsian Global Justice: Beyond the Law of Peoples to a Cosmopolitan Law of Peoples," *Political Theory*, 28: 640–74.

(2002). "More Than Charity: Cosmopolitan Alternatives to the 'Singer Solution'," *Ethics and International Affairs*, 16/1: 107–20.

Kymlicka, Will (1989). *Liberalism, Community and Culture* (Oxford University Press, Oxford).

(1990a). *Contemporary Political Philosophy: An Introduction* (Oxford University Press, Oxford).

(1990b). "Two Theories of Justice," *Inquiry*, 33: 99–119.

(1995). *Multicultural Citizenship* (Oxford University Press, Oxford).

(2001a). *Politics in the Vernacular* (Oxford University Press, Oxford).

(2001b). "Territorial Boundaries: A Liberal Egalitarian Perspective," in David Miller and Sohail Hashmi (eds.), *Boundaries and Justice* (Princeton University Press, Princeton, NJ).

(2002). *Contemporary Political Philosophy*, 2nd edn (Oxford University Press, Oxford).

Kymlicka, Will and Wayne Norman (1994). "The Return of the Citizen," *Ethics*, 104: 352–81.

Lichtenberg, Judith (1998). "How Liberal can Nationalism Be?," in Beiner (1999).

Linklater, Andrew (1999). "Cosmopolitan Citizenship," in K. Hutchings and R. Dannreuther (eds.), *Cosmopolitan Citizenship* (St. Martin's Press, New York), 35–59.

Lu, Catherine (2000). "The One and Many Faces of Cosmopolitanism," *Journal of Political Philosophy*, 8/2: 244–67.

Lukes, Steven (1995). "Equality and Liberty: Must they Conflict?," in Held (1991).

McCorquodale, Robert and R. Fairbrother (1999). "Globalization and Human Rights," *Human Rights Quarterly*, 21/3: 735–66.

MacIntyre, Alasdair (1984). *Is Patriotism a Virtue?*, The Lindley Lectures (Department of Philosophy, University of Kansas, Lawrence, KS).

McKim, Robert and J. McMahan (eds.) (1997). *The Morality of Nationalism* (Oxford University Press, Oxford).

McMahan, Jeff (1997). "The Limits of National Partiality," in McKim and McMahan (1997).

Mahbubani, Kishore (1998). *Can Asians Think?* (Times Books International, Singapore).

Mapel, David and T. Nardin (1998). *International Society* (Princeton University Press, Princeton, NJ).

Mason, Andrew (1997). "Special Obligations of Compatriots," *Ethics*, 107: 427–47.

Mayall, J. (1998). "Globalization and International Relations," *Review of International Studies*, 24/2: 239–50.

Michie, James and J. G. Smith (eds.) (1999). *Global Instability: The Political Economy of World Economic Governance* (Routledge, London).

Mill, John Stuart (1977a [1861]). *Considerations on Representative Government*, in *The Collected Works of John Stuart Mill*, vol. XIX, ed. John M. Robson (University of Toronto Press, Toronto).

(1977b [1861]). *Utilitarianism*, in *The Collected Works of John Stuart Mill*, vol. X, ed. John M. Robson (University of Toronto Press, Toronto).

Miller, David (1988). "The Ethical Significance of Nationality," *Ethics*, 98/4: 647–62.

(1995). *On Nationality* (Oxford University Press, Oxford).

(1996). "Secession and the Principle of Nationality," in Couture et al. (1998).

(1998). "The Limits of Cosmopolitan Justice," in Mapel and Nardin (1998).

(1999a). "Justice and Global Inequality," in A. Hurrell and N. Woods (eds.), *Inequality, Globalisation and World Politics* (Oxford University Press, Oxford).

(1999b). "Bounded Citizenship," in Hutchings and Dannreuther (1999).

(2000). *Citizenship and National Identity* (Polity Press, Cambridge).

Miller, David and M. Walzer (eds.) (1995). *Pluralism, Justice, and Equality* (Oxford University Press, Oxford).

Miller, Lynn (1994). *Global Order* (Westview Press, Boulder, CO).

Miller, Richard (1998). "Cosmopolitan Respect and Patriotic Concern," *Philosophy and Public Affairs*, 27/3: 202–24.

Milward, B. (2000). "What is Structural Adjustment?" in Mohan et al. (2000).

Mohan, Gill et al. (2000). *Structural Adjustment: Theory, Practice and Impacts* (Routledge, London).

Moellendorf, Darrel (2002). *Cosmopolitan Justice* (Westview Press, Boulder, CO).

Moody, Peter (1996). "Asian Values," *Journal of International Affairs*, 50: 166–92.

Moody-Adams, Michele (1997). *Fieldwork in Familiar Places* (Harvard University Press, Cambridge, MA).

Murphy, Liam and Thomas Nagel (2002). *The Myth of Ownership* (Oxford University Press, New York).

Nadkarni, A. (1999). "World Trade Liberation," in Michie and Smith (1999).

Nagel, Thomas (1979). *Mortal Questions* (Cambridge University Press, Cambridge).

(1986). *The View from Nowhere* (Oxford University Press, New York).

(1991). *Equality and Partiality* (Oxford University Press, Oxford).

(1999). "Justice, Justice, Shalt Thou Pursue: Review of Rawls, *Collected Papers*, *The Law of Peoples* and *A Theory of Justice* (revised ed.)," *New Republic*, 25 October.

Nickel, James (1993). "How Human Rights Generate Duties to Protect and Provide," *Human Rights Quarterly*, 15: 77–86.

Nielsen, Kai (1991). "Global Justice, Capitalism and the Third World," in John Arthur and William H. Shaw (eds.), *Justice and Economic Distribution*, 2nd edn (Prentice Hall, Englewood Cliffs, NJ), 228–41.

(1999). "Cosmopolitan Nationalism," *Monist*, 82/3: 446–68.

Nussbaum, Martha (1996). "Patriotism and Cosmopolitanism," in J. Cohen (1996).

(1997). *Cultivating Humanity* (Harvard University Press, Cambridge, MA).

(2000a). *Women and Human Development* (Cambridge University Press, Cambridge).

(2000b). "The Costs of Tragedy: Some Moral Limits of Cost-Benefit Analysis," *Journal of Legal Studies*, 29/2 (part 2): 1005–36.

(2000c). "Duties of Material Aid: Cicero's Problematic Legacy," *Journal of Political Philosophy* 8/2: 176–206.

O'Cleireacain, Seamus (1990). "Introduction," in *Third World Debt and International Public Policy* (Praeger, New York).

O'Neill, Onora (1986). *Faces of Hunger: An Essay on Poverty, Development and Justice* (George Allen and Unwin, London).

(1989). *Constructions of Reason: Exploration of Kant's Practical Philosophy* (St Martin's Press, New York).

(1991). "Transnational Justice," in Held (1991).

(2000). *Bounds of Justice* (Cambridge University Press, Cambridge).

Oxfam (2002). *Rigged Rules and Double Standards*: www.makefairtrade.com.

Palast, G. (2000). "Keeping Our Tablets (No One Else's): The WTO's Response to Africa's AIDS Crisis is a Chilling Reminder of Where Power Lies," *Guardian Weekly*, 27 July: 14.

Palley, Thomas (1999). "Toward a New International Economic Order," *Dissent*, Spring: 48–52.

Parekh, Bhikhu (1998). "The Incoherence of Nationalism," in Beiner (1999).

Pogge, Thomas (1986). "Liberalism and Global Justice," *Philosophy and Public Affairs* 15/1: 57–81.

(1988a). "Rawls and Global Justice," *Canadian Journal of Philosophy*, 18/2: 227–56.

(1988b). "Moral Progress," in Steven Luper-Foy, *Problems of International Relations* (Westview Press, Boulder, CO).

(1989). *Realizing Rawls* (Cornell University Press, Ithaca, NY).

(1992a). "Cosmopolitanism and Sovereignty," *Ethics*, 103/1: 48–75. Revised and reprinted in Pogge (2002).

(1992b). "An Institutional Approach to Humanitarian Intervention," *Public Affairs Quarterly*, 6/1: 89–103.

(1992c). "O'Neill on Rights and Duties," *Grazer Philosophische Studien*, 43: 233–47.

(1994). "An Egalitarian Law of Peoples," *Philosophy and Public Affairs*, 23/3: 195–224.

(1997). "Migration and Poverty," in Bader (1997).

(1998). "The Bounds of Nationalism," in Couture et al. (1998). Revised and reprinted in Pogge (2002).

(1999). "Economic Justice and National Borders," *ReVision*, (Fall) 22/2: 27–34.

(2000). "The Moral Demands of Global Justice," *Dissent* 47/4: 37–43.

(2002). *World Poverty and Human Rights* (Polity Press, Cambridge).

Railton, Peter (1993). "Alienation, Consequentialism, and the Demands of Morality," in Scheffler (1993).

Rawls, John (1971). *A Theory of Justice* (Harvard University Press, Cambridge, MA).

(1980). "Kantian Constructivism in Moral Theory," *Journal of Philosophy*, 77: 515–72.

(1993). "The Law of Peoples," in Stephen Shute and Susan Hurley (eds.), *On Human Rights: The Oxford Amnesty Lectures 1993* (Basic Books, New York).

(1996 [1993]). *Political Liberalism*, paperback edition (Columbia University Press, New York).

(1999a). *The Law of Peoples* (Harvard University Press, Cambridge, MA).

(1999b). *Collected Papers*, ed. Samuel Freeman (Harvard University Press, Cambridge, MA).

(2001). *Justice as Fairness*, ed. Erin Kelly (Harvard University Press, Cambridge, MA).

Raz, Joseph (1986). *The Morality of Freedom* (Oxford University Press, Oxford).

Reidy, David (2004). "Rawls's International Justice: A Defense," in *Political Theory* (forthcoming).

Robinson, Fiona (1999). *Globalizing Care: Ethics, Feminist Theory, and International Relations* (Westview Press, Boulder, CO).

Rousseau, Jean-Jacques (1915). *The Political Writings of Rousseau*, ed. Charles Vaughan (Cambridge University Press, Cambridge).

Sachs, Jeffrey D. (1998). "The IMF and The Asian Flu," *American Prospect* 9/37: 16–21.

Sandel, Michael (1992). "The Procedural Republic and the Unencumbered Self," in Avineri and de-Shalit (1992).

(1996). *Democracy's Discontent* (Harvard University Press, Cambridge, MA).

Sassen, Saskia (1998). *Globalisation and its Discontents* (New Press, New York).

Satz, Debra (1999). "Equality of What Among Whom?" in Shapiro and Brilmayer (1999).

Scanlon, Thomas (1975). "Rawls's Theory of Justice," in Daniels (ed.), *Reading Rawls* (Basic Books, New York).

(1982). "Contractualism and Utilitarianism," in Amartya Sen and Bernard Williams, *Utilitarianism and Beyond* (Cambridge University Press, Cambridge).

(1997). *The Diversity of Objections to Inequality*, The Lindley Lectures (Department of Philosophy, University of Kansas, Lawrence, KS).

(1999). *What We Owe To Each Other* (Harvard University Press, Cambridge, MA).

Scheffler, Samuel (1982). *The Rejection of Consequentialism* (Oxford University Press, Oxford).

(ed.) (1988). *Consequentialism and its Critics* (Oxford University Press, Oxford).

(2001). *Boundaries and Allegiances* (Oxford University Press, New York).

Schlereth, Thomas (1977). *The Cosmopolitan Ideal in Enlightenment Thought* (University of Notre Dame Press, Notre Dame).

Sen, Amartya (1979). "Equality of What?" Tanner Lectures on Human Value (University of Utah Press, Salt Lake City).

(1981). *Poverty and Famines: An Essay on Entitlement and Deprivation* (Oxford University Press, Oxford).

(1992). *Inequality Reexamined* (Harvard University Press, Cambridge, MA).

(1999). *Development as Freedom* (Knopf, New York).

Shapiro, Ian and L. Brilmayer (eds.) (1999). *Global Justice* (New York University Press, New York).

Shue, Henry (1984). "The Interdependence of Duties," in P. Alston and K. Tomasevski (eds.), *The Right to Food* (M. Nijhoff, Boston).

(1988). "Mediating Duties," *Ethics*, 98: 687–704.

(1996 [1980]). *Basic Rights*, 2nd edn (Princeton University Press, Princeton, NJ).

(1997). "Eroding Sovereignty: The Advance of Principle," in McKim and McMahan (1997).

Simmons, A. John (1996). "Associative Political Obligations," *Ethics*, 106/2: 247–73.

(2001). *Justification and Legitimacy: Essays on Rights and Obligations* (Cambridge University Press, New York).

Singer, Peter (1979). *Practical Ethics* (Cambridge University Press, Cambridge).

(1996). "Famine, Affluence and Morality," in Aikens and LaFollette (1996), 26–38. Originally in *Philosophy and Public Affairs* (1972) 1/3.

(2002). *One World* (Yale University Press, New Haven, CT).

Smith, Anthony (1991). *National Identity* (University of Nevada, Reno, NV).

Smith, J. G. (1999). "A New Bretton Woods: Reforming the Global Financial System," in Michie and Smith (1999).

Smith, Rogers (2002). *Stories of Peoplehood: The Politics and Morals of Membership* (Cambridge University Press, Cambridge).

Stiglitz, Joseph E. (2002). *Globalization and its Discontents* (W. W. Norton, New York).

Sumner, L. W. (1987). *The Moral Foundation of Rights* (Princeton University Press, Princeton, NJ).

Tamir, Yael (1992). *Liberal Nationalism* (Princeton University Press, Princeton, NJ).

(1997). "Pro Patria Mori! Death and the State," in McKim and McMahan (1997).

Tan, Kok-Chor (1995). "Military Intervention as a Moral Duty," *Public Affairs Quarterly* 9/1: 29–47.

(1997). "Kantian Ethics and Global Justice," *Social Theory and Practice*, 23/1: 53–73.

(1998). "Liberal Toleration in Rawls's Law of Peoples," *Ethics*, 108/2: 276–95.

(2000). *Toleration, Diversity, and Global Justice* (Pennsylvania State University Press, College Park, PA).

(2004). "Justice and Personal Pursuits," *The Journal of Philosophy* 101/7: 331–62.

(forthcoming). "Nationalism and Democracy," in Deen Chatterjee (ed.), *Globalisation and Democracy* (Rowman and Littlefield, Lanham, MD).

Taylor, Charles (1989). "Cross-Purposes: The Liberal-Communitarian Debate," in Nancy Rosenblum (ed.), *Liberalism and the Moral Life* (Harvard University Press, Cambridge, MA), 159–82.

(1992). "Atomism," in Avineri and de-Shalit (1992), 29–50.

(1996). "Why Democracy Needs Patriotism," in J. Cohen (1996).

Teson, Fernando (1995). "The Rawlsian Theory of International Law," *Ethics and International Affairs*, 9: 79–99.

Thompson, Dennis (1996). "Democratic Theory and Global Society," *Journal of Political Philosophy*, 7/2: 111–25.

Toulmin, Stephen (1992). *Cosmopolis* (University of Chicago Press, Chicago).

Ul-haq, Mahbub (1995). *Reflections on Human Development* (Oxford University Press, New Delhi).

United Nations Development Program (UNDP) (1996). *Human Development Report 1996* (Oxford University Press, New York).

(1997). *Human Development Report 1997* (Oxford University Press, New York).

(1999). *Human Development Report 1999* (Oxford University Press, New York).

(2000). *Human Development Report 2000* (Oxford University Press, New York).

(2001). *Human Development Report 2001* (Oxford University Press, New York).

Van Parijs, Philippe (1995). *Real Freedom for All* (Oxford University Press, Oxford).

Vincent, Andrew (2002). *Nationalism and Particularity* (Cambridge University Press, Cambridge).

Waldron, Jeremy (1992). "Minority Rights and the Cosmopolitan Alternative," *University of Michigan Journal of Law Reform*, 25/3: 751–93.

(2000). "What is Cosmopolitan?" *Journal of Political Philosophy*, 8/2: 227–43.

(2003). "The Primacy of Justice," *Legal Theory* 9/4: 269–94.

(forthcoming). *Cosmopolitan Right* (Oxford University Press, Oxford).

Walzer, Michael (1980). "The Moral Standing of States," *Philosophy and Public Affairs*, 9/3: 209–29.

(1983). *Spheres of Justice* (Basic Books, New York).

(1990a). "The Communitarian Critique of Liberalism," *Political Theory*, 18/1: 6–23.

(1990b). "Nations and Universe," *The Tanner Lectures on Human Values XI* (University of Utah Press, Salt Lake City).

(1994). "Comments," in Gutmann (1994).

(1995). "Response," in David Miller and Michael Walzer (eds.), *Pluralism, Justice, and Equality* (Oxford University Press, Oxford).

(1999). "The New Tribalism," in Beiner (1999). Originally in *Dissent*, Spring 1992.

Weinstock, Daniel (1999). "National Partiality: Confronting the Intuitions," *The Monist*, 82/3: 423–41.

Wellman, Christopher Heath (2000). "Relational Facts in Liberal Political Theory: Is There Magic in the Pronoun 'My'," *Ethics*, 110: 537–62.

Wenar, Leif (2002). "The Legitimacy of Peoples," in P. De Grieff and C. Cronin (eds.), *Global Justice and Transnational Politics* (MIT Press, Cambridge, MA), 53–76.

Whiting, Jennifer E. (1991). "Impersonal Friends," *The Monist*, 74/1: 3–29.

Williams, Bernard (1981). *Moral Luck: Philosophical Papers 1973–1980* (Cambridge University Press, Cambridge).

Woodiwiss, A. (1999). *Globalisation, Human Rights and Labour Law in Pacific Asia* (Cambridge University Press, Cambridge).

World Bank (2000). *World Development Report 2000/2001* (Oxford University Press, Oxford).

Yack, Bernard (1999). "Myth of the Civic State," in Beiner (1999).

Young, Iris (2000). *Inclusion and Democracy* (Oxford University Press, Oxford).

Zack-Williams, A. (2000). "The Long Road to Structural Adjustment," in Mohan et al. (2000).

Zolo, Danielo (1997). *Cosmopolis: Prospects for World Government* (Polity Press, Cambridge).

(1999). "A Cosmopolitan Philosophy of International Law? A Realist Approach," *Ratio Juris*, 12/4: 429–44.

Index